INFORMIX® *Press*

INFORMIX

DATABASE

ADMINISTRATOR'S

SURVIVAL GUIDE

D1613603

Joe Lumbley

PRENTICE HALL PTR, ENGLEWOOD CLIFFS, N.J. 07632

Library of Congress Cataloging-in-Publication Data

Lumbley, Joe.
      INFORMIX database administrator's survival guide /
      Joe Lumbley.

          p.   cm.
      Includes index.
      ISBN 0-13-124314-4
      1. Database management.   I.   Title
      QA76.9.D3L86   1995   94-22197
      05.75'65 -- dc20   CIP

© 1995 Prentice Hall P T R. Some programs © 1990–1993 The Tigon Corporation.

Prentice Hall PTR
Prentice-Hall, Inc.
A Simon & Schuster Co.
Englewood Cliffs, New Jersey 07632

INFORMIXPress

Informix Press
Informix Software, Inc.
4100 Bohannon Drive
Menlo Park, CA 94025

Cover design director: *Jerry Votta*
Cover design: *Karen Marsilio*
Acquisitions editor: *Mark L. Taub*
Editorial assistant: *Marcy Levine*

Manager, Informix Press: *Todd Katz*
Founder, Informix Press: *Suzanne Fuery*

The publisher offers discounts on this book when ordered in bulk quantities. For more information: Corporate Sales Department, PTR Prentice Hall, 113 Sylvan Avenue, Englewood Cliffs, NJ 07632.　Phone: 1-800-382-3419 FAX: 201-592-2249. E-mail (Internet): dan_rush@prenhall.com.

Printed in the United States of America

10 9 8 7 6 5 4 3 2 1

ISBN 0-13-124314-4

Prentice-Hall International (UK) Limited, *London*
Prentice-Hall of Australia Pty. Limited, *Sydney*
Prentice-Hall Canada Inc., *Toronto*
Prentice-Hall Hispanoamericana, S.A., *Mexico*
Prentice-Hall of India Private Limited, *New Delhi*
Prentice-Hall of Japan, Inc., *Tokyo*
Simon & Schuster Asia Pte. Ltd., *Singapore*
Editora Prentice-Hall do Brasil, Ltda., *Rio de Janeiro*

Contents

CHAPTER 6
HOW DO I?   133

CHAPTER 7
COMMON DBA TASKS   189

CHAPTER 9
DBA TOOLS

Preface

You're the new database administrator. Whether you got there as the result of years of maneuvering and planning or whether the job was thrust upon you, the results are the same. You need to hit the ground running and take control of the system as though you knew what you were doing. You will either be stepping into an absolutely chaotic mess that was made worse by the last DBA, or you'll be starting up the job function for the first time. Either way can be a challenge.

You're probably feeling a little overwhelmed. Good, that's a sane response given the circumstances. You've just discovered that there are about twenty manuals that you need to read just to discover where to start. Unfortunately, they are computer manuals. Computer manuals seem to have been written by someone who doesn't understand English and translated into English by someone who doesn't understand computers. Either that, or they assume that you know everything already and are just using the manual for a syntax reference.

The purpose of this book is to help you ease your transition into being a DBA. All too often, technical people such as programmers and other computer people tend to view everything as a programming problem. Problem? Fix the code. This is a trademark approach of the computer nerd, and a lot of us fall victim. The secret of being a good DBA, in fact of being successful in just about anything, consists of being very good at the technical parts of your job, being very good at communicating, and of being aware of the political environment in which you work.

This book talks about specific versions of Informix® software. The information contained here applies to INFORMIX®-OnLine database engines prior to Version 6.0. Some mention is made of features in Version 6.0 and 7.0, but this information comes from second-hand information and has not been personally verified. Some of these techniques may be applicable to INFORMIX®-SE engines, but this has not been verified.

What's in this book? You'll find an approach to the DBA function that attempts to cover the technical and the political aspects of the job. You'll find source code on the same page with suggestions on how to handle different types of people. You'll find tips on using utilities next to tips on handling office politics. The code and the technical material is as accurate as I can make it. The rest is opinion. Take what's useful to you.

Acknowledgments

A book is almost never the product of just one person. I thought that I had written this book until I got to writing this acknowledgment section. The truth of the matter is that I just put the words on paper.

A group of enthusiastic, talented individuals played a major part in turning this project from a discussion at the Informix World Users Conference in 1993 into a book published about a year later. If I miss anyone, I'll try to make it up to you.

My editor at Informix® Press, Mark Taub, has been instrumental in making this book happen. I attended a "birds of a feather" session at the 1993 Informix World User's Conference in which Mark was making a presentation on "So You Want to be a Computer Book Writer." I went into the session with a lot of questions and left with a determination to do this book. Thanks, Mark. Your help has been greatly appreciated all along the way.

A thank you is in order for my previous manager, Glenn Jenkins, of the Tigon Corporation. Glenn kindly agreed to let me include many DBA scripts that I had created on Tigon's time. Thanks also to my current manager at BancTec, John Fox. John has been very supportive of this project and I appreciate it.

Many thanks go to my technical reviewers, Elliott Danziger and Mary Schulte, of Informix Corporation, and Lisa Manno of AT&T. I hope it was not too painful.

To all of the Informix gurus, UNIX wizards, kernel hackers, and other various denizens of the Internet, you have my eternal thanks. I am especially indebted to all the users of the `comp.databases.informix` USENET user group on Internet. Your hints, suggestions, and criticisms have shaped both my understanding of the OnLine products and the contents of this book.

Thanks to my daughter Katherine, who for too many nights tolerated my hogging the computer. You can have it back now. Finally, I am deeply indebted to my wife, Jayne, for putting up with me during this whole project. She tolerated far too many 3 a.m. bedtimes and probably never wants to hear "Not tonight dear, I have a modem" again in her life.

Thanks to all of you.

Chapter 1

The Database Administrator: Doing the Job

There are probably as many different descriptions of the database administrator's job function as there are DBAs. Depending upon the complexity and culture of the firm, the database administrator can be anything from a developer who just happens to also wear a DBA hat all the way up to a member of a team of DBAs, all of whom have different responsibilities. Most will fall somewhere in the spectrum between the two extremes.

I'm not sure that I've ever seen a proper definition of a database administrator. Perhaps the broadest definition would be: "The person or persons in charge of the database." Oftentimes, though, what this really means is: "The person who's read the DBA manual."

In the hierarchy of database consumers, there's usually an identifiable division between developers and end users. As we move more into empowering the end users, this dividing line becomes less distinct. Is a user who is using INFORMIX®-WingZ to pull data into his own spreadsheet a developer? Who's developing the spreadsheet? What about a user who is using INFORMIX-ViewPoint™ and INFORMIX®-DBA to write reports? In many shops, generating reports is strictly an Information Services "glass house" application. The further we move into the client/server model, the more blurred these distinctions become.

Likewise, as more tools become available for managing the database, the line between developer and DBA begins to blur. Developers and systems analysts regularly design database schemas and address application performance questions. They often create their own tables and indexes as well as develop the application code. Database administrators often write application code, especially when they are not full-time DBAs.

Actually, there is a continuum that begins at end users and works up through developers, analysts, DBAs, and Information Service managers. One of the more challenging aspects of working in this field is deciding if and where to draw the lines.

TYPICAL DBA JOB FUNCTIONS

No matter where the lines are drawn, there are certain functions that need to be part of the overall management of any database system. This list is not comprehensive. Every organization will have it's own quirks and peculiarities, but these are the basic items.

Keeping the database running

This is the primary function of the database administrator in production environments. Especially in mission-critical applications that run 24 hours a day, 7 days a week (24x7), the database administrator is judged first on system downtime. In some situations, the cost of minutes of downtime can be more than the annual salary of the DBA.

In most applications, whether mission-critical or not, database downtime impacts just about everyone associated with the database. Order entry personnel, service and help line personnel, data entry staff, and software developers need to have the database up and running to get any work done.

Downtime is not only when the database is completely down. It's perceived downtime that hurts. If the database is running slowly, no matter what the cause, the effect is just about as bad as if it is not running at all. In fact, when the database is running slowly, it is often as bad as or worse than when it is not running at all.

Have you ever been standing waiting for an elevator that is running slowly? Chances are, you've pushed the button several times, hoping that repeatedly pushing the button will somehow make the elevator get to you faster. Computer users exhibit the same type of superstitious behavior. They will put jobs in the background, use the UNIX `nice` command, open additional terminal windows and database jobs, fill their keyboard buffers with useless keystrokes, or hit a series of breaks, all in the hope that something will make the database go faster. Usually this just makes things worse. What started as a slowdown ends up as a crash.

What this means to the DBA is that you must communicate with your users. If the database is slow, let the users know. Believe me, they already know. What you're doing is telling them that you know there's a problem and you're working on it. If it's possible, plan your downtime in advance. Give everyone lots of notice. If you can negotiate scheduled downtime, do so. The users will get used to it and your life will be easier.

Often, the DBA will be the cause of the slowdowns. This you can almost certainly control. If you're using any of the Informix utilities, be aware of their effects on the database. Certain options in `tbcheck` can cause tables to lock. Using `tblog` on an active logfile can freeze up the database. Know your tools.

If the database does inexplicably freeze up, look first for problems with the checkpoints. This is a common cause of database hangs. Often, a checkpoint may hang while it is blocked by some other system activity. The checkpoint hang may very well be a symptom of some other problem. As an example, a checkpoint that is requested while the `tbtape` archive is waiting for a new tape will freeze up until the new tape is inserted. Beware of such interactions between programs.

Training the users

The user community can make or break the DBA. If the users are knowledgeable about the database, they'll make fewer demands on the DBA and do more for themselves. The DBA will spend less time fighting fires and more time in more constructive activities if he devotes the necessary time to helping the users get up to speed.

Of course, different users have different needs. If most of your users are using "canned" software, meaning that all of their dealings with the database are through well-tested and well-debugged programs, they'll need a lot less training. As long as they don't engage in impatient or superstitious behavior, they will need little database training. Users of such "canned" programs quite often just view it as a "black box" anyway. They don't realize that they're dealing with a database. They just deal with screens and keystrokes.

More sophisticated users need more training. When you begin to give users unstructured access through various access tools, there's more that can go wrong. If they use SQL, they need to be schooled in how to compose their queries, especially in how to compose the WHERE clauses. A *disjoint query* is a query using multiple tables that do not join properly. Rather than restricting the number of rows that the query returns, this type of query often returns a number of rows equal to the product of the number of rows in each table. Thus, a disjoint query on two tables, each with ten rows, could return one hundred rows. Disjoint queries on large tables can quickly overwhelm the database with millions of rows of output. Likewise, queries that join on unindexed tables or that generate unreasonable query plans can take forever to complete. The user will often wait for thirty minutes or so, realize that it's taking too long, and then try to kill the job. This often results in long transactions, database rollback, or database crashes if the job is killed incorrectly. If you have these somewhat sophisticated users, get them some training. If you have software developers, try to get *them* to train the ad hoc users. It'll help both of them.

Software developers are often the most challenging training problem for DBAs. Most often, developers are building highly specialized applications. They'll know much more about the applications than you do. They'll probably know a lot more about the database structure than you do. These sophisticated developers can be a valuable resource when it comes to going very deep into the database. Quite often, though, developers will be weak on either extreme of the database. They often know the structure of the data, but many times they know a lot less about the contents of the data than the data entry people do. On the other end of the spectrum, the developers will know a lot about how individual parts of the database behave, but they'll be weak on how it all fits together.

Often, developers are not aware of the effects of long transactions, logfile use, resource contention, and latch contention. They will code their software until it gives them the results they want. They're usually under such time pressures that they don't spend a lot of time trying to optimize the code. Produce, produce, produce! Of course these are generalizations. No users are the same. If you're lucky, you'll have developers who can view the overall picture and create finely crafted code that fits in well with the overall system. If you don't have these kinds of developers, it's the DBA's job to try and create them. If you can, get them to develop some code for you. Teach them about the things you need to monitor and let them work on it for a while. You'll get some good tools as well as a better-trained developer community.

There's nothing better for developers than teaching them how to run and interpret the SET EXPLAIN output. If they know how the optimizer is interpreting their queries, they'll write better queries.

Another area that developers and system analysts often can use help with is developing a concept of a data life cycle. Often, much attention is paid to getting data into a database, with little or none paid to getting rid of the data when it's out of date. If the developers don't develop plans for archiving and removal of obsolete data, guess who finally gets the job? When you suddenly get to 95 percent capacity, you'll start frantically trying to clean out the junk, and you'll be fighting a hopeless battle. If your organization has a formal program for software specifications, lobby very hard to have every new query or other SQL statement that is included in new code be accompanied by the output from the SET EXPLAIN command. If the software specification calls for creating new data or inserting data into tables, the specification should include a plan for the archival or deletion of old data.

Providing services to users

The DBA needs to be seen as a resource person for the users. She needs to be aware of the overall structure of the database system and needs to know how the parts fit together. Often, the DBA tends to inherit the job of documenting the database, especially if the organization has been somewhat lax in documentation in the past. Users need to know the structure of the tables and indexes, where source code is located, which utilities are available, and which scripts have been written to make their jobs easier.

If your organization uses an 3GL language such as INFORMIX®-ESQL/C, the DBA will often be the resource person who helps the developers when their programs don't compile. Hint: look first at their makefiles.

It's usually good procedure to prohibit all but a few of the more sophisticated users from ever killing an SQL job or backend. As this is a major cause of system crashes, it's usually better to let the DBA be the "executioner" of runaway jobs.

The DBA should also be available to help developers interpret `sqlexplain.out` files to help them tune their queries. Here, the DBA needs to understand in detail the operations of the optimizer.

Often, the DBA needs to be the person who grants access and privileges in the database. Along with this comes the job of providing the correct environmental variables to access the database and to compile ESQL/C code. The DBA often needs to be able to provide synonyms and aliases for the user. It's better if the DBA and system administrator cooperate in this area and that they have scripts or other programs designed for the task. This task is made more complex if the system utilizes a distributed database across a network. Here, the DBA and system administrator need to insure that all of the above items occur, not only on one computer system, but on many.

Disaster recovery

System crashes are an unfortunate fact of life for all those who deal with computer systems. No matter how fault-tolerant the system is, no matter how good the database is, no matter how good the DBA plans, the system will crash. Take that as a given. If you're lucky it will be recoverable. If you're unlucky, your entire computer center will disappear into a hole in the earth some night.

We're all subject to the "it can't happen here" syndrome, which says that all bad things happen to someone else. Next time you see a disaster scene on the news, look around and you'll probably find someone's computer system at the bottom of one of the piles of rubble. What would you do if it were yours?

That's the worst of the disaster recovery scenarios. Your more common occurrences will usually be of a less catastrophic nature, simple things like disk errors, hardware failures, and user errors. If you plan for the end of the world scenarios, you'll always be able to handle the simple problems.

Your disaster recovery plan needs to begin with the simple recovery of the database. Usually this means setting up and following a plan for periodic archives of the database. Regular archives, combined with database logging, can be an almost foolproof means of recovering from just about all kinds of errors. The only drawback is the time needed for performing the archives and the time necessary to recover the system from the archives. Crashes are usually chaotic times, and a well-practiced plan is a necessity. This is not the right time to begin reading up on database recovery in the manual!

Although archives and logs will suffice most of the time, you need to keep the catastrophic situation in the back of your mind. Disaster recovery entails recovering from a partial or complete destruction of *everything* in your computer room. Look at your backup tapes right now. Where are they? If they're sitting on top of the computer in the computer room, the airliner that crashes into your computer center will probably take them out too. What about communications? What'll you do if the phones are down? Or the power? Where are the telephone numbers of your critical staff members? In the computer?

Devising a good disaster recovery plan is an exercise in paranoia. You need to think about these things. Imagine that your computer center's in that hole in the ground. It may not be practical to devise contingencies that will cover the end of life on earth as we know it, but you'll be surprised how some simple precautions can let you sleep better at night.

Planning for the future

The DBA is often the person in the organization who has the broadest view of the data management function. Individual developers and project leaders usually view a piece of the overall application, but the DBA's viewpoint must be more global and wide-ranging. The DBA must maintain this global view and must participate in planning how to best meet the organization's data management needs.

This planning function is often pretty far down the DBA's list of priorities. The DBA can get into a firefighting mode in which it seems that 90 percent of her time is spent handling emergencies. This is probably due to someone's failure to plan adequately. While firefighting is usually the most visible and often the most exciting part of the DBA's functions, the ideal situation is to avoid the fires.

The DBA needs to participate in planning for such items as hardware and software upgrades, maintenance schedules, facilities management, communications capabilities, and project plans. If the enterprise is of any size at all, most of this planning will be the responsibility of someone else. Even so, the DBA must represent the realities of the database to those who are doing the planning. Failure to do so will result in unworkable plans, unreasonable expectations, and much frustration down the line.

The DBA should also take the lead in planning for the integration of new products and tools. As more third-party tools become available that work with the Informix family of products, the DBA has a wider range of options.

Historically, Informix has been accessed through character-oriented tools, reflecting its origin in the UNIX world. Until recently, there have been few graphical or GUI tools available to Informix. While users of such databases as Oracle® have had access to sophisticated graphical tools, the Informix user has been restricted to tools that run on dumb terminals. This, however, is changing. Informix has released their INFORMIX®-HyperScript® toolset which allows PC applications to utilize the graphics capability of personal computers to work against either SE engines located on the PC itself or against SE or OnLine engines across a network. These applications are enabled by the use of the Informix data transport programs, INFORMIX®-STAR and INFORMIX®-NET.

Many of these graphical tools are end-user tools that allow users to compose their own queries, build their own forms, and write their own reports. These tools can provide a mixed blessing to the DBA. On the one hand, they allow the DBA to shift some of the development out of the IS department and into the hands of the users. Balancing this benefit is the risk of allowing inexperienced users access to the database.

The DBA needs to assist in plotting a course that will allow these new classes of tools to fit into the existing IS structure. The DBA's perspective is crucial in insuring that such areas as database security, resource monitoring and controls, and data validity are considered in the integration of new tools.

Tuning the database

Monitoring and improvement of database system performance is a constant part of the DBA job function. Although we are classifying this as "tuning the database," the function really encompasses:

- Tuning the hardware
- Tuning the operating system
- Tuning the database engine
- Design and structure of the database schema
- Tuning the application, and
- Monitoring daily operations

Of these, tuning of the hardware and operating system is usually considered to be the System Administrator's bailiwick. These two functions, though, are absolutely critical if we are to wring the best performance out of the entire system. The DBA should endeavor to become familiar with tuning the UNIX operating system and with the parameters that can affect the speed of the operating system. Of particular interest from the hardware and operating system viewpoints are:

- Disk layout
- Disk striping
- Single vs. multiprocessors
- Shared memory parameters
- Other resource limitations in the kernel

Tuning the database engine is usually the sole responsibility of the DBA. If not, it should be. The DBA should be the one point of contact for any parameter changes to the OnLine system. The DBA is constantly monitoring system performance and tweaking the parameters until the system is matched well to the types of tasks it is asked to perform.

The DBA should also be responsible for maintaining the structure and layout of the tables. Although system analysts and developers most often specify the tables and structure, the DBA needs to be the person who actually creates the tables and indexes. If the DBA is attempting to create and maintain an enterprise-wide data dictionary, this is even more important, as the data dictionary needs to know about new tables and indexes.

Maintenance of indexes is a large part of the overall performance of the database system. You will find that most of the time, performance problems can be traced back to improper indexing.

Running a close second to poor indexing as a performance bugaboo is inefficient application design. Often, the queries can be made much more efficient by analyzing them with SET EXPLAIN. It is sometimes advisable to restructure the application to access its data in a completely different way, especially if the old way requires unindexed scans of large tables. There are some types of queries, such as correlated subqueries, that are inherently inefficient. Sometimes it is possible to significantly speed up SQL statements by using temporary tables to force the optimizer to evaluate the SQL statement in a preferred manner.

A final part of the speed enhancement function calls for the DBA to monitor and correct resource hogging and other disruptive activities of the users. The DBA should be alert for instances in which users create disjoint queries or engage in excessive locking or long transactions. Most often, the user is not even aware that his activities are a problem to others. Usually all that the DBA has to do is point out the problem and make the user understand why his activities are causing a problem. Users who continue to create problems usually need a little more prodding.

Maintaining security

The data in a firm's computer system is often one of the most valuable of the company's assets. Among other things, the database often contains:

- customer information
- vendor information
- accounting and credit information
- mailing lists

- marketing data
- planning data
- product information
- personnel and salary information.

A good way to visualize the value of your database data is to imagine it placed in the hands of your company's biggest competitor. If this thought scares you, your data is probably worth protecting.

Security administration consists of protecting the data from loss and misuse. Your logging and archive plans probably handle the loss contingency, but how well are you protected from theft or misuse? More databases are being backed up onto DAT helical scan tapes. One of these tapes can hold up to 25 gigabytes of data. This means that someone could walk out of your computer room with all of your company's critical data in a shirt pocket.

If your system has connections to the outside world, either through modems, LANs, WANs, or Internet, you have potential security problems. The primary defense against security breaches is your operating system. This is analogous to locking your front door. Once this security is in place, the database itself must be made secure. By granting and limiting access using the GRANT command in SQL, you can further limit data that can be accessed by someone who gets into the operating system.

The primary purpose of the Informix security is provide secure access within an organization. The standard example is salary information. This information is sensitive and is usually available only to a few users. Since Informix SQL allows a table's owner to grant privileges on a table by column, it is possible to restrict access to certain columns for certain users. You can also use views to allow certain users to access only part of the data. Views, which are essentially "canned" queries, can be created by either DBAs or users and look just like tables to the users. In most instances, the user never realizes that he is dealing with data from multiple tables. By creating a view, the DBA has made details of the table layout irrelevant to the user.

An example of using a view to restrict access to certain information often arises when it is necessary for someone to only be able to view a subset of a table:

```
create table salary (name char(30), dept char(5),
                            salary int);
create view dp_salary as select * from salary where
                         dept="DP";
```

The manager of the Data Processing department could be granted select privileges on the view `dp_salary` and be able to view his own employees' salaries, but no others. (Of course, the DP people probably have total access to the system anyway, so you really can't keep anything secret from them!)

INTERFACING WITH YOUR PEERS

In any organization in which the DBA is not in total control of the entire computer system (all but the absolutely smallest applications), the DBA will have to work with and become interdependent with other professionals. As the organization becomes larger and more complex, the job functions often become narrower and more specific.

In a small operation, the DBA is often the UNIX system administrator, the development staff, the technician, and the troubleshooter. As the organization gets larger and more complicated, the DBA is forced to wear fewer hats. In the largest organizations, the DBA may be part of a team of DBAs. These DBAs may have their duties divided by function or divided by systems. In these larger organizations, it becomes more important that the DBA communicate and cooperate with many other professionals. The following list is not exclusive, but it includes the major players in the DBA's professional life.

The system administrator

The UNIX system administrator can be a tremendously valuable resource to the DBA. He can be a source of information about the inner workings of the computer system and can help guide the DBA around potential problems and pitfalls. Especially in areas of initial database setup and subsequent performance tuning, the system administrator can be a lifesaver. Often, the only person who really understands the file system and the raw devices is the system administrator. As you begin to design the disk layouts and to make decisions about striping and mirroring of the Informix database chunks and devices, you'll begin to appreciate the value of a good system administrator. If your initial installation requires UNIX kernel modifications, you'll probably have to have the system administrator do it. They're protective of such things as kernel configuration.

The system administrator is usually conversant with the performance monitoring and tuning tools available with your flavor of the operating system. As you begin to tune for maximum performance, you'll need to be able to differentiate between performance problems at the operating system level and at the Informix level.

Get on and stay on good terms with your system administrator. One good way to work is to cross-train with him or her. Let the system administrator learn enough about the database to serve as a backup DBA. Likewise, learn enough about the operating system to be able to serve as a backup system administrator. Together you'll be able to solve problems that neither of you could tackle alone.

Computer operators

If your organization is large enough to need and afford operators for your computer systems, these people can make your job much easier. Set up well documented written procedures for such day-to-day activities as doing database archives and handling logging tapes. Give them simple, user-oriented menus for the operational tasks that they can do. You'll appreciate having an operator available when you have a logfile or an archive problem at 3:00 A.M. It's much easier on the DBA if she can call into an operations center and walk someone through a fix instead of driving into the office.

Operators should know how to start and stop the database, how to start and stop applications, how to handle the archives and logs, and how to detect problems with the system. One of the most important things they need to know is when to call the DBA. It is important to set some guidelines and to make sure everyone knows when the problems need to be escalated to the DBA 's attention.

Informix support

Informix support policies change, so anything you read here may or may not still be in effect, but the general features remain the same.

If you're not participating in the InformixLink® bulletin board system, you should be. Informix has just recently included InformixLink with all of their support options. With InformixLink, you can call a common carrier telephone number and connect with an Informix system. This system contains e-mail, release information, bug lists, and a read-only access to the `comp.databases.informix` USENET group. You should be using this service regularly, even when you don't have problems. Pay special attention to the "tech alerts," which bring up items that could potentially become serious. This database is a limited version of the database that Informix support uses. The difference is that you can access it at any time and get immediate information. If you can get access to the Internet or to the USENET UNIX newsgroups, look into becoming a regular on the comp.databases.informix newsgroup. If you don't have access, there are several options for getting Internet access. Check with your system administrator or local UNIX gurus. Someone will probably know the best deal in your area. Questions or problems posted to comp.databases.informix often get multiple responses with detailed solutions, frequently containing programs or code fragments.

Your primary source of "real person" Informix support will probably be the support 800 number. As support hotlines go, this is pretty decent. You'll get a voice mail application that will walk you through to a real live person. You'll need your software serial number. It's probably a good idea for the DBA to have the Informix serial numbers tattooed on his arm. They'll get a lot of use. One thing about the hotline that is not immediately obvious is that there's a 911 feature. On dialing in, immediately punch 911 and you'll get to a support person quickly. Informix wants you to use this in emergencies only. They define an emergency as a production system down or seriously impaired. Use some discretion in taking this option. Don't cry "wolf" unless you really have an emergency.

Assuming that you're not taking the 911 option, you'll probably get a support person whose job is to log your call and put you in a queue to talk to another support person. When they give you a problem number, be sure and write it down. It'll make it much easier to follow up later. If you're lucky, you'll get to a technical support person on this call. If not, they'll have that person call you back. At some point in the process, you will probably be requested to rate the severity of your problem. If your system is down or seriously impaired, let them know it. They will put the more serious problems at the top of their queue. Don't be shy about requesting faster response or special services. Just about everyone in the support system has the ability to escalate your problem to a higher level. It doesn't hurt to ask, but be nice about it. You will be dealing with these people again.

Your first technical contact may or may not be tremendously helpful. Their usual response is to read sections of the manual to you. These people usually don't have access to the source code and pretty much have to follow the "company line." They do, however, have access to the complete Informix bugs database. If your problem has shown up before, they may have a quick solution for you. It's a good idea to prepare before talking to these first-line technical folks. Think about how you think Informix would classify your problem. The support staff will be looking up keywords in the database. Give them several options. You'll have a better chance of getting an answer.

In any questionable situation, they'll often recommend that you either reinstall or restore from your archive tape. If you're not pleased with this, don't be afraid to ask to speak to a manager or to escalate the problem to a higher level.

Your Informix account representative

The salespeople who handle your Informix account can be valuable resources as well. They will have access to local technical personnel who can help you solve problems with your systems. Salespeople have a much greater vested interested in keeping you happy as a user, and thus will often knock themselves out to help you out of a problem. If your account is of any significant size, they'll be able to provide evaluation copies of new software in the hope that you'll buy a ton of them. If you have temporary needs for software, such as special tools for conversion, they can often provide "loaner" software to help you out of a bind. Just remember how helpful they were when it comes time to write up purchase orders.

Hardware and operating system vendors

These are an often-neglected source of help for Informix-related solutions. Many vendors have close relationships with database vendors such as Informix. If your hardware or operating system vendor has such a relationship, and if you know how to get to the proper people, they can often be the best source of solutions to problems. Inquire about their other installations running Informix. Even if you're a small operation, your vendor may have other, larger accounts running Informix on the same hardware. Piggyback on top of the big guys. It doesn't hurt to check.

Users' groups

If you have a local Informix users' group, by all means get involved with it. You can usually find out about users' groups through your Informix account reps. If they don't know, check out the users' group sections on InformixLink. If there's not a local group, consider starting one. If you live in an area with many Informix users, this can become a most valuable resource. A users' group is a great tool for networking and providing mutual support and assistance with problems. It's a good source of information on new techniques and new products. It's also a good way to keep your eyes on the Informix job market, whether you're looking for another position for yourself or whether you're looking to hire someone. Don't be too blatant about soliciting employees or employers at users' groups. It's not considered good form to come in and try to hire everyone in sight!

Internet and the general user community

One of the major untapped resources out there is the collective knowledge of the twenty or so million Internet users. For those of you who are not familiar with the Internet, it is a network of thousands of computer systems tied together with communication lines. The Internet originated as a resource connecting academic and research institutions. As it expanded, it included military, government, and commercial interests. Up until recently, access to Internet was more or less restricted to those who had access through one of these member sites.

The Internet is now expanding into a more business and commercial role. This vast infrastructure is being opened to businesses and to private individuals as part of the "Information Superhighway" concept. Many of the online services such as Bix®, Compuserve®, Prodigy®, and NetCom® are offering inexpensive connections to the Internet without your having to go through the time, effort, and expense of actually connecting your computer systems to the network. For most of the reference tasks you'll be needing, this dial-up Internet access will be enough.

One of the big draws of the Internet is access to more than 6000 newsgroups that are part of the USENET news facility. These newsgroups are essentially bulletin board systems that cater to specific interests. Many of the newsgroups are exercises in anarchy or attempts to see how far the users can push the bounds of bad taste. Ignore them. If you look hard enough, you'll find plenty of hard, useful data.

Among the most valuable newsgroups to the Informix DBA is the `comp.databases.informix` newsgroup. You'll find discussions of new and old products, bug reports, workarounds, theoretical discussions, and much peer-to-peer interaction in this newsgroup. No matter what kind of problem or question you have, you can post it to this newsgroup and probably have three or four answers to it within the next day or two. You'll find many Informix employees active in the group and they are almost all helpful. For the DBA, access to this newsgroup is reason enough to join Internet.

Whenever you connect to the `comp.databases.informix` newsgroup, one of the first documents you need to locate is `informix.faq`. This file is the *frequently asked questions* file. This is a common service that is found in newsgroups on USENET. Reading the *faq* file in a newsgroup will give you a feeling for the types of information that is available in the newsgroup and will help you become familiar with the customs and procedures of the group. The `informix.faq` file contains many helpful hints for setting up, maintaining, and troubleshooting your OnLine system.

Also available on Internet are thousands of programs available for download for various operating systems. Most of them have source code and you'll have to tweak them a little for your own system and compile them, but this is a great source of software and ideas for software. There are also several places on the Internet where you can get Informix-specific software. Check the newsgroup for current archive sites.

Chapter 2

Inside the Black Box:

Understanding the OnLine Architecture

Database Administrators need an understanding of all of the factors that affect their systems. This includes appropriate operating system information, general information about Informix OnLine internal operations, and specific information regarding the individual site's setup.

This basic knowledge prepares the DBA for effectively managing the operations of an OnLine database. These items can be considered the prerequisites for becoming an effective DBA.

The actual day-to-day operations of an OnLine database are straightforward and relatively simple. Keep the system up. Make backups. Kill a few runaway jobs occasionally. When things are going smoothly, anyone can be the DBA. For the most part, OnLine is a reliable black box. You make requests of it. It gives you back data.

It's when things start to go wrong that the DBA needs to understand what's really going on inside the black box. When the system crashes, nobody wants to be the DBA. If you survive the encounter with angry users who've had the database blow up in the middle of **THE MOST IMPORTANT JOB THEY'VE EVER RUN**, you'll have to answer to management types who want to know what went wrong with the system and who to hang for doing it. Unless you are able to get inside the database and avoid the crash in the first place, or at least be able explain what happened, you'll be the most likely candidate for the lynch mob's noose.

I'm making a distinction between understanding the architecture of the database and understanding the data flow. Actually, these two areas of knowledge are so closely associated that they are effectively the same skill set. To understand how the data is managed within OnLine, one has to understand the architectural entities that manage this flow. Similarly, to understand the architectural entities, you must know how they are used and what they are used for, that is, how the data flows through the database architecture.

UNDERSTANDING THE DATA FLOW

We'll look at the data flow first. This will allow us to get an overall view of the needs that are met by the architectural elements. Once the general needs are understood, it is much easier to understand why Informix is doing what it does.

You'll find that the overall OnLine system architecture is a trade-off between multiple factors. Some decisions are made to enhance speed. Others sacrifice speed for security. Still others sacrifice speed and security for memory or disk savings. Like any vendor, the people at Informix have tried to present a product that offers trade-offs that are reasonable to the largest possible audience. In some cases, the DBA can work around these trade-offs by tuning the database or the application. Sometimes, though, the DBA just has to admit that the database has some weaknesses that need to be worked around. Although some of the limitations and constraints seem to be arbitrary, most often they make sense when viewed in the context of database operations as a whole.

INFORMIX-OnLine is a multiuser relational database that supports transactions. Understanding what these two terms really mean will make understanding the data flow much easier.

OnLine: a multiuser RDBMS

A multi-user relational database management system (RDBMS) must do much more than simply store and retrieve data. It must maintain the integrity of the data and ensure that the user is using the "cleanest" data available.

Most of the finer points of the multi-user design are there to help act as a traffic cop when different users want to work with the same data at once. OnLine has implemented a series of locks and isolation levels that manage these multi-user conflicts.

Locks are internal data flags that determine who gets to modify or read data at any particular time. OnLine has locks available at many levels, depending upon the user's needs. These locks are available at the database level, locking an entire database. Locks are available at the table level, locking an entire table. They are also available at the page level within a table. Page-level locking is the default in INFORMIX-OnLine. If you don't specify locking levels, you will get page-level locking. For the finest control of locking granularity, OnLine allows locks to be placed at the row level.   There are also locks at the index and at the byte level that are used internally by OnLine.

Along with locking comes the concept of isolation levels. Isolation levels are transaction-level commands that specify the levels of "cleanness" the user will accept. The least clean isolation level is *dirty read*, in which the user really doesn't care if someone is changing the data while the user is working with it. Isolation levels range up to *repeatable read* in which the database has to insure that a query will return the same rows if it is run twice in a row with no other actions in between. We'll go further into these items in the section on tuning.

OnLine: supports transactions

OnLine also supports the concept of transactions. Supporting transactions begins with the admission that lots of things can go wrong in an RDBMS. Most of these things can have disastrous results if the data is left in an inconsistent state.

The textbook example of transactions is designing a database to handle the accounting transactions at a bank. Such transactions consist of two balancing debit and credit transactions to two separate tables.   Suppose you have two tables, bank_cash_on_hand and customer_account. To simplify matters, consider that each table has one column, balance. When the customer comes in and withdraws $1000, the following two SQL statements are generated:

```
update bank_cash_on_hand set balance=balance - 1000;
update customer_account set balance=balance - 1000;
```

(Ignore the credits and debits, DBAs aren't accountants!)

Clearly if one of the above SQL statements completes successfully and the other fails, the bank's books will be out of balance. What kind of failure could cause this?

DBAs are finding new kinds of failures daily. A needed table could be locked. The disk could fill up. The system could crash after completing the first SQL statement. If the database were distributed over two machines, one machine could crash or the network connection between the two could fail. Possible failure modes could fill a book.

What transaction processing does is to consider the separate SQL statements as a single entity. Any changes made to the database while inside a transaction are not made permanent until the transaction is committed with an SQL statement. The database designer and application designers build their systems to assure that both parts of the transaction are completed before the program issues the commit statement. If the transaction is not committed, the changes will be rolled back to the original status.

If the particular database is using transactions, any changes are logged to logfiles as they are made. If, for some reason, the user decides either to not commit or to rollback the work, the logfiles are used to restore the data to its original status. The purposes and uses of these mechanisms will become clearer as we track the flow of data beginning from when the user makes a query.

TRACKING THE FLOW OF DATA

This is a greatly simplified view of the flow of data to, from, and inside an OnLine database server. We are assuming that the query initiates from a client application such as I-SQL or ESQL/C. Don't worry too much about the details now. Just get a feel for how the data flows. We're glossing over such items as data concurrency, transactions, and isolation levels for the time being. In this simplified view, we are also glossing over the differences between simply reading data and performing an update or an insert.

The data flows something like this:

- Client program formulates its SQL request. The client generates SQL requests to be presented to the server.

- Transmits it to the server. The request is transferred through UNIX pipes, in the case of the client and server being on the same machine. When the client and server are on different machines, the transmission is via UNIX pipes and a transport program such as I-Net or I-Star.

- Server optimizes the query and formulates a plan
  to retrieve the data.   The server process uses
  its cost-based optimizer to calculate the most
  effective order in which to access the database
  tables and which indexes to use.

- Server requests a page from the database. This
  may be a data page or an index page. The query
  may need the entire page or only one row. Either
  way, it still pulls in an entire page.

- Server searches for the page in the shared memory
  buffer pool.

- If the page is in the buffer pool, server tries to get
  a lock on the buffer page. If the lock succeeds,
  server process can read and/or modify the buffer.

- If the page is not in the buffer pool, look for a free
  buffer. If there is no buffer free, go to the LRU
  (Least Recently Used) queue and look for a free
  buffer. If no free buffer is found, flush out the
  oldest buffer and load the data into it.

- Server writes a copy of the unchanged original
  page to the physical log buffer.

- If logging is turned on and if data has been
  modified, the changes are logged to the logical
  log.

- Returns data to the client The server returns the
  data either over UNIX pipes, using I-Net or I-Star
  if the client and server are on separate machines.

- Server updates its disk with the new data. At
  some time, either through a foreground process or
  through the actions of the page flushers, pages in
  shared memory that have been modified are

flushed to the hard disk. These flushes do not
empty the buffer, they just copy it to disk.

To fully understand the flow of data, remember that just about everything is
buffered in shared memory and that access to any resource requires obtaining a latch on
the resource.

UNDERSTANDING THE PHYSICAL ARCHITECTURE

The DBA's goal is to understand what is going on inside the database. Informix OnLine
can be an intimidating, complex creation that uses as much shared memory as the disk
capacity of some personal computers. Shared memory sizes of 50 to 100 megabytes are
not uncommon. All of the files are usually invisible to the computer's operating system
and cannot be inspected as ordinary files.

Most of the workings of the database will show up as `sqlturbo` on a UNIX `ps`
listing, yielding very little data about what the process is really doing. Understanding
what's really happening means learning how to use the Informix tools provided for
peeking into the database and knowing how to interpret the data provided by these tools.

Processes and daemons

The OnLine system uses a *two-process* architecture. The database process, or
server process, does the actual manipulation of data within the system. This manipulation
consists of retrieving (querying) and modifying (inserting or updating) the data within the
database tables. This process is named `sqlturbo`. The other process is the *client*
process. This process is often I-SQL or ESQL/C. The client process is the interface
between the user and the database system. It interprets user input and commands, passing
the requests to the server process and receiving appropriate responses from the server.

Even when the client process is operating against a single database on a single
machine, the client/server model is in effect. When a transport mechanism such as
INFORMIX-Star or INFORMIX-Net is added to the OnLine system, the client and server
applications can be on different machines connected by a network. Thus, the OnLine
database is designed from the beginning as a client/server database.

Although the division of labor between client and server processes is efficient, one of the drawbacks is that each client, or *frontend* process must have a corresponding server, or *backend* process. Since these backend processes can use over a half megabyte of RAM, performance can deteriorate when available RAM begins to get low. This problem is often addressed by third-party "middleware." Middleware, also known as transaction monitors, accepts requests from multiple clients and calls the server only once. Informix Version 6.0 will eliminate or reduce the need for some middleware, as this new version will support a dynamic server environment that will allow the DBA to choose to start a given number of back-ends that will serve the requests of all the frontend processes. Version 6.0 will thus become a *multiprocess* architecture, rather than a two-process architecture.

Unlike the Oracle database, which allows the frontends to communicate with the backends using different methods, OnLine uses UNIX pipes to transmit the data from the frontends to the backends.

References to UNIX in general are full of discussions of *daemon* processes. In OnLine these daemon processes run in the background and are responsible for such jobs as handling the checkpoints and maintaining the shared memory. The daemon processes for the OnLine system will show up first in the `tbstat -u` output and can be identified by the trailing "D" (for daemon) or "F" (for page flusher) in the flags field. These daemons will show up in `ps` listings as `tbinit`.

Disk storage

To understand how OnLine deals with the data on the disk, the DBA needs to understand the differences between physical and logical storage. Physical storage refers to the actual devices or files that Informix uses to talk to the hardware by way of the UNIX operating system. Logical storage refers to the method in which the database views the data structure internally.

Units of disk storage

OnLine can address the disks directly, bypassing the UNIX filesystem. This results in efficiencies because the Informix disk access routines can be much more specialized than UNIX routines. These processes are designed strictly for database access, while the

UNIX routines have to be able to handle everything from disk input and output (I/O) to device I/O. Use of these raw devices by OnLine can take advantage of the fact that these raw devices are large, contiguous blocks. This allows OnLine to use more efficient I/O methods such as *big reads* and direct memory to disk transfers. The disk subsystem is just another resource to the OnLine system.

Disk space is made available to OnLine through the `tbmonitor` or `tbspaces` utilities. Using `tbmonitor` is somewhat safer for the DBA, as `tbmonitor` will respond with verification prompts on the line of "Do you really want to do something as stupid as this?"

Throughout this book, we will be using the `tbmonitor` command, because it is simple and intuitive and because it provides a menuing interface. Most if not all of the functions of `tbmonitor` can be called individually by using the underlying programs and the reader should realize that most of the work can be done directly from the command line should it be necessary.

`Tbmonitor` allows the DBA to assign parts of a raw UNIX device or a UNIX file to a dbspace. It will also allow the DBA to specify offsets into the device to be used. An offset is a certain number of kilobytes that OnLine is instructed to skip at the beginning of a device. OnLine does not place any data within the offset. In some systems, the formatting of a disk will place system data in the first few tracks of a device. If Informix writes over this, the disk format is blown. Specifying an offset allows the DBA to map around areas such as this.

Using offsets also can allow OnLine to place several chunks within the same UNIX device. If separate data areas are needed, this can be a boon to the DBA, as reformatting a hard disk is often quite a chore. Even if it were easy, the wise DBA will avoid making such UNIX-level changes lightly.

Chunks

The actual unit in which disk storage is made available to overall database access is the *chunk*. Chunks are sections of the hard disk. Chunks can be either actual UNIX files or portions of the disk outside the UNIX file system. Using the non-UNIX, or *raw* chunk is preferable to using UNIX files because the additional overhead of managing the UNIX file system will slow the system down.

Note that both raw and UNIX filesystems will show up in a listing of /dev. The difference is that the raw devices are never mounted and do not show up in a UNIX df output. They also never have a makefs done on them, as it is the makefs command that creates the UNIX file system.

For the most part, OnLine is happy with a chunk if it can identify it through a UNIX device. OnLine does not know whether the device is a single disk partition or a virtual device composed of multiple disks, perhaps striped and mirrored. It's all the same to Informix. Anything that the DBA can do to speed up access to the chunk will help Informix. If your UNIX supports striped or mirrored disks or RAIDS and if you have the option of using them, they will provide payoffs in the area of fault tolerance. There's seldom any reason not to use the UNIX disk striping, as striping generally provides overall improvements in disk performance. Mirroring and RAIDs can greatly increase your fault tolerance, but there is often a cost to balance against the improvements. Mirroring will usually slow down disk operations a bit, whether you are using the operating system's or Informix's mirroring. Using a RAID can also slow down writes to a disk. For some areas of high write activity, such as physical and logical logfile spaces, the DBA may want to explore using lower levels of RAID to optimize the write speeds.

The speed and efficiency of disk access is a powerful indicator of overall database speed. A little effort spent at the time the system is installed will pay you back many times over in better performance.

The OnLine manuals recommend that the actual names of the partitions that comprise a chunk not be used, but that they be linked to a more descriptive name. Thus, you may have a chunk that is physically known to UNIX as /dev/rdisk23h but known to Informix as /dev/chunk1. The DBA has used the UNIX ln command as follows:

```
ln /dev/rdisk23h /dev/chunk1
chown informix /dev/chunk1
chgrp informix /dev/chunk1
chmod 660 /dev/chunk1
```

Using links rather than actual device names serves more than a mnemonic purpose. If you ever lose a disk or have to rearrange your system's disk layout, the links will be much easier to set up than the actual devices. For instance, in the above example suppose you have a disk crash on /dev/rdisk23h. If you have called your chunk /dev/rdisk23h, you will be down until you physically replace /dev/rdisk23h.

The chunk name and its path are stored within the chunk reserved page for the OnLine system. When the system comes up, it will always look for chunks and paths found on this reserved page.

If you have used links, you can scrounge around and find another device to link to /dev/chunk1. This is important because disk problems usually lead to the need to restore your system from a tape archive. The tape archive program requires that the device names of the target system match the source system. The sizes of the target system's chunks must be at least as large as those of the corresponding source system's. They can be larger.

The ownership and group ownership is critical. If you have it wrong, you will often have no problems as long as user informix is using the system, but you will get error messages when another user tries to use the system.

Notice also that the UNIX /dev/rdisk*** devices are used. These are the character-based devices, not the block-based devices such as the /dev/disk*** devices. If you have accidentally created your raw devices on block devices, you may find that the initial process of disk initialization takes a long time. Subsequent accesses to the disk will take much longer than usual. This is because of the additional overhead of using the UNIX kernel services. Using the block devices will use the UNIX kernel buffer cache while using the character device will not. To guarantee that writes are flushed to disk in a timely manner, you must use the character device.

Chunks can be further divided into tablespaces and pages. Many chunks can be joined together to form dbspaces, which can be joined together to form databases. Lets look at the differences between these terms.

Pages

The smallest, most atomic unit of disk storage is the page. Page sizes are either 2K or 4K, depending upon your architecture. This page size is not changeable. Most of the reports generated by tbcheck and the other utilities express size in number of pages. SQL CREATE TABLE statements refer to sizes in kilobytes. Remember the difference.

Extents

Extents are groups of pages that are contiguous on the disk. The first extent is allocated to a tablespace at table creation time. When a table is created in the database, the table creator can specify the FIRST SIZE and NEXT SIZE in the CREATE TABLE statement. The tablespace is initially created with one extent with a size of FIRST SIZE (in kilobytes, not pages) As the table grows, additional extents of size NEXT SIZE (in kilobytes) are allocated. Although the space within an extent is contiguous, when additional extents are allocated they are not necessarily contiguous with the previous extent(s). OnLine attempts to allocate subsequent extents contiguously, but it there is not enough available space to add an extent of NEXT SIZE, OnLine will look elsewhere for the space. OnLine defaults to four pages FIRST SIZE and four pages NEXT SIZE if the table builder does not specify the sizes.

Tablespaces

A tablespace is a collection of all of the extents that are allocated for a given table. These extents hold the table's data and indexes and any free space that may be in the table. A tablespace can gain extents, but it never loses them unless the table is rebuilt, either as an explicit rebuild or by use of an ALTER INDEX TO CLUSTER statement or by issuing any ALTER TABLE statement that affects the structure of the table.

Dbspaces

A `dbspace` is a collection of chunks. Additional chunks can be added to a dbspace at any time if there is adequate disk space and an available UNIX device or file, and provided that there are adequate slots in the chunks pseudotable. Adding chunks can be done without bringing the database down.

The chunks are known as the *primary* chunk for the first chunk in a dbspace and as *secondary* chunks for any additional chunks added. There are also *mirror* chunks if you have chosen to use Informix mirroring. Databases and tables are created in particular `dbspaces`. Tables cannot span multiple `dbspaces`, but databases can span multiple `dbspaces`. If you run out of space in a dbspace, you must add another chunk. In a pinch, create a chunk out of a UNIX file until you can get your system cleaned out.

It is important to note that once added, a chunk cannot be dropped. The DBA has to drop the entire dbspace to clear up its chunks. This will change in Version 6.0, which will allow you to drop unused chunks from a dbspace.

Blobspaces

A blob is a "binary large object." Blobs are used to store text or binary data. Blob storage can be used for such items as compressed picture files, encoded voice data, word processing documents, and the like. Blob data can be stored either in ordinary tablespaces or in dedicated blobspaces. In most cases, using blobspaces is more efficient, since the blobspace creator can specify the page sizes for the blobspace. Using larger page sizes for blobspaces is a good way to reduce the number of locks required for updating the blobs. This will also allow the engine to handle the large I/O requests that are used to access blobs much more efficiently. Thus, blobspaces can be tailor-made to hold particular types of blob data.

HOW UNIX MANAGES MEMORY

The UNIX operating system is responsible for allocating sufficient memory resources for all processes running on the system. UNIX operating systems allocate three separate areas in memory for each process.

Text segment

Contains machine-level instructions for the program or process's operation. These instructions can be used by multiple processes without loading individual copies of the code if the code is written to be *reentrant*. Such reentrant code is code that is written to resolve multi-user conflicts caused by several processes calling the shared code simultaneously.

Programs running under UNIX use shared text segments and therefore share code. This greatly cuts down on memory requirements, as multiple client processes can access the same code without having multiple copies of the code in memory. Multiple server programs also share common code.

Data segment

Contains global variables, buffers, and other data structures to be accessed by the process. These data segments are private to each sqlturbo.

Stack space

Contains internal storage for individual processes. Largely invisible to the user. OnLine processes maintain individual stack spaces and these areas of memory are not shared.

HOW ONLINE MANAGES SHARED MEMORY

Shared memory is an area of the system's memory that is available to all OnLine users. Much of the shared memory is used by buffers. Using shared memory for these buffers enables OnLine to pool its memory resources for multiple servers rather than set aside individual buffer areas for each process.

These buffers are used to buffer pages to and from the physical disk storage on the system. Only the most recently used pages are kept in the shared memory buffers. Thus, if a needed disk page is in the buffers, it will be the latest version and can be accessed quickly. As the buffers begin to fill or as the system detects the need to flush the buffers, buffered pages are written back to disk. When the system needs to read data from the disk, it looks for the page in the buffers first. If it's there, the page is accessed from the buffer, saving on time-consuming disk I/O. If the needed page is not in the buffers, the system chooses a free buffer, if there is one. If there is no free buffer, the system forces the oldest page (the *least recently used*, or *LRU*) to flush to disk, freeing up that page.

OnLine shared memory segments are allocated by database instance. Each instance will maintain its own shared memory and each instance will require adequate resources to be allocated for its use. The DBA has control over many parameters that determine the size and division of the shared memory.

The `tbmonitor` utility allows for the sizing of the shared memory. As different parameters are changed, the program will indicate how much shared memory is needed.

If your UNIX kernel has been configured with adequate shared memory resources, you can alter the amount of shared memory used by changing the parameters in tbmonitor. Always add a little "fluff factor" to the suggested shared memory. For instance, if tbmonitor indicates that 13 megabytes shared memory is needed, make sure that UNIX is ready to give you an extra megabyte or so. This will allow you to have some flexibility for later tuning of the OnLine parameters without having to rebuild the kernel.

CONTENTS OF ONLINE SHARED MEMORY

OnLine uses its shared memory to store system information as well as to buffer actual pages from the database. This system information keeps track of system resources and their availability to the user.

This data is stored in arrays and other data structures within OnLine shared memory. These data structures are created and sized at the time the shared memory is initialized. The parameters come from the $TBCONFIG file for that particular database instance. The tbmonitor utility writes to the $TBCONFIG file as its parameters change. These data structures are accessible to the DBA only through the use of OnLine or other utilities, mainly tbstat.

These data structures, or *pseudotables* contain information that is critical to the DBA. A large portion of the task of understanding what is going on in the database consists of understanding how to use tbstat to decipher the contents of the pseudotables. The major areas and pseudotables in the shared memory structure are:

Latches

An inherent problem with a multi-user database is the situation in which multiple users need concurrent access to a system resource. Shared memory is such a resource, and OnLine needs to consider what happens when there are conflicts in accessing shared memory resources.

Even though a pseudotable itself may contain locks that grant access to a database resource, access to the pseudotable itself must be controlled. OnLine does this through *latches*.

A latch is a data mechanism that allows a user to modify a system resource. Before a user or process is allowed to modify a system resource, it must first acquire the latch that is associated with the resource. There is not actually a separate pseudotable for latches. because the latch data element is the first item in its respective lock table.

Latches can be viewed by using the `tbstat -s` command:

```
joe 53> tbstat -s
RSAM Version 5.01.UC1    -- OnLine -- Up 8 days 17:34:19 -- 18704 Kbytes


Latches with lock or user set
name       address   lock wait user
bbf[0]     e075adb8 1    0    e0002770
physlog    e0001670 1    1    e0002e30
physb2     e0001694 1    1    e0002470
bf[3276]   e072dcac 1    0    e00024d0
pt[33]     e067afa0 1    0    e0002590
pt[48]     e067bdec 1    0    e0002a10
bbf[0]     e075adb8 1    0    e0002a10
bh[4749]   e06e9cb0 1    0    e0001e70
bbf[0]     e075adb8 1    0    e0002a10
bbf[0]     e075adb8 1    0    e0002a10
tblsps     e00000f8 1    0    e0001e70
LRU13      e000046c 1    0    e0002230


(Note:  This is a composite run over several tbstat -s invocations.
 The data is not necessarily consistent.  It's just a format sample)
```

Locks

The locks pseudotable is one of the busiest of the pseudotables. The lock table is broken down into a number of linked lists, each controlled by its own latch. The server uses a hashing mechanism based upon the lock requested to control access to the correct linked list. As access to this locks table is controlled by a a small number of latches resource, the locks table can become a bottleneck in active systems. There is one lock for every OnLine resource that is shared or is otherwise in use. Entries in the lock table are cheap, they use only a small amount of shared memory. Configure your system for as many as you can, within reason. Lock configuration depends on the level of locking that you are using for your tables. If you have a 200,000 row table with row level locking, you will need 200,000 locks to do an update to every row in that table. If you are using the default page-level locking you can get by with fewer locks.

One lock space in the lock table is used for each lock, whether that lock is a very high-level lock like a database lock or a very low-level lock like a row lock. Suppose you were doing an insert of a million rows into a table. The target table is set for row-level locking. Attempting this insert would cause an overflow of the locks table and would cause the job to crash unless you had a million lock table entries. There is a simple rule that helps you avoid this locking problem:

Always lock the target table in exclusive mode, if you can.

The "if you can" is an important caveat here. Locking the target table means that no other users can access the table while the table is locked. If this causes a concurrency problem with your operations, you'll have to split the insert into several separate jobs or, better yet, use the dbload utility to load the rows without having to worry about locks (or long transactions).

Here's an example:

```
insert into new_table (select * from million_row_table);
```

This would use a million locks if new_table had been created or altered to row level locking, but the following would use just one lock (assuming no indexes):

```
begin work;
lock table new_table in exclusive mode;
insert into new_table (select * from
million_row_table);
commit work;
```

Locks can be viewed by using the tbstat -k command:

```
joe  42>tbstat -k

RSAM Version 5.01.UC1   -- OnLine -- Up 7 days 23:48:24 -- 18704 Kbytes
Locks
address  wtlist   owner     lklist   type    tblsnum  rowid   size
e0057628 0        e00020b0 0         HDR+S   1000002  201     0
e0058e68 0        e0002230 0             S   1000002  202     0
e0059a28 0        e0002bf0 0             S   1000002  202     0
   3 active, 200000 total, 16384 hash buckets
```

Chunks and dbspaces

The chunk pseudotable is actually two pseudotables, one for the primary and one for the mirrored chunks. The chunk pseudotable keeps track of each chunk that has been allocated in an OnLine system. The total number of allowable chunks is the tunable parameter CHUNKS in tbmonitor and in the $TBCONFIG file.

One latch controls access to the chunk pseudotable. The dbspaces pseudotable registers all dbspaces in the system. Access to this table is also controlled by one latch.

There are two tbstat options that can view chunk and dbspace information. To see the space utilization of the database, use the tbstat -d command:

```
joe  43>tbstat -d
RSAM Version 5.01.UC1   -- OnLine -- Up 7 days 23:48:38 -- 18704 Kbytes


Dbspaces
address  number  flags   fchunk   nchunks  flags   owner     name
e0016e88 1       1       1        3        N       informix  rootdbs
e0016eb8 2       1       4        2        N       informix  logspace
e0016ee8 3       1       5        2        N       informix  dbspace1
e0016f18 4       1       7        2        N       informix  logspace2
e0016f48 5       1       10       1        N       informix  slowdbspace
   5 active, 20 total
```

```
Chunks
address   chk/dbs offset    size      free      bpages    flags pathname
e0014e78 1    1    0         135000    35718               PO-   /dev/rootdbs3
e0014f10 2    1    0         57000     56997               PO-   /dev/rootdbs1
e0014fa8 3    1    0         75000     74997               PO-   /dev/rootdbs2
e0015040 4    2    0         147500    24542               PO-   /dev/log1
e00150d8 5    3    0         812500    74310               PO-   /dev/chunk1
e0015170 6    3    0         677000    78338               PO-   /dev/chunk2
   6 active, 27 total
```

To see read and write information regarding your database's chunks, use the tbstat -D command:

```
joe   44>tbstat -D
RSAM Version 5.01.UC1   -- OnLine -- Up 7 days 23:48:53 -- 18704 Kbytes

Dbspaces
address   number   flags    fchunk   nchunks  flags    owner     name
e0016e88 1         1        1        3        N        informix rootdbs
e0016eb8 2         1        4        2        N        informix logspace
e0016ee8 3         1        5        2        N        informix dbspace1
e0016f18 4         1        7        2        N        informix logspace2
e0016f48 5         1        10       1        N        informix dbspace3
   5 active, 20 total

Chunks
address   chk/dbs offset    page Rd   page Wr   pathname
e0014e78 1    1    0         731422    1030390   /dev/rootdbs3
e0014f10 2    1    0         114001    0         /dev/rootdbs1
e0014fa8 3    1    0         150001    0         /dev/rootdbs2
e0015040 4    2    0         233963    120000    /dev/log1
e00150d8 5    3    0         8498773   238186    /dev/chunk1
e0015170 6    3    0         10034058  178169    /dev/chunk2
e0015208 7    4    0         341480    173365    /dev/log3
e00152a0 8    2    0         239961    120000    /dev/log2
e0015338 9    4    0         193767    164848    /dev/log4
e00153d0 10   5    0         1628350   114065    /dev/chunk3
   10 active, 27 total
```

Users

Every time a server process starts up, it attaches to the shared memory of the OnLine system. When this occurs, the user obtains an entry in the users pseudotable and certain information, such as process ID and user name, are stored. Besides server processes, some OnLine administrative functions occupy a user slot. This data can be seen using `tbstat`.

You can also see some information about OnLine users by using the UNIX `ps` command. There is always a `tbinit` process running. It started up the shared memory in the first place. If your system is using page cleaners, you will see one user `tbpgcl` for every page cleaner that you have configured. With some versions of UNIX, the page cleaners will be identified as `tbinit` rather than as `tbpgcl`.

OnLine has a "trapdoor" built into its user table that often saves the DBA when the user table fills. It saves the last user entry for a `tbmonitor` process, whether there are existing `tbmonitor` processes running or not. The DBA can always get into the system as a user through `tbmonitor`.

To see the contents of the users pseudotable, use the `tbstat -u` command:

```
joe   46>tbstat -u

RSAM Version 5.01.UC1    -- OnLine -- Up 7 days 23:49:06 -- 18704 Kbytes

Users
address   flags    pid    user      tty      wait   tout locks  nreads nwrites
e0001b70 ------D 555     informix console  0       0    0      6746    2607
e0001bd0 ------D 0       informix console  0       0    0      0       0
e0001c30 ------F 556     informix          0       0    0      0       0
e0001c90 ------F 557     informix          0       0    0      0       0
e0001cf0 ------F 558     informix          0       0    0      0       0
e0002890 ------- 4143    dba       -       0       0    1      2907    148
e00028f0 ------- 16460   dba       -       0       0    1      54972   4767
e00029b0 ------- 12247   support   -       0       0    1      100726  6677
e0002b90 ------- 12245   support   -       0       0    1      100554  6651
e0002bf0 --B---- 12246   support   -       0       0    1      101859  6650
e0002c50 ------- 13547   dba       -       0       0    1      6522    1741
e0002e30 --A---M 2740    informix ttyi02   0       0    0      0       0
  42 active, 150 total
```

Transactions

OnLine versions beginning with version 5.0 include transaction information in the `tbstat -u` output. This is useful in looking at distributed transactions across different databases on different machines. It's not too useful for simple applications, since each user will have only one transaction going at a time. To see users and their transactions (OnLine 5.0 and later) use the `tbstat -u` command:

```
joe  27>     tbstat -u
RSAM Version 5.01.UC1     -- OnLine -- Up 6 days 06:40:42 -- 12976 Kbytes
Users
address  flags   pid    user     tty      wait      tout locks nreads
nwrites
e0001bbc ------D 3954    informix ttyp8    0         0    0     1348      16
e0001c28 ------D 0       informix ttyp8    0         0    0     0         0
e0001c94 ------F 3956    informix          0         0    0     0         0
e0001d00 ------F 3957    informix          0         0    0     0         0
e000227c ------- 16936   dba      -        0         0    1     0         1
e00022e8 ------- 16965   dba      -        0         0    1     0         19
e0002354 ------- 16957   dba      -        0         0    1     0         16
e00023c0 ------- 16948   dba      -        0         0    1     0         1
e000242c ------- 22832   tony     -        0         0    1     0         0
e0002498 ------- 23247   dba      ttyp1    0         0    1     158       18
e0002504 ------- 23246   dba      ttyp1    0         0    1     510       33
   11 active, 110 total


Transactions
address  flags user       locks log begin isolation retrys coordinator
e0004a24 A---- e0001bbc 0       0           NOTRANS   0
e0004c04 A---- e0001c28 0       0           NOTRANS   0
e0004de4 A---- e000242c 1       0           COMMIT    0
e0006464 A---- e000227c 1       0           COMMIT    0
e0006644 A---- e00022e8 1       0           COMMIT    0
e0006824 A---- e0002354 1       0           COMMIT    0
e0006a04 A---- e00023c0 1       0           COMMIT    0
e0006be4 A---- e0001d6c 1       0           COMMIT    0
e0006dc4 A---- e0002498 1       0           COMMIT    0
e0006fa4 A---- e0002504 1       0           COMMIT    0
   10 active, 110 total
```

Tblspaces

The tblspace pseudotable tracks open tablespaces in the system. All tables are tracked here, whether they are permanent or temporary. Temporary tables that are created because of ORDER BY clauses also receive entries in this table. If multiple processes are accessing the tablespace, a single entry will be in the pseudotable.

To see the tablespaces in use, use the `tbstat -t` command:

```
joe  30>    tbstat -t
RSAM Version 5.00.UC2    -- OnLine -- Up 6 days 06:41:15 -- 12976 Kbytes


Tblspaces
n address   flgs ucnt tblnum    physaddr npages nused  npdata nrows   nextns
0 e00b85f4 1    1    1000001   10000e   5405   408    0      0       1
1 e00b88b8 1    1    2000001   200004   905    2      0      0       1
2 e00b8b7c 1    1    3000001   300004   10005  940    0      0       1
3 e00b8e40 1    1    4000001   500004   1355   2      0      0       1
4 e00b9104 1    19   3000002   300005   64     59     35     627     8


5 active, 1100 total, 512 hash buckets
```

Buffers

OnLine buffers are by far the largest portion of the shared memory. The internal data structure for the buffer is a three-fold structure.

First, there is the actual page from the disk itself. The buffer holds the entire page, so another structure is used to track the information about the page itself. This is the buffer header table. The third structure is a hash table to simplify locating an individual buffer.

The `tbstat` command comes in two flavors, depending upon whether you want to see just the buffers in use or whether you want to see all buffer data. To see the status of buffers currently in use by OnLine, use the `tbstat -b` command:

```
joe  31> tbstat -b
RSAM Version 4.10.UD4   -- OnLine -- Up 8 days 17:26:14 -- 18704 Kbytes


Buffers
address  user    flgs pagenum  memaddr  nslots pgflgs xflgs owner
waitlist
```

address	user	flgs	pagenum	memaddr	nslots	pgflgs	xflgs	owner	waitlist
e070976c	0	0	651566	e0937000	29	1	400	e00023b0	0
e06fff6c	0	6	50479c	e0807000	23	1	0	0	0
e07052ac	0	0	504894	e08ad800	77	10	400	e00020b0	0
e071c7ac	0	2	50af71	e0b97800	101	90	100	0	0
e072ae6c	0	0	5047b1	e0d65000	29	1	400	e00020b0	0
e073feac	0	0	50661f	e1005800	1	90	400	e00026b0	0
e072876c	0	0	537ffb	e0d17000	51	90	400	e0002530	0
e072986c	0	2	56c416	e0d39000	48	90	100	0	0

```
 2526 modified, 4750 total, 8192 hash buckets, 2048 buffer size
```

(NOTE: this output is a composite output from several runs of tbstat.
There may be inconsistencies because of this. It's just a sample)

To see the status of *all* the buffers, use the `tbstat -B` command:


```
joe 35> tbstat -B
RSAM Version 4.10.UD4   -- OnLine -- Up 7 days 23:51:48 -- 18704 Kbytes


Buffers
address  user    flgs pagenum  memaddr  nslots pgflgs xflgs owner waitlist
```

address	user	flgs	pagenum	memaddr	nslots	pgflgs	xflgs	owner	waitlist
e06fa9ac	0	6	69c58b	e075b800	27	1	0	0	0
e06faaac	0	6	57a379	e075d800	144	10	0	0	0
e06faaec	0	6	60f8e3	e075e000	36	90	0	0	0

```
..
..  (continues for all of your defined buffers)
..
```

address	user	flgs	pagenum	memaddr	nslots	pgflgs	xflgs	owner	waitlist
e06facac	0	6	66d87f	e0761800	82	90	0	0	0
e06facec	0	6	69beac	e0762000	75	90	0	0	0
e06fad2c	0	6	69c49f	e0762800	27	1	0	0	0

```
 284 modified, 4750 total, 8192 hash buckets, 2048 buffer size
```

LRUs

The Least Recently Used (LRU) queues are data structures that track usage of the buffer pool. The queues are allocated in pairs, one for *clean* data and one for *dirty* data. Data is clean if the buffer is not flagged as having been modified. The queues are arranged so that the most recently used buffers are found at the head of the queue.

When a buffer is accessed, it is moved to the beginning of the queue. Buffers at the least recently used end of each queue (dirty queue and clean queue) are the ones that are used first for storing new data from disk or for flushing to disk.

There is one latch for each queue, making two latches for every queue pair. The number of LRU queues is determined by the $TBCONFIG parameter LRUS.

To see the status of the LRU queues use the tbstat -R command:

```
joe  57>tbstat -R

RSAM Version 4.10.UD4    -- OnLine -- Up 7 days 23:53:44 -- 18704 Kbytes

16 buffer LRU queues
LRU  0:     6 ( 0.9%) modified of  643 total
LRU  1:     6 ( 1.0%) modified of  631 total
LRU  2:     8 ( 1.2%) modified of  674 total
LRU  3:     6 ( 1.1%) modified of  557 total
LRU  4:    13 ( 2.4%) modified of  551 total
LRU  5:     6 ( 1.0%) modified of  601 total
LRU  6:     8 ( 1.4%) modified of  569 total
LRU  7:     4 ( 0.8%) modified of  524 total

57 dirty, 4750 queued, 4750 total, 8192 hash buckets, 2048 buffer size
start clean at 60% dirty, stop at 50%; first pass search 70%
```

Page cleaners

As the buffer pool fills with data, it becomes necessary for some buffers to be reused to hold new data. It is advantageous for there to always be some clean buffers on the queue. If OnLine needs to bring data in from the disk into a buffer, it is most efficient if the target buffer is a clean buffer, since clean buffers can be overwritten with the new data.

A dirty buffer is another thing. If there are no clean buffers, OnLine has to use a dirty buffer. First, the dirty buffer needs to be written out (flushed) to disk. Then OnLine brings the new data into the newly-clean buffer. This creates more load for the engine, as the engine has to perform the flush. This is known as a foreground (fg) write. If you are getting many foreground writes, the buffers need cleaning more often.

The preferred way of cleaning the buffers is through the actions of the page cleaner daemons. Their actions are controlled by the Informix parameters, LRU_MAX_DIRTY and LRU_MIN_DIRTY. As each LRU queue becomes populated with dirty buffers, it will eventually reach the LRU_MAX_DIRTY percentage. When the buffer reaches this percentage of dirtiness, the page cleaner daemon is awakened and it begins cleaning the buffers. When the dirtiness is down to the LRU_MIN_DIRTY percentage, the page cleaner goes back to sleep.

The defaults are usually 60 percent for MAX and 50 percent for MIN. These parameters are tunable. The object is to reduce the foreground writes to a minimum, as these are engine processes. We'll talk extensively about tuning these parameters in Chapter 8.

To see the status of the page cleaners (flushers), use the `tbstat -F` command:

```
joe  59>tbstat -F

RSAM Version 5.01.UC1  -- OnLine -- Up 7 days 23:53:56 -- 18704 Kbytes

Fg Writes       LRU Writes     Idle Writes      Chunk Writes
0               279744          5142            471793

address  flusher  snooze   state    data
e0001c30 0          60        I        0         = 0
e0001c90 1          60        I        0         = 0
e0001cf0 2          60        I        0         = 0
e0001d50 3          60        I        0         = 0
e0001db0 4          60        I        0         = 0
e0001e10 5          60        I        0         = 0
         states: Exit Idle Chunk Lru
```

Logs

There are two types of logs in the OnLine system, physical logs and logical logs. The physical logs store pages of data or indexes from the buffer pool as the pages are modified.   The physical log is used primarily in the fast recovery process that accompanies the startup of the database. It also coordinates with the `tbtape` archiving processes when an archive is running.

Access to the physical log is through two physical log buffers, which are periodically flushed to the actual physical log. There is one latch controlling access to each of the two physical log buffers.

The logical logs are areas of the disk (often in their own dbspace) in which OnLine stores records of transactions that are in progress or are completed. OnLine begins with three logs in the root dbspace. The size of these logs is a tunable parameter in `tbmonitor`. It is very important to give thought to the sizing of your logical logs before you begin to initialize your OnLine system. The sizing of the logical logs can only be changed by reinitializing the entire database. This is a major task, so it is important to get the sizing right the first time. Additional logs can be added and become available for use only after an archive is done. Access to the logical logs is through three built-in logical log buffers, each controlled by its own latch.

To see the status of your logs, use the `tbstat -l` command:

```
joe  62>tbstat -l

RSAM Version 5.01.UC1     -- OnLine -- Up 7 days 23:54:27 -- 18704 Kbytes

Physical Logging

Buffer bufused  bufsize   numpages numwrits pages/io
  P-1  69        128       713655   5901       120.94
       phybegin physize  phypos    phyused  %used
       117202   6000     2999      69         1.15
```

```
Logical Logging
Buffer  bufused  bufsize  numrecs    numpages numwrits recs/pages pages/io
  L-1   8        64       31030148   668262   21047    46.4       31.8
```

address	number	flags	uniqid	begin	size	used	%used
e06d25d8	1	F------	0	400b8e	30000	0	0.00
e06d25f4	2	F------	0	4080be	30000	0	0.00
e06d2610	3	F------	0	40f5ee	30000	0	0.00
e06d262c	4	F------	0	10126e	30000	0	0.00
e06d2648	5	F------	0	10879e	30000	0	0.00
e06d2664	6	F------	0	10fcce	30000	0	0.00
e06d2680	7	F------	0	416b1e	30000	0	0.00
e06d269c	8	F------	0	800003	30000	0	0.00
e06d26b8	9	F------	0	700a94	30000	0	0.00
e06d26d4	10	F------	0	707fc4	30000	0	0.00
e06d26f0	11	F------	0	70f4f4	30000	0	0.00
e06d270c	12	F------	0	716a24	30000	0	0.00
e06d2728	13	F------	0	900003	30000	0	0.00
e06d2744	14	U---C-L	2296	907533	30000	14897	49.66

Profiles

The profile pseudotable contains various items related to the performance of the OnLine system. It includes items such as cache hit ratios for reading and writing, number of different types of calls to the database, number of times pseudotables overflowed, and number of times a process had to wait for different resources.

This is one of the most important pseudotables, as this is just about the only source of data about the performance of the database. You'll be doing `tbstat -p` in your sleep the more you work on tuning the database.

For an overall performance profile, use the `tbstat -p` command:

```
joe  63>tbstat -p

RSAM Version 5.01.UC1    -- OnLine -- Up 7 days 23:54:38 -- 18704 Kbytes

Profile
dskreads pagreads bufreads %cached dskwrits pagwrits bufwrits %cached
14970755 22166265 498552631 97.00    543747   2139408   49870693 98.91


isamtot   open     start    read     write    rewrite  delete   commit   rollbk
424714409 5813437  23348999 175473799 10989374 5499045  2603325  8699910  101


ovtbls    ovlock   ovuser   ovbuff   usercpu  syscpu    numckpts flushes
0         0        0        0        387006.97 41611.33 294      587


bufwaits lokwaits lockreqs deadlks  dltouts  lchwaits ckpwaits compress
21748    8046     476500421 9        0        1594907  1664     2220019
```

SUMMARY

This has been an overview of the contents of the OnLine shared memory. As we look more at tuning and troubleshooting in future chapters, you will become much more familiar with the meanings of the data returned by the various tbstat options.

Chapter 3

Understanding Logging

GENERAL LOGGING CONCEPTS

OnLine keeps track of changes to its data by the use of physical and logical log files. There are two types of logfiles, physical and logical. Each log file is accessed through buffers in the shared memory. You need to make the distinction between the log buffers, which are areas of shared memory and the log files, which are areas of the disk that receive data from the buffers. The shared memory is by definition transitory. If the system goes down, this data is lost. The logfiles on disk are persistent. Assuming there are no hardware problems with the disk, their contents survive system crashes.

The essential point of difference between the physical and logical logs is really indicated by their names. The physical logs are simply images of the pages as they come in from the disk system. They are essentially reference points to bring the system back to a known state. The logical logs represent a chronological record of data changes that occur within the database. Should the engine receive a ROLLBACK WORK command, it is able to go to the logical logs and undo any transactions that are affected by the ROLLBACK WORK command.

Whenever a data page is needed by a process, the engine first looks in its shared memory. If the data page is not found in shared memory, it is pulled in from the disk into a page buffer in shared memory. As soon as any data on this page is scheduled for modification, the page is copied into the physical log buffer. This occurs only on the first update to the particular pages. This before image data in the physical log buffer is then flushed out to the physical log on disk. This flushing of the physical log buffer to the physical log on disk occurs when the buffer is full, during checkpoints, or when a page in both the shared memory buffers and the physical log buffer is flushed to disk.

The physical log buffer is actually a pair of buffers in shared memory, each of which is the size indicated in the `tbconfig` file. This "double buffering" allows the system to switch between the first and second buffers so that no time or data is lost while the other is flushing to the physical log on disk. These buffers are identified as `P-1` and `P-2` in the `tbstat -l` output.

Likewise, the logical log buffer is actually three separate buffers in shared memory, each the size indicated in the `tbconfig` file. This "triple buffering" allows one buffer to flush while one of the others fills, and provides an additional buffer in case the active buffer fills up before the first buffer is completely flushed.

Flushing the physical log buffer to the physical log on disk occurs in three separate circumstances. In the first instance, the physical log buffer becomes full. When this occurs, the system switches to the other physical log buffer and flushes the full buffer to disk.

The second instance is somewhat more subtle. This flush must occur before any page cleaner activity flushes pages in the buffer back to the disk. Here, it is possible that a page in the buffer pool has been modified, causing its before image to be written to the physical log buffer. If a page cleaner fires up in this case, it is possible for the modified page to be on disk while the original before image is still in the physical log buffer. This gives rise to the rule that flushing a before image of a page to disk must occur before the actual modified page can be flushed to disk.

The third instance in which the physical log buffer is flushed is at a checkpoint. The first step of a checkpoint calls for this flushing of the buffer.

When any data is changed in the shared memory page buffer, the engine checks to see whether or not anything needs to be logged to the logical logfile. In addition to changes that are either specifically or implicitly part of a transaction, the engine also logs SQL data definition language (DDL) statements, changes to the OnLine configuration such as changes in chunks, `dbspaces`, and blobspaces, and any checkpoint events. All of these loggable events are first placed into the logical log buffer and then flushed back to disk.

The physical and logical logs are used by the engine in three major situations:

Transaction rollback

If a SQL command or a series of SQL commands is executed within a BEGIN WORK/COMMIT WORK structure, the engine will not commit any of the transactions until it receives the OK to "commit work." If something fails, either in a SQL statement or for outside reasons, the engine uses the information in the logical logfiles to roll back the transaction. This brings the database back to a consistent state as though the transaction had never begun.

Restoring from tape

In the event that the data is completely lost as the result of mechanical or human error and it is necessary to recover the entire system from tape, the tbtape program first loads the data from the last archive. This is either one tape from a Level 0 archive, or a combination of Level 0, Level 1, and Level 2 archive tapes. After the last archive tape is loaded, the engine then applies data contained in the logfiles that have been saved to tape. This brings the database up to its condition before the crash. After all of the logged data is back in the system, any transactions that were not yet committed at the time of the crash are rolled back to insure the consistency of the instance. If the instance was using buffered logging, it is possible that some of the last transaction data will be lost due to the loss of data in the buffer.

Fast recovery

Most of the time when the system goes down, it is not necessary to recover from tape. OnLine has a robust recovery process that is part of its shared memory initialization process. When the shared memory is initialized upon restart after a crash, the engine goes into *fast recovery* mode, which is automatic and not under control of the DBA. In fast recovery, the instance is first brought back into a known good status as evidenced by the condition at the last checkpoint by restoring data from the physical log. After this known status is attained, OnLine then goes to the logical log files and finds the location of the last checkpoint. From that point onward, the engine applies all of the transactions that it finds in the logical log files. Finally, it rolls back any changes that were made inside a transaction and for which it finds no COMMIT WORK entry in the log.

When the system is halted properly, the physical logfile is flushed to disk as part of a final checkpoint that occurs when the system leaves online status and becomes quiescent. When the system crashes, the physical logfile is left with data in it. This is what tells the `tbinit` process that the physical recovery is necessary.

Often the fast recovery process is not fast at all. The speed of the fast recovery depends upon many factors, including the length of time from the last checkpoint and the amount of work that has been done since then. This time can often be estimated by checking the number of active logfiles. Whenever you are forced into a fast recovery, it helps to note the number of logs that it has to go through and to note the amount of time it takes to recover. Whenever your system crashes in real life, one of the most pressing questions you'll receive is "How long until the database is up?" Any time you find yourself waiting through a fast recovery, note how many logfiles are involved and time the recovery. Developing such a rule of thumb based on logfiles is better than just answering with an "I dunno."

LOGGING MODES

The OnLine engine provides for three modes of logging operation. The selection of logging mode is important to the issue of data recovery in the event of a system crash.

Until the contents of the logical log buffer are flushed to disk, the transaction log records that the buffer holds are at risk should the system go down. If the system crashes with data in the logical log buffers, any changes to the database held in the buffer will not be recoverable. Thus, the three logging modes represent increasing degrees of data survivability.

No logging

If the database is created with no logging, there is still a small amount of activity directed towards the logical logs and logical log buffers. Any statement that uses the data definition language (DDL) will result in entries into the logical logs, as will some internal activities of the engine.

In fast recovery of a non-logging database, only the physical log records are read back into the system during fast recovery. After these pages are read back into shared memory, the system does an automatic checkpoint as part of the fast recovery process. This brings the database into consistency as of the last checkpoint prior to the crash. In databases that use logging, this checkpoint is followed by rolling forward the transaction data from the time of the last checkpoint, followed by rolling back the non-committed transactions. These final two steps do not occur in the case of a database created with no logging. The effect of this is that without the use of logging, you can never recover any further than your last checkpoint. Work that occurred between the last checkpoint and the crash will be lost.

Non-logging databases are useful in cases where the data flow is such that transactions can be recreated in the event of a crash. Often, batch operations against a non-logging database will meet this criteria. Also, non-logging databases are useful for the initial loading of database rows from other sources. Loading tables into a non-logging database will save the overhead of logging and will make the loads go much faster.

Changing of logging modes can occur only when the engine is quiescent. Also, any change from non-logging to any form of logging require completing an immediate archive. A `tbtape` archive to `/dev/null` is a useful tool here.

Buffered logging

If a database is created with buffered logging, the contents of the logical log buffer are flushed to the disk logfiles only when the buffer is full. This results in more efficient database operations because expensive disk I/O operations are avoided.

Buffered logging also results in more efficient use of logical logfile space on disk. Writes from the logical log buffer to the logical logs on disk occur in page units. Whether there is a full page of transaction entries or only one entry occupying just a small part of a page, the entire page gets written to the disk file. Since no writes occur to the disk logfile until the buffer is full, the logfiles on disk will hold a higher percentage of useful information. The logfile data on disk will thus be more efficiently packed than with unbuffered logging.

All databases in an instance share the same buffers and disk logfiles. Thus, if some of your databases use buffered logging and some use non-buffered logging, the non-buffered databases could still force high I/O rates to the disks. When a non-buffered database completes a transaction, it will force the buffer to flush whether or not the buffer is full. The other databases will just sort of be dragged along.

The cost of buffered logging is the risk of losing data in the case of a crash. Although not as costly as crashing a non-logging database, crashing a buffered-logging database will result in loss of any transactions in the buffer that have not been flushed to disk. Although not as bad as losing all data changed since the last checkpoint, this data loss can still be costly. It's up to the DBA to make the judgement call as to whether the improved performance is worth the risk of data loss.

Unbuffered logging

In a database created with unbuffered logging, the logical log buffer flushes every time a transaction completes. Note that this includes jobs that are included in a BEGIN WORK/COMMIT WORK section as well as *singleton* transactions that are implicitly considered as transactions. A singleton transaction is any SQL statement that inserts or modifies data. It either completes or fails. It cannot partially complete. You can count on a log flush every time a loggable SQL transaction completes.

There is one drawback to using unbuffered logging. Since the logical log buffers flush with essentially every transaction, the buffers often contain only a small amount of data when they flush. Since the flushing occurs in page increments, the empty space is written to the logfiles, causing the logfiles to fill up more rapidly. This can happen if you have only one database set up for unbuffered logging, as every time it flushes, it will flush for all the databases. Log flushing is for the entire instance, not just for particular databases.

Unbuffered logging offers the ultimate in data survivability, at a cost of disk I/O and some bloating of your log files. Again, this requires a judgement call by the DBA.

SAVING THE LOG FILES

In the event that the worst happens and the database needs to be recovered from tape, it's essential that the log files be regularly copied to tape. They can also be stored on other media. Such saving to disk or optical disk can be kludged together, but the `tbtape` program is really designed to be used with a tape device, preferably two.

There are really two good reasons to get the logs copied to tape rapidly. The first is the obvious reason of getting them safely stored off-line. The other reason is that once a log file has filled up with data, it cannot be reused unless it has been marked as "backed up" and copied to tape (or some other medium).

OnLine provides two methods for saving the log files to tape, automatic backup and continuous backup. Automatic backup is not really automatic. It just backs up all existing log files to tape. It's almost useless except for instances where you need to back up a batch of logs in a one-time situation. After an automatic backup, you need to change tapes in the tape device because `tbtape` will write over them the next time it backs up logfiles. The really useful backup is the continuous backup option. Under continuous backup, whenever a logfile fills up, it is automatically backed up to the tape device and the process waits for the next log to fill up. Continuous backup provides an almost invisible method of assuring that the tape backups get done. Under continuous backup, the tape device is not closed and the backups of the logfiles occur one after another on the tape.

It's recommended that you have two tape devices available for each OnLine instance. This can be a major problem if you are running multiple instances. It usually means that it becomes very hard to automate database archives and logfile backups with multiple instances unless you have a lot of tape devices. Consider this if you are considering going to multiple instances of the database. Version 6.0 of OnLine promises significant improvements in this area, but does not provide any relief for needing separate tape devices for separate instances.

For a single instance, it is still best to have two tape drives, one for the archives and one for the logfile backups. Working with one drive is possible, but it means that you'll have to do some manual intervention. Actually, this is not all bad. The temptation, especially with large DAT drives, is to just pop in a logfile backup tape, turn on continuous logfile backups, and wait till the end of the tape. This is not advisable for several reasons. First, `tbtape` does not reliably handle end of tape conditions and it's best to avoid getting that far on a tape. Second, if you have gigabytes of logfiles on one tape, you're putting a lot of your eggs in one eight-millimeter basket. If you're on your hundredth logfile and the tape breaks, you've just lost numbers one through ninety-nine.

The most important reason is that if you ever have to apply the logfiles in a restore situation, you'll have to run through the entire logfile backup tape, which may take forever. Suppose you have a logfile backup tape that starts with logfile number 1 and goes through number 100, with each logfile taking 20 megabytes. Your last archive occurred at logfile number 75. If you should have to restore from tape, you'll first have to load the archive tape, then you'll have to apply the logs from number 75 to number 100. Since all of your logfiles are on one tape, you'll have to run through tapes number 1 through number 74 before you get to the first usable logfile. The amount of time that it takes to do this will be magnified greatly if you have users asking you "When will the system be back up?" every five minutes.

It's best to rotate your logfile tapes on a regular basis along with your archive tapes. If you're using one tape drive for both archives and log file backups, you're forced to do this anyway since you have to restart the logging after the archive is done.

LONG TRANSACTIONS

One of the most critical things that can happen to an OnLine instance is a long transaction. A long transaction occurs when a transaction begins in one logfile and spans multiple logfiles. If it gets to a certain point of logfile usage, the transaction begins to roll back. If there is not enough logfile space available for the rollback, OnLine cannot make the database consistent. If this happens, the database needs to be reinitialized and restored from an archive. If you get into this problem, pray that your OnLine support contract is up to date. Support may be able to help you out. Otherwise, you'll have to reinitialize the data spaces and reload from an archive.

This is almost the worst thing that can happen to the database. You'll certainly lose a lot of time. You'll probably lose data. Before Version 4.1, the situation was much easier to get into. The later versions have several `tbconfig` parameters that are meant to avoid the problem, but their defaults are not conservative enough and need to be changed. In versions later than 4.1, the configuration file has two critical parameters.

> LTXHWM: This is the *long transaction high water mark*. The Informix default value is 80 percent. When the total number of filled logs reaches this amount, any transactions that started in the oldest logfile are marked as long transactions and are forced to begin to roll back. This parameter's default is 80 percent and it is often way too high. Set it at about 60 or 70 percent in most cases. You need to give the transaction enough room to roll back as well as give other jobs room to log.

LTXEHWM: This is the *long transaction exclusive high water mark*. The Informix default value is 90 percent. When the total number of filled logs reaches this amount, all processes except long transactions that are rolling back are prevented from logging to the logfiles. These processes are effectively frozen. When you reach this stage of fullness, all of the logspace is needed to assure that the long transactions can roll back. It's defaulted at 90 percent and should probably be 75-80 percent.

The long transaction is the culprit that fills up the logfiles. There are several types of long transactions, most of them easily understood and one that is less obvious. Let's start with the one of the more obvious ones.

When you are working within a database that supports logging, either explicitly or by virtue of being a MODE ANSI database, the BEGIN WORK statement may precede a series of SQL statements. The BEGIN WORK statement is logged in the logfile. Until the corresponding COMMIT WORK statement is entered into a logfile, the engine will consider that the all of the logfiles beginning with the one holding the BEGIN WORK and ending with the currently active logfile are needed in case the transaction does not complete and the engine needs to roll it back The classic long transaction occurs when a user or a program is performing an update, insert, or delete on a large set of rows from a very large table. Each row affected generates a logfile entry. It is possible that one SQL statement on a table with hundreds of thousands of rows can swamp the logfiles, even if nothing else is being logged within the system. This type of situation often occurs when initially loading the database or when loading or unloading large tables.

The less obvious situation is when a user is doing a short transaction and fails to commit work. In this case, the BEGIN WORK statement is logged. The job does very little work, but the COMMIT WORK statement is not issued. Everything else that is logged into the logfiles then constitutes the long transaction. The engine does not care what is being done between the BEGIN WORK and the COMMIT WORK statements. Until it sees a matching COMMIT WORK statement it thinks it's in a long transaction. Suppose a user issues a BEGIN WORK statement from within `isql` for a short transaction and neither issues a COMMIT WORK nor exits from `isql`. That person then goes to lunch, or on a long weekend, or maybe on vacation. You've got a long transaction working. It will continue until the user either commits or exits `isql`. If the user exits `isql`, the program will prompt for action on the commit before `isql` exits memory. As long as that `isql` instance is running, it will be looking for the COMMIT WORK statement. The lesson here is to train your users to be aware of their transaction usage.

SIZE, NUMBER, AND LOCATION OF LOGFILES

When OnLine is first installed, all logfiles are in the root dbspace. OnLine defaults to three logfiles, so unless changes are made in the `tbconfig` file, you will start out with three logfiles in your `root` dbspace. OnLine does not allow you to change the size of the logfiles, although it does allow you to change the number and location of the logfiles. All logfiles will be the same size. In the initial configuration, the engine will calculate the total size requested for the logfiles (number times size of each one) and will assume that all of these logfiles go into the root dbspace. If this space is larger than the size of the `root` dbspace, OnLine will not initialize. This is a common cause of problems during installation because the DBA will often specify his maximum number of desired logfiles in the `tbmonitor` process and the initialization program will try to actually allocate space for all the requested logfiles in the root dbspace.

One of the major questions in the original setup of the OnLine system concerns the anticipated size and number of logfiles. Generally, you need to have sufficient logfiles to allow logging of a transaction in your largest table. If you do not have adequate logs for this, you will get long transaction errors and will not be able to complete your maximum size transaction.

Adding additional logfiles in a simple procedure. Changing the size of logfiles is a complex undertaking. To increase the size of logfiles the entire OnLine system must be reinitialized and your data must be rebuilt from an export or from other flatfiles. Changing the logfile size, reinitializing, and then restoring from an archive does not work. The RESTORE command in `tbmonitor` performs an initialization itself. It initializes the system to the parameters that were in effect at the time of the ARCHIVE. If you try to use the RESTORE in this manner, you will end up with the same size logfiles that you started with.

The Informix manual recommends a total logfile allocation of approximately 20 percent of total database space. Depending upon the nature of your transactions, this may or may not be enough. Note that a maximum size transaction by definition takes quite a bit of time to complete. If other loggable transactions are occurring at the same time, the logging requirements must take into account ALL of the logging load simultaneously, not just the largest. Since both the number and the location of the logfiles can be changed, only the size represents an unalterable (without reinitializing the disk) decision. There is only one constraint to consider, and that is the maximum number of logfiles allowed. A system using a 2-kilobyte page size can have about 60 logical logfiles. Size the logfiles such that a total of 60 logfiles will take up about 20 to 25 percent of the maximum anticipated database size. If your database grows at such a rate that reach the maximum number of logfiles, you'll probably be reinstalling on bigger hardware before then anyway. Don't worry too much about trying to predict years into the future. Get the system tuned for now with a little bit of room to expand.

One factor to consider in deciding on logfile size is the speed of your tape backup device. Keep the logfile size down if you have a slow backup device. The real solution is, as usual, hardware. Get a faster tape device. As a system gets larger, the capacity of the archive tape device and the logging tape device often become the limiting factor in how large the database can grow. When your archive devices are running constantly in an attempt to archive your system, you are reaching the limit of manageable size. Version 6.0 should go a long way towards alleviating this problem because it will allow parallel archiving to multiple backup devices. There will be provisions for a maximum of 99 parallel devices in Version 6.0.

New logfiles do not come into use until after an archive is done. The level of the archive does not matter. If the DBA is just adding or moving logfiles, the trick here is to do the archive to /dev/null.

The location of logfiles is also important. Logfiles usually have a relatively heavy write activity. This usually consists of efficient sequential writes. Still, Informix recommends that logfiles be optimized for writing. If you have a preferred disk location that allows more efficient writes, this is a good place to place your logs. An example would be in a UNIX-mirrored rather than a RAID 5 disk partition. RAID 5 is optimized for reading. Depending upon your implementation, writing to a RAID 5 partition can be significantly slower that writing to a mirrored partition. The DBA should also look at placing the logfiles on a separate disk to minimize disk contention.

One thing to consider is moving the initial three logfiles out of the root dbspace. If there is a lot of temporary table creation, and if the temp tables are created in the root dbspace (the default) relocating the logfiles is often a good idea. Since OnLine requires a minimum of three logfiles at all time, moving the initial three is more complicated than simply dropping the old ones and adding the new ones. You must always have three logfiles available at all times.

To move the logfiles, you need to be logged in as user `informix` or `root`. The `informix` login is preferred, because all activities as `root` need to be done through the command line rather than through `tbmonitor`. First, you have to create at least three more logfiles in another dbspace. To activate them, do an ARCHIVE to `/dev/null`. The `/dev/null` archive occurs very quickly, as OnLine handles archiving to `/dev/null` differently than it handles archiving to a real device. This dummy archive convinces OnLine that a real archive has been done and activates the new logfiles for use.

Now, using `tbstat -l`, see which logfile is currently in use. You can use the `tbmode -l` command from the command line to cause the current log to advance to one of the new, non-rootdbs logfiles. You may need to execute the `tbmode` command several times until the current logfile is one of the newly created ones. You then need to do a backup of any of the logfiles you want to drop. Even if you skipped over them with the `tbmode` command, they need to be backed up to a real tape device, not to `/dev/null`. After the logs are backed up, go to quiescent mode and drop the three logfiles that are in the root dbspace. If you are using `tbstat -c` to force continuous backup of logfiles, these logfile backups will be happening automatically and you won't have to do them manually. Finally, do an actual Level 0 archive to tape to establish a baseline for future recoveries.

If you already have an OnLine system running, it is very informative to watch your disk I/O statistics to see exactly how your application reads and writes to disk. This simple c-shell script called `watch_hot` will do the job:

```
#!/bin/csh
while ( 1 == 1 )
   tbstat -D
   tbstat -z
   sleep 5
end
```

Since this script reinitializes the `tbstat` statistics every five seconds, make sure that it does not interfere with any long-term `tbstat` statistics collection that you or someone else may be doing. The script will output numbers representing the incremental reads and writes to database chunks every five seconds.

One thing that you'll find with this script is that your highest rate of writing is probably to your physical logs. This is where you need to watch your disk placement to optimize for writing speed. The physical log can be a bottleneck for the entire system, so place it carefully.

Another thing that this script can show you is where you are in completing an archive. If you run it while an archive is running, you'll see a running bulge of heavy read activity in your chunks as the archive program walks through your database structure.

Chapter 4

Understanding Archives

One of the main duties of the database administrator is insuring the safety of the data. Although OnLine is a very robust product, a number of factors can cause the system to go down. Often, these problems arise from user errors such as killing engine processes with a UNIX `kill -9` command. Other things that can crash the system are hardware problems and UNIX problems that crash the entire computer.

In most instances, OnLine will recover from the error during the fast recovery process that occurs automatically when the shared memory is first started. In most cases, user errors and software problems cause no physical damage to the data and this fast recovery is adequate to bring the system back up. It is the hardware crashes that most often cause the database administrator to have to recover the database from the archives. When this happens, the DBA quickly realizes that the only thing between him and the deep blue sea is a flimsy length of recording tape. It behooves the DBA to be absolutely certain of the Informix archive and recovery system. This chapter will explain the archive and recovery system and point out some of the ways that the DBA can assure the integrity of this system.

LIMITATIONS OF THE `tbtape` PROGRAM

In addition to the UNIX filesize limits noted in the previous section, there are several more items that can cause serious problems with the archiving process.

The Informix manuals recommend that a terminal be dedicated to the `tbtape` program and that someone watch that terminal for notices that it's time to change the tape. If you do this, the terminal should actually be in the same room as the tape drive, so that the operator can visually check the status of the drive and change the tapes quickly. Although this looks good on paper, it is not always the best method from an operational standpoint. Sometimes, the DBA needs to have these processes working in the background or as a part of a management script. This can be done as in the following script:

```
#!/bin/csh
tbtape -s << EOF
0
^M     (note, this is a control M
EOF
```

This script runs the `tbtape` program and answers "0" to the Level? prompt and then enters a carriage return when prompted to hit enter when the tape is mounted. Please note that running `tbtape` from a script or in the background is DEFINITELY NOT RECOMMENDED by Informix. You're doing it at your own risk, but the risk is manageable.

What's so risky about this? Problems arise if you exceed the capacity of your tape archive device. This capacity is set with the `tbmonitor` program. This tape size parameter, as well as the names of the archive and log devices, are changeable without having to restart the engine. When `tbtape` thinks you've reached the end of your tape, it will send a prompt to the standard output requesting you to change tapes and hit ENTER. If `tbtape` is running in the background or as part of a script, you cannot hit ENTER, and `tbtape` continues to wait for you to change tapes. This creates a problem when your system needs to perform a checkpoint. Whether the checkpoint is needed because the checkpoint interval has elapsed or because the physical logs have reached 75 percent full, the checkpoint program will try to write out data to the archive tape. (Remember, the archives, logs, and checkpoints all work together and know of each other's status.) This write cannot occur when the archive is waiting for a tape change, so the checkpoint cannot occur. This causes the engine to freeze up and allows processes to perform nothing but data reads. The only way out is to kill the `tbtape` process. (Kill it with a UNIX `kill -15` command, not with the very dangerous `kill -9` command.)

You can feel relatively comfortable with running `tbtape` either in a script or in the background as long as you are *absolutely sure* that your entire archive will fit within a single archive tape.

Another thing to do if you're running `tbtape` in this way is to redirect the output into a file. Since `tbmonitor` and `tbtape` both use UNIX standard input and standard output, standard UNIX redirection methods work. If you redirect the output into a file, you can then access this file and check on the status of the archive without having to be at a dedicated terminal. You can also use the file output in other scripts. This is done in the `status` script included with this book. Note that `tbtape` uses the UNIX curses library and that it addresses the screen directly. The output file is difficult to read with the `vi` editor, as `vi` thinks it is all one line. Use the UNIX `cat` command and pipe it to `more` and you'll be able to see the output better. The `status` script runs a UNIX `tail` command on this output file to print the progress messages from `tbtape`.

GENERAL ARCHIVE CONCEPTS

Archiving in OnLine is done with the `tbtape` program. This program performs both the data archiving when invoked as `tbtape  -s` and the logfile archiving when invoked as `tbtape  -c` or `tbtape  -a`. The `tbmonitor` Archive menu options invoke the `tbtape` program.

One of the more compelling features of the OnLine database is that archives can be run without shutting down the database. In an environment such as a large transaction processing system, this becomes a critical point. There is just no time available to take the database offline for long enough to complete an archive.

When you consider exactly what is happening in backing up a database that is being accessed and modified at the same time, you will better understand some of the limitations of the archive process. At the same time the archive process is trying to take a snapshot of the database, users and batch jobs are trying their best to make that snapshot out of date. The archive process has to cooperate with checkpoints and logging processes to maintain the integrity and consistency of the data.

ARCHIVE DEVICES

OnLine has somewhat of a split personality with regard to archive devices. The `tbtape` program theoretically can use any UNIX device as an archive destination, but it's really designed to archive to tape. Actually, tape is the only option that makes sense, especially if your disk space is limited. Archiving to tape reduces your exposure to catastrophic disk crashes. If you are archiving to disk and crash an OnLine raw disk because of hardware problems, you may well also crash the disk device you are using for the archive. With tape, you spread your exposure to mechanical problems across two totally separate types of devices, most often controlled by different controller boards. In a pinch, you can archive to a UNIX file, but it takes some manual intervention, especially if the archive is larger than one file.

For a system of any size, you can't beat a large DAT drive. These drives, although expensive, can give you tremendous data capacity and a high transfer speed. Some DAT drives can also use data compression to cram even more data onto an archive tape. The combination of fast reading and writing speeds and tremendous storage capabilities is hard to beat. Given the difference in price between DAT drives and drives of lesser capacity, one can often justify going to DAT simply by calculating the differences in media cost.

If you are using logging with your OnLine engine, it is preferable to have two separate tape drives, one for the archives and one for the logs. That way, your log tapes can continue their continuous backups to tape while the archive is going on. It's possible to get by on one tape drive if you are willing to do a lot of tape swapping. Tape drives seem to have a higher failure rate than other components, so having at least two drives available for OnLine makes sense.

If you plan on using multiple instances of Informix, remember that their archiving and logging needs should also be considered. The preferred but costly solution is to have two separate tape drives per instance, if the multiple instances will both be doing a lot of archiving and logging.

ARCHIVE SCHEDULES

OnLine provides a three-level archive schema. A full archive is a Level 0 archive, and it corresponds to an epoch level UNIX dump. Everything is dumped to tape. A Level 1 archive will back up any database pages that have changed since the last Level 0 archive. Likewise, a Level 2 archive will back up any changes since the last Level 1 archive.

In deciding on an archive schedule, the DBA needs to balance several factors. Obviously, if the DBA has two fast DAT drives available, he will handle the archives differently than if he is backing up to one 9-track tape. How volatile is the data? Does it change often, or are some of the tables very large and relatively static? How valuable is the data? Can it be easily recreated from other sources? How much time is available to do the archives? Are there people available to change tapes? Can you dedicate a terminal just for archiving?

For a system that has large capacity tape drives with the entire archive being well below the UNIX filesystem size unit, the answer is easy. Simply do Level 0 archives daily. As the database gets larger, the archive process must become more complicated. At some point it becomes necessary to begin to do Level 1 and maybe Level 2 archives.

One of the major factors to consider when deciding on an archive schedule is what will happen in the event that you actually have to use the archives to recover the database. Archive tapes are sort of like atomic bombs. You keep them around but hope you never have to use them. If you are doing only Level 0 archives, the recovery process consists of loading the Level 0 tape and then applying any subsequent log tapes. Systems using Level 1 and Level 2 archives require loading the Level 0 tape first, followed by any Level 1 tape, followed by any Level 2 tape, then followed by any log tapes.

The process of applying the log tapes after restoring the archive is the most time-consuming part of the process. For this reason, it is best to schedule your archives so that you do not allow an excessive number of logs to accumulate between archives. For example, on a Pyramid multi-processor system using 60 megabyte logs, it takes about 15 to 20 minutes to apply each log tape. At a TAPESIZE of about 2 gigabytes per tape, a full tape could take close to ten hours to apply all of the logs if the tape were totally full and if all logfiles were used.

Problems with an archive usually do not show up until you try to recover the data. The fact that tbtape completed an archive without errors and without complaint does not mean that the archive has completed properly. When setting up your system, at some point you need to schedule a test of your recovery process. The test should be as realistic as possible. If you are using multiple levels of archives, create them and try to recover from them. Let several logfiles accumulate after the last archive. When you recover, time the process, note the size of the database, note the size of the archives, and note how long it takes for each activity of the recovery. This data will help you to fine-tune your procedures.

Having to recover from an archive is usually a traumatic event, accompanied by confusion, angry users and managers, and much finger-crossing by the DBA. Recoveries also seem to occur after midnight on holidays. You want to make the process as simple and as fast as possible. Remember, though, that the most important part is actually getting the data back.

Chapter 5

Understanding the Utilities

Tbstat

The tbstat utility is the most important of the entire suite of OnLine utilities. It is used to inspect the pseudotables that are held in shared memory structures. This information cannot be determined without using the tbstat utility, at least in versions of OnLine prior to Version 6.0. In 6.0, much of this information will be available in actual tables. Until then, the only way to view this critical information is to use tbstat.

Why is this information important? The main reason is that this is where the operations of the OnLine "black box" are recorded and controlled. For a regular user, the engine is simply the mechanism that translates his SQL statements into actual data returned from the database. This level of detail is enough for most users. The database administrator needs much more detailed information to troubleshoot problems, improve performance, and generally know what is going on inside the engine itself. For the same reasons that it is important for the DBA to understand the architecture and internal operations of the engine, the database administrator needs to understand all of the options, output codes, and interrelations of the tbstat program. The tbstat program is well documented in the *Informix OnLine Administrator's Guide*, and the reader is urged to become familiar with the relevant sections of the Guide. What the Guide doesn't cover, however, is the "why" and "how does this relate to my problem" type of question. The guide's information needs to be assimilated and used, but in order for the DBA to use the tool effectively, the administrator needs to know how the pieces fit together.

Using tbstat

The tbstat program gives you instantaneous data about the contents of the shared memory structures. It takes very little CPU time and locks no tables and creates no latches. As such, you can consider that tbstat is essentially "free," that is, it has a minuscule effect on database performance. You can let it run continuously in the background if you wish, collecting performance data and usage data with little or no performance cost.

There is only one option that could possibly cause you any problems, and that is the `tbstat -o filename` option. This option places the *entire* contents of shared memory into a file specified by `filename`. If you have a large shared memory, be sure that you have sufficient room in your UNIX file system to save the file. This option will also cause significant I/O in the system if you have it saving a large shared memory file to disk.

The `tbstat` utility is often used as a troubleshooting tool. When you encounter problems in the engine such as unexpected freeze-ups, long transactions, deadlocks, and the like, you will turn to the `tbstat` utility to tell you what's happening in the engine. Usually, this is an effective technique, but sometimes your problem will be transient.

Since `tbstat` gives you an instantaneous snapshot, by the time you enter the correct `tbstat` command, the problem may be gone. If you are looking for solutions to these transient problems, you may need to use the `tbstat -o filename` option. The trick is to catch the database in the act of doing whatever it is doing and save the shared memory to a file.

If you can get the output file saved before the problem goes away, you can then inspect the output file at your leisure and run any or all of the `tbstat` options against the file without worrying about the transient problem going away. To do this you would use the following series of `tbstat` commands:

```
tbstat -o any_filename                          (takes the snapshot)
tbstat -"any_options" "filename"        (reports from snapshot file)
```

The first step in fully understanding the `tbstat` utility is understanding what all of the options mean. This is the help screen for `tbstat` (Most commonly used items are marked with an asterisk):

```
joe  60>tbstat --
usage: tbstat [-abcdklmpstuzBDFPRX] [-r secs][-o file][infile]
    * --      print this help screen
    * -       print just the tbstat header (undocumented feature)
      -a      print all info (options: bcdklmpstu)
      -b      print buffers
      -c      print configuration file
    * -d      print dbspaces and chunks
    * -k      print locks
    * -l      print logging
      -m      print message log
    * -p      print profile
    * -s      print latches
    * -t      print tblspaces
    * -u      print users
      -z      zero profile counts
      -B      print all buffers
      -D      print dbspaces and detailed chunk stats
      -F      print page flushers
      -P      print profile, including BIGreads
      -R      print LRU queues
      -X      print entire list of sharers and waiters for buffers
    * -r      repeat options every n seconds (default: 5)
      -o      put shared memory into file (default: tbstat.out)
  infile use infile to obtain shared memory information
```

tbstat - -

Using this option displays the help screen for the tbstat command. This is actually the "minus" option, not the "minus minus" option. The first minus sign indicates that a command options follows, the second minus is the actual option.

This convention is followed by most of the OnLine utilities. Just enter commandname   -- and you'll see the help text.

```
tbstat -
```

Using just the first minus and a null option will show just the header of the
tbstat series of commands. This header looks like:

```
RSAM Version 5.01.UC1    -- On-Line -- Up 7 days 23:54:27 -- 18704 Kbytes
```

This header includes five important sections. The first section gives the version
number of the OnLine engine. The second section shows the current operating mode.
Possible values of the mode are:

Offline: Engine not running

Quiescent: No user can start a server process. User
                    informix can use administrative options of
                    tbmonitor. Any user can use tbstat or view
                    options of tbmonitor

Online: Fully usable by all users

Shutdown: System is in transition from online to quiescent or
                    from quiescent to offline. Cannot be canceled.

Recovery: Moving from offline to quiescent. Fast recovery is
                    performed here.

The third section is the (checkpoint) indicator. If applicable, this section can
contain:

(CKPT REQ) Some process has requested a checkpoint, and the
           engine is trying to initiate the checkpoint. This
           flag is often seen if the database is hung waiting
           for a checkpoint.

(CHKT INP) Checkpoint is in progress. Users have read-only access to the database. No changes to data are allowed until the checkpoint ends.

The fourth section shows the real time that the database has been running, i.e., the time since the last database startup. The fifth and final section shows the amount of shared memory in use by OnLine in kilobytes. This is roughly the size of the output file generated by the `tbstat -o command`.

`tbstat -d`

The `tbstat -d` command provides several important pieces of information. the most important being the disk and chunk usage for the database. The output is divided into two sections, Dbspaces and Chunks.

```
joe  43>tbstat -d

RSAM Version 5.01.UC1    -- On-Line -- Up 7 days 23:48:38 -- 18704 Kbytes

Dbspaces
```

address	number	flags	fchunk	nchunks	flags	owner	name
e0016e88	1	1	1	3	N	informix	rootdbs
e0016eb8	2	1	4	2	N	informix	logspace
e0016ee8	3	1	5	2	N	informix	dbspace1
e0016f18	4	1	7	2	N	informix	logspace2
e0016f48	5	1	10	1	N	informix	

```
slowdbspace
 5 active, 20 total
```

address	The dbspace's address in the shared memory table
number	The dbspace's unique ID number. Dependent upon the order in which the dbspaces were created.
flags	First series of flags describes mirroring, status, and/or blobspace status: 1 0x0001 Not mirrored 2 0x0002 Mirrored 3 0x0004 Dbspace is down 4 0x0008 Newly mirrored dbspace 5 0x0010 Blobspace
fchunk	The unique identifying number of the first chunk in the dbspace
nchunks	Total number of chunks in this dbspace
flags	Second series of flags gives essentially the same information as the first only using alphabetic codes: First position: M Mirrored N Not Mirrored Second position: X Newly mirrored Third Position: B Blobspace
owner	User name of the owner of the dbspace
name	The name of the dbspace

`tbstat -d` **output (dbspace section)**

```
Chunks
address   chk/dbs offset   size      free      bpages    flags pathname
e0014e78 1    1    0        135000    35718               PO-   /dev/rootdbs3
e0014f10 2    1    0        57000     56997               PO-   /dev/rootdbs1
e0014fa8 3    1    0        75000     74997               PO-   /dev/rootdbs2
e0015040 4    2    0        147500    24542               PO-   /dev/log1
  4 active, 27 total
```

address	The address of the chunk
chk	The unique ID number of the chunk
dbs	The number of the dbspace containing this chunk. Corresponds to the `number` field in the `dbspaces` output of this command.
offset	The number of pages that this chunk is offset into the device, if any.
size	Size of the chunk in pages
free	Number of free pages in this chunk. This is the number of pages that are not part of any allocated tablespace. It does not take into account any unused pages within extents that are allocated to tablespaces.
bpages	Number of free blobpages. Blobpages can have their own page sizes. Don't confuse this number with free pages. They don't necessarily correspond.

flags	The status flags for the chunk, using the following codes:
	    Position 1: P Primary chunk
	                  M Mirror chunk
	    Position 2: O Chunk Online *
	                  D Chunk Down *
	                  R Recovering
	                  X Newly mirrored
	    Position 3: B Blobspace
	                  - Dbspace

pathname	Either the device name or the path name of the UNIX cooked file that contains this chunk

`tbstat -d` output (chunks section)

On most terminals, the screen displays for the O and the D letters are easily confused. It's often hard to tell from the screen whether a chunk is up or down. Versions prior to 5.0 can run with a chunk down, so it's important to watch your status.

Usage tips

If you're like most DBA's, you'll spend a lot of time fighting the database "battle of the bulge." Murphy's Law says that any database will expand to fill the amount of space available. OnLine does not bother to warn you when you're beginning to fill up your disks.

The first sign of a problem will be when users get messages saying that OnLine cannot allocate more extents for a table. Especially when you're using raw devices, there is no easy way to tell how much disk space you are using.

The `tbstat -d` program is your most powerful tool for monitoring the usage of your disks. This invocation of `tbstat` is used to develop percentage full statistics for various `dbspaces` in the `status` script that we develop later in Chapter 6. You'll probably develop various scripts on your own to massage the output of all the utilities. With `tbstat -d`, you'll find yourself writing scripts to answer such questions as "How much space is there left in dbspace X?"

Here it becomes important to have some naming conventions for your chunks and `dbspaces`. If all of the chunks contained in dbspace `dbs1` begin with the letters `dbs1`, for example, it will be a simple matter to `grep` for `dbs1` followed by the UNIX command, `awk '{print $6}'` to get the free space in `dbs1`. If you have the luxury of creating your databases from scratch, keep in mind this consistency in naming. Do the same with the names of your `dbspaces` dedicated to logfiles and with the names of your tables too if possible.

You may notice that the examples in this book do not always exhibit this level of foresight. I don't have the excuse of having inherited the databases. I developed many of these databases before I began developing DBA scripts to manage them. If you follow these recommendations, you'll do a better job. I know that doing so would have made my life as a scriptwriter a lot easier.

If you're not familiar with the capabilities of the UNIX commands `grep`, `sed`, and `awk` and with the operations of UNIX regular expressions, it may make some sense to learn them early in the game. Using these UNIX tools on the outputs of OnLine utilities can allow you to generate just about any sort of reports and data.

```
tbstat -D
```

This is a useful variant of the `tbstat -d` command. It provides exactly the same output as the `tbstat -d` command, with the exception that in the Chunks section the `size` and `free` statistics are replaced by `page Rd` and `page Wr` numbers representing the numbers of pages read from and written to in each of the chunks.

This option provides a very useful tool for locating "hotspots" in your databases, areas that have abnormally high I/O activity. Since disk I/O is most often the slowest activity your computer system will perform, the elimination or minimization of these hotspots can go a long way towards improving the performance of your databases.

One minor drawback to `tbstat -D` is that it reports cumulative data rather than instantaneous data. The statistics shown cover the time period beginning when OnLine was either last started or when the statistics were zeroed out. While it would be easy to write a script that subtracts out the last totals and only shows you the differences from the last time the script was run, there is an even easier way to do this. Write a little script and name it `hotspot`:

```
joe 51>  cat hotspot

#!/bin/csh
tbstat -D
tbstat -z
```

Every time you run the `hotspot` script, it will zero out the `tbstat` statistics when you finish. Each subsequent run will show the actual activity that has occurred since the last run. This is suitable for running hotspot repeatedly in one sitting or over a short period of time. It could be modified to save the date and statistics of the last run, but why get complicated? Just remember that running hotspot will zero out *all* of the `tbstat` statistics. If you (or any other user) are running cumulative statistics monitoring, the `tbstat -z`'s will interfere with this statistics gathering.

The most important thing I've discovered by running `hotspot` is the tremendous amount of activity that occurs to the physical logfile. Conventional wisdom says to locate the logfiles in an area that is optimized for heavy write activity. I had taken this advice to mean the logical log files. Study of hotspot output will show that it's the physical log file that needs to be optimized. It is relatively easy to relocate and/or resize the physical log file (the database does need to come down however). Watch your hotspots for a while and then experiment with relocating and resizing the physical log. You'll see how much activity it gets. It is also possible to experiment with the size of the physical log buffers as a way to optimize the writing activity.

```
tbstat -z
```

Since we just used `tbmode -z` in a script, this may be a good time to talk about this command option. There's not much to say. It just zero's out everything. This does not affect anything in the database. You can zero it out all day long if you wish. Don't confuse these statistics with the statistics kept by the OnLine UPDATE STATISTICS command. That's a completely different subject. Just be aware of the fact that you may interfere with other statistics-gathering programs. I discourage my users from using any of the OnLine utilities, preferring to give them access through scripts that I control. That way, they won't be stepping on my toes.

If your OnLine system stays up for long periods of time without zeroing out the `tbstat` statistics, you'll eventually reach your UNIX limits on integer sizes and some of the numbers will roll over, showing negative numbers. To correct this, just run the `tbstat -z program`.

```
tbstat -u
```

This option gives you an overview of the database processes that exist at any particular time. This option gives you data from the user pseudotable in the shared memory. It is useful as a debugging tool when the system has inexplicably frozen up and the DBA is attempting to find out what is going on. In the case where everything is frozen, you will need to compare information from this option with data from other `tbstat` options to trace down the offending process. This usually takes some time because you have to track the transactions through several invocations of the utility. If the database is hung up, probably nothing in the user table is changing and you can run multiple `tbstat`'s against the shared memory and get the same data. If the database is not frozen, you often run into a problem because the data in the user table is changing. In this instance it is often useful to take a snapshot of the shared memory by running the `tbstat -o file` command and then running your `tbstat` options against `file`.

With a hung database in a production environment, it is often tempting to simply restart the database and hope the problem goes away. While this is often a viable solution to the problem, there are instances when the recovery time would be excessive and when it would be better to try to track down the specific problem.

You can expect such excessively long recovery times in recovery from such problems as long transactions interrupted while in rollback or other occasions in which much logfile data has not been released. Whether to try to debug or restart the database is a judgement call. Even if you decide to shutdown the database, do a `tbstat -o debug.filename` so that you can later try to find out what caused the problem.

If you learn nothing else of `tbstat`, learn how to read the `tbstat -u` output. OnLine is a black box and `tbstat` is the main way of looking into this black box. This data is impossible to decipher from a UNIX `ps` output. It just shows up as `sqlturbo`. You'll note that many of the flags correspond with the invocation flags for `tbstat`. Keep working with it. Soon you'll be reading these outputs in your sleep.

The output of `tbstat -u` changed from OnLine Version 4.11 to Version 5.0. Both 4.11 and 5.0 have the same first section. OnLine 5.0 gives you a second section, `Transactions`, that applies to the X/A environment and to transactions that are running under INFORMIX-Star.

Here is a greatly abbreviated sample of the output from the `tbstat -u` utility:

```
joe  46>tbstat -u

address  flags   pid     user     tty      wait      tout locks nreads  nwrites

e0001b70 ------D 555     informix console 0         0    0     6746    2607
e0001f30 ------- 21059   dba      -        0         0    1     31538   3813
```

address	Address of user in user table in shared memory. This is the only point of contact between user addresses found from other `tbstat` command forms. As you trace a problem using the -s output (latches), the -b -B and -X outputs (buffer status), and the -k output (locks held), you will eventually trace it to a user address. Then match the address with a PID or user name.

flags	Probably the most important output of this command. Tells you what the process is doing. Has a four-position alpha output:
	
	Position 1: B Waiting for Buffer
	                   C Waiting for a Checkpoint
	                   L Waiting for a Lock
	                   S Waiting for a Latch
	                   X Long trans. Awaiting rollback
	                   G Waiting for loG buffer
	                   T* Waiting for transaction*
	Position 2: B Transaction w/ Begin work
	                   T In trans. Logging occurred
	                   R In Rollback
	                   A Archive process
	                   C* Committed or is committing*
	                   H* Heuristically aborted or aborting*
	                   P* Prepare state. Precommitted*
	                   X* X/A prepared or is doing so*
	Position 3: R Reading from the database
	                   X Inside a CRITICAL section
	Position 4: M Running tbmonitor program
	                   D Running a Daemon
	                   C Corpse. Dead process awaiting cleanup
	                   F Page Flusher daemon

pid	The UNIX process identification number
user	The name of the user running the process
tty	TTY associated with the process, if any
wait	Latch or lock ID being waited for, if any
tout	How many times a lock timeout has occurred for the process
locks	Number of locks held by this process
nreads	Number of read calls executed by this process
nwrites	Number of write calls executed by this process

* NOTE: Items marked with * used in Online V.5.0 and above only

Explanation of fields of the Users section of the `tbstat -u` command.

Versions 5.0 and above include this `Transactions` section in the output of the `tbstat -u` command:

```
Transactions
address  flags user    locks log begin isolation retrys coordinator
e0004a24 A---- e0001bbc 0      0        NOTRANS   0
e0004c04 A---- e0001c28 0      0        NOTRANS   0
e0005384 A---- e0001eb0 1      0        COMMIT    0
e0005564 A---- e0001f1c 1      0        COMMIT    0
```

address	Address of the transaction in transaction pseudotable
flags	A five-position alpha flag of which #1, #3 & #5 are used:
	Position 1: A Attached to a server process
	C Cleanup. Probably crashed
	Position 3: B Begin. Work has been logged.
	Writable operation has occurred. Not the same as a BEGIN WORK.
	C Transaction being committed
	H Heuristic rollback in progress
	P Prepared to commit
	R Rollback in progress.
	Position 5: C This transaction is Coordinator
	G Global transaction
	P Participant transaction
user	Address of the user process that owns the transaction
locks	Locks owned by the transaction and thus by its owner process
log begin	ID of the logical log where this transaction begins
isolation	Transaction Isolation Level:
	COMMIT Committed Read
	CURSOR Cursor Stability
	DIRTY Dirty Read
	REPEAT Repeatable Read
	NO TRANS Processes that don't own transaction, or Databases with no logging
retrys	Number of times this transaction has exceeded the timeout (TXTIMEOUT)
coordinator	Name of the transaction coordinator

Explanation of the fields in the Transactions section of the `tbstat -u` command

We will not attempt to delve deeply in this volume into the operations of INFORMIX-Star and INFORMIX-Net. As an introductory text for DBA's, we'll concentrate mainly on the operations of single OnLine instances. As such, I will refer you to the *Informix OnLine Administrator's Guide, Database Server Version 5.0* for further details on debugging INFORMIX-Star problems. The pertinent information is in Chapter 9.

```
tbstat -t
```

This invocation of the `tbstat` utility provides information from the `tblspace` pseudotable in shared memory. These may be regular database tables currently in use, temporary tables created by users, or temporary tables created implicitly by the OnLine system for such tasks as SORT or ORDER BY. Each table in use will have only one entry.

```
joe:/devel/usr/joe> tbstat -t

RSAM Version 5.00.UC3    -- On-Line -- Up 2 days 08:09:41 -- 16080 Kbytes

Tblspaces
```

n	address	flgs	ucnt	tblnum	physaddr	npages	nused	npdata	nrows	nextns
0	c0095c98	1	1	1000001	10000e	2214	2214	0	0	3
1	c0095da8	1	1	2000001	200004	1285	71	0	0	1
2	c0095eb8	1	1	3000001	300004	245	245	0	0	1
3	c0095fc8	1	1	4000001	400004	115	2	0	0	1
4	c00960d8	1	1	5000001	500004	285	2	0	0	1
5	c00961e8	1	2	6000001	700004	15	2	0	0	1
6	c00962f8	1	2	7000001	800004	15	2	0	0	1

```
7 active, 1500 total, 512 hash buckets
```

n	counter of the number of open tablespaces
address	address of the tablespace in the tblspace pseudotable

flgs	Status of the tablespace:
	    0x1 1 Busy
	    0x2 2 Dirty, needs to be written

ucnt	Usage count. How many users are using the tablespace?
tblnum	Tablespace number (hexadecimal). Corresponds to hex(partnum) from the system table, `systables`, for the database. The first digit (leftmost 8 bits) of the tblnum will always tell you the dbspace that contains the table (cross-reference to the `tbstat -d` output). The remaining portion gives you the order in which the tables were created in the dbspace. The internal table known as `tablespace tablespace` will always be X000001, where X is the number of the dbspace. This `tablespace tablespace` is always considered to be an active table and will be included in each `tbstat -t` output, one for each dbspace you may have created, whether it is in use or not.
physaddr	Physical address on disk of the tablespace
npages	Total number of pages allocated to the tablespace. This includes data and index pages as well as empty space that is left over in any allocated extents.
nused	The number of pages in the tablespace that have been used.
npdata	Number of data pages used. Does not necessarily correspond with npages because an extent may have empty pages. This does not differentiate between data and index pages, although the heading (npdata) may seem to indicate so. This refers to DATA + INDEX pages.
nrows	Number of rows in the tablespace
nextns	Number of noncontiguous extents allotted. Even though the table grows larger and new extents may be added, if these extents can be created contiguous to the last extent, this number does not get bigger. This is a good indicator of the level of fragmentation of a tablespace.

Explanation of the fields in the `tbstat -t` output.

The final line of the `tbstat -t` output is:

```
2 active, 1100 total, 512 hash buckets
```

The `active` represents the number of tablespaces that are currently active, while the total figure is the configuration parameter found in the `$TBCONFIG` table.

A *hash bucket* is part of an algorithm to speed up access to the tblspace table. It's a method of dividing up all of the possible values and cross-referencing them to values in the *hash table*. The cross-referencing is done by an internal mathematical algorithm that takes each entry in the `tblspace` table, performs some math on it, and relates it to an entry in the hash table. Each entry in the hash table is called a hash bucket.

```
tbstat -s
```

The `tbstat -s` invocation provides information on the active latches in the OnLine system memory. An active latch represents a user process that is modifying a shared memory structure. In normal operations, latches are granted and released rapidly. At any particular time, a run of `tbstat -s` will most often reveal no latches held.

A latch is a type of lock that is placed on shared memory. Most often, latches are placed on the pseudotables in shared memory. When a user needs to access one of these pseudotables, he first must acquire a latch on the table, then makes his changes, and then release the latch. If the user cannot obtain the latch, the user process will wait for that latch to be freed. If for some reason it can never obtain the latch, the user process will hang.

When the database is hung, the DBA usually runs `tbstat -s` to see if someone is frozen on a latch. If anything is found, this is usually a good place to start looking for the bottleneck.

```
joe 53> tbstat -s

Latches with lock or user set
name       address   lock wait user
bbf[0]     e075adb8  1    0     e0002770
bf[2070]   e071af2c  1    0     e0002a10
pt[33]     e067afa0  1    0     e0002590
bh[4749]   e06e9cb0  1    0     e0001e70
```

name	The name of the structure that is being latched by this latch.	
	`locks`	lock table latch
	`tblsps`	tblspace table latch
	`ckpt`	checkpoint latch
	`archive`	archive latch
	`chunks`	chunk table latch
	`loglog`	logical log buffers latch
	`physlog`	physical log latch
	`users`	users table latch
	`trans`	transaction table latch
	`flushctl`	flush table latches
	`flush%d`	flush process control latches
	`flushr`	page cleaners
	`LRU%d`	LRU queue latch
	`pt[%d]`	partition latch
	`pt`	tablespace tablespace latch
	`bh[%d]`	buffer hash latch
	`bf[%d]`	buffer latch
	`bbf[%d]`	big buffer latch
	`altlatch`	alter table count latch
	`physb1`	physical log buffer 1 latch
	`physb2`	physical log buffer 2 latch
	NOTE: the `%d` in the above codes will be an integer representing a subscripted value of the structure.	
address	The address of the latch in shared memory. This address corresponds to the `wait` field in `tbstat -u` output if the process is waiting for this latch.	
lock	Machine-dependent flag indicates if the latch is locked and set.	
wait	Indicates if any other processes are waiting for this lock.	
user	The address in shared memory of the owner of the latch. This corresponds to the address in the `tbstat -u` output	

`tbstat -u` output codes.

Tips on using the `tbstat -s` output:

Should a persistent latch be found in the `tbstat -s` output, it is a straightforward job to track down the culprit. A definite sign of a problem is a persistent latch that has many other users waiting for the latch. If the database is frozen, you can expect to see quite a few users stacked up waiting for this latch to release. The information given in the name field will provide detailed information about what kind of latch is giving the problem. Knowing the type of latch that is hung up can point to the underlying problem in the database.

Once the latch is identified and the fact noted that several users are waiting on the latch, you can run `tbstat -u` and note which users have this latch address in their `wait` field. If these users and processes are the ones that are hung up, you've found your problem. Going back to the `tbstat -s` output for the offending latch, you can check its `user` field and get the address of the user process that is blocking everything. Going back to `tbstat -u` will identify the process and give you a UNIX process ID number. You can then decide whether or not to kill the offending process.

This process is the heart of troubleshooting with `tbstat`. You usually poke around until you find something that is out of place or just doesn't seem right. Then you backtrack using the `tbstat -u` command along with specific commands that seem to be related to the problem. The eventual goal is to find a user process of a job that can be killed to clear up the problem.

Of course, the DBA should be certain that the user process is neither holding a latch nor in a critical part of the code before killing a `sqlturbo` process, as either case will cause OnLine to abort, crashing the system.

The `tbstat -s` output can also alert you to possible bottlenecks and resource limitations in your OnLine system. If you find yourself with an abnormally high percentage of jobs waiting for a short time to get latches, you may be able to improve your performance by increasing the numbers of the structures that are controlled by the latch. You cannot alter the number of latches themselves because they are set based upon the size of the resource's parameters.

There are several statistics in the `tbstat -p` output that can point to problems with inadequate resources. When we get to that section, I'll point out several ratios that are listed and several ratios that you can derive from the statistics that can give you an early warning to some resource inadequacies.

The `status` script presented in Chapter 6 makes use of several of these ratios and will give you a central place to look to evaluate the performance of your OnLine database engine.

```
tbstat -k
```

The `tbstat -k` invocation of `tbstat` provides information about the state of the locks in the shared memory lock table. The lock table is accessed through a lock hash table in much the same way as the `tblspace` table. Access to the lock table itself is controlled by a single latch.

Before a process can modify the lock table, it must first acquire the latch. Once the modification is complete, the latch is released. Likewise, each entry in the lock hash table is also guarded by one latch that much be acquired before modifications can be made to any particular hash bucket.

Locks are on tablespaces. Their types and scope (table lock, page lock, row lock, key lock, or byte lock) can be deciphered by using the data and a few rules.

```
INFORMIX  206>tbstat -k

RSAM Version 5.01.UC1  -- On-Line -- Up 5 days 04:09:22 -- 18752 Kbytes

Locks
address   wtlist   owner     lklist    type     tblsnum   rowid   size
11056e48  0        110024b0  0           S      1000002   206     0
11056ea8  0        1100243c  0           S      1000002   206     0
11056f08  0        1100209c  11057548  HDR+IX   200035a   0       0
11056f28  0        11002354  110572c8  HDR+IX   200035f   0       0
11056f48  0        11002768  110574c8  HDR+IX   2000354   0       0
11056fc8  0        11002184  110577a8  HDR+IX   200035e   0       0
11057008  0        11002524  0           S      1000002   206     0
11057048  0        110024b0  11056e48  HDR+IX   2000359   0       0
110570a8  0        11001f40  110571a8  HDR+IX   2000355   0       0
110570c8  0        110023c8  0           S      1000002   206     0
110570e8  0        11002028  11057308  HDR+IX   2000361   0       0
110571a8  0        11001f40  0           S      1000002   206     0
110571c8  0        110026f4  0           S      1000002   206     0
110571e8  0        110023c8  110570c8  HDR+IX   2000360   0       0
11057208  0        110027dc  0           S      1000002   206     0
11057288  0        1100243c  11056ea8  HDR+IX   200035c   0       0
110572c8  0        11002354  0           S      1000002   206     0
11057308  0        11002028  0           S      1000002   206     0
11057388  0        11002524  11057008  HDR+IX   2000356   0       0
 28 active, 200000 total, 16384 hash buckets
```

address	Address of the lock in the lock table. Corresponds to the `wait` field in the `tbstat -u` output if a process is waiting on this lock.
wtlist	Address of first process that is waiting for this lock.
owner	Shared memory address of the owner of the lock. If this value is zero, it means that the server process that owned the transaction is dead but that it continues to hold a lock. In this case, the lock will be almost impossible to clear up and if it's in the way, you'll probably have to restart the database. A valid entry (other than zero) corresponds to the owner's address in the `tbstat -u` output.
lklist	If the owner of this lock holds other locks, the address of the owner's next lock.
type	HDR — header lock (lock hash table) B — Bytes lock (for VARCHARS) S — Shared lock X — Exclusive lock U — Update lock IX — Intent Exclusive IS — Intent Shared SIX — Shared, intent exclusive A lock can be any combination of the above, its elements are joined by a "+."
tblsnum	The tablespace number for the locked resource. The name can be derived by comparing this number with the `tblnum` in the `tbstat -t` output. The first digit represents the dbspace that the tablespace occupies.
rowid	The `rowid` identifies the row being locked. The `rowid` can be used to identify the scope of the lock by using the following rules: Table Lock — `rowid` = 0 Page Lock — `rowid` ends in 00 Row Lock — `rowid` is six digits or less and does not end in 00 Key Lock — hex number with more than six digits Byte Lock — `rowid` ends in 00, and the "size" field is not zero
size	Number of bytes locked for VARCHAR locking (see Byte Lock)

Explanation of the `tbstat -k` output.

`tbstat -b` **and** `tbstat -B`

These two options will print information about buffer utilization by the OnLine engine. The difference between the two is that the lowercase `tbstat -b` will list information only about buffers that are in use by engine processes, while the uppercase `tbstat -B` will print out information about all buffers provided for in the configuration file, whether in use or not. Buffers may and probably will contain data even though they are not currently being accessed by an engine process. The fields reported by both commands are identical. An OnLine buffer structure is actually composed of three separate components:

Buffer pool	Contains copies of pages from disk exactly as they come from disk. These pages can be the contents of any disk structure such as data pages, index pages, system data, etc. Each page in this buffer pool is exactly one page in size, so there is no room left to put housekeeping information.
Buffer header table	This header table is where the housekeeping information is kept. This header table includes information that OnLine needs to manage the related buffer pool entry. It contains entries for the address of the user using the buffer, the state of the buffer (dirty or clean), and the address of the buffer.
Buffer hash table	Used to facilitate faster access to the buffer pool.

Each of the three elements of the buffer has latches that must be acquired before the buffer can be modified. These latches will show up in the tbstat -s output. Each buffer has an individual latch. The buffer header table has a single latch that controls access to the table. Each hash bucket has an individual latch.

```
joe  31> tbstat -b

RSAM Version 4.10.UD4  -- On-Line --Up 8 days 17:26:14 - 18704 Kbytes


Buffers
address   user      flgs pagenum  memaddr  nslots pgflgs xflgs owner waitlist


e070976c 0         0    651566   e0937000 29     1      400   e00023b0 0
e06fff6c 0         6    50479c   e0807000 23     1      0     0        0
 2526 modified, 4750 total, 8192 hash buckets, 2048 buffer size
```

address	Address of the buffer header in the buffer table		
user	Address of the current user or the most recent user to access the buffer.		
flgs	0x01	Buffer contains modified data	
	0x02	Buffer contains data	
	0x04	Buffer on LRU list	
	0x08	I/O error on this page	
	0x10	Buffer is in near table	
	0x20	Buffer is being flushed	
pagenum	The physical page number the page comes from		
memaddr	The address of the buffer page in memory		
nslots	Number of slots on the page. The number of rows stored on this page		
pgflgs	Flag that indicates the type of data held on the page.		
	0x0001	data page	
	0x0002	partition page (`tablespace tablespace`)	
	0x0004	free list page	
	0x0008	chunk free list page	
	0x0009	remainder data page	
	0x000b	partition resident blob page	
	0x000c	blobspace resident blob page	
	0x000d	blob chunk free list bit page	
	0x000e	blob chunk blob map page	
	0x0010	B-tree node page (index)	
	0x0020	B-tree root node page (index)	
	0x0040	B-tree branch node page (index)	
	0x0080	B-tree leaf node page (index)	
	0x0100	logical log page	
	0x0200	last page of logical log	
	0x0400	sync page of logical log	
	0x0800	physical log page	
	0x1000	reserved root pages	
xflgs	Access flags showing how the buffer can be accessed:		
	0x0100	Access buffer in share mode	
	0x0200	Access buffer in update mode	
	0x0400	Access buffer in exclusive mode	
	0x0600	Process is waiting for all other users to finish	
owner	User process that locked the buffer with above `xflgs`		
waitlist	First of the list of users waiting to access the buffer.		

Explanation of `tbstat -b` output, continued.

```
tbstat -R
```

This invocation mode is used to display information about OnLine's Least Recently Used (LRU) queue structures. These queues are a means that OnLine uses to distribute the allocation of the buffer pool in as even a method as possible. When OnLine determines that it needs to place a page into the buffer pool from disk, it needs to be able to find a free buffer in which to place the page.

Since OnLine tries to keep pages in shared memory that may be useful, it uses a least recently used (LRU) algorithm. Depending on the OnLine configuration parameters, there are between three and thirty-two pairs of LRU queues. These queues are in pairs, consisting of a clean queue and a dirty queue. When a page is initially brought into shared memory, it is on a clean queue. When it is modified, it is moved to a dirty queue. Every time a buffer is accessed, it is moved to the head of its queue, called the MRU (most recently used) end.

This movement from the LRU end to the MRU end is done in two steps. First, a latch on the queue is acquired and the buffer is removed from the queue. The latch is then released. Now, OnLine attempts to reobtain the latch. If the latch is reobtained, the buffer is placed on the MRU end of the queue. If OnLine cannot obtain the latch for the second time, it tries the next available queue (either clean or dirty as the case may be). It keeps trying to obtain latches on subsequent queues until it gets one, at which time it places the buffer on the MRU end of the queue.

The effect of this queue dance is that buffers may move from queue to queue in an attempt to balance the load between the queues. The `tbstat -R` command lets the DBA see how often the queues are being accessed and how their cleaning is going on. This is more of a tuning tool than a debugging tool. The DBA will use this command to decide whether or not he has enough queues allocated and to decide threshold points for the page cleaner daemons. See the section on tuning in Chapter 8 for more details.

```
joe 58> tbstat -R

LRU  0:     6 ( 0.9%) modified of  643 total
.... (several lines deleted)
```

```
57 dirty, 4750 queued, 4750 total, 8192 hash buckets, 2048 buffer size
start clean at 60% dirty, stop at 50%; first pass search 70%
```

The first line of the output gives the total number of queues allocated by the LRUS parameter in $TBCONFIG. For each pair, the output gives you a raw number of modified buffers, its percentage of the whole, and the total number of buffers on each queue. In the last line, the start clean is the $TBCONFIG LRU_MAX_DIRTY parameter and the stop at is the LRU_MIN_DIRTY parameter. Notice that the "total" buffer counts are not necessarily equal for each queue pair. This is because of the "queue dance" just discussed in which the buffers move from queue to queue to balance the load.

```
tbstat -F
```

The tbstat -F invocation provides information about the page cleaners or *page flushers* allocated to your OnLine system. It gives you historical data on the different types of writes which have been used to flush your buffers off to disk. It also tells you instantaneous status on the page cleaners currently allocated for your engine.

Different types of writes are more or less efficient than others. By noting the types of writes that your system is performing, you may be able to affect your overall throughput by minimizing some and maximizing others. The tbstat -F command provides you with your raw data.

```
joe  59>tbstat -F
Fg Writes      LRU Writes      Idle Writes    Chunk Writes
0              279744          5142           471793


address  flusher  snooze   state    data
e0001c30 0        60        I        0        = 0
e0001c90 1        60        I        0        = 0
      states: Exit Idle Chunk Lru
```

Fg Writes	These writes are performed by the server process itself. If your system is doing a lot of these writes, your server is constantly having to interrupt itself and go off and do the page cleaner's job. Either increase the number of page cleaners or start them working earlier by lowering `LRU_MAX_DIRTY` .
LRU Writes	These are writes performed by the page cleaners when woken up by the engine, not during the normal operations of the page cleaners. The page cleaners can have their sleep time overridden by the engine in two ways. First, if 16 `fg` writes occur the engine will assume that the page cleaners need to have their sleep interrupted and will wake them up. The other reason is when the percentage of dirty buffers on the LRU queue goes above `LRU_MAX_DIRTY` before the cleaner's snooze time is up, the engine will awaken the page cleaners and have them begin cleaning the buffers. In this example, this is the case, as `LRU_MAX_DIRTY` is set at 60%.
Idle Writes	Idle writes are writes performed by the page cleaners as part of their normal operations as they wake up at the expiration of their snooze time.
Chunk Writes	These are writes that happen during checkpoints. Chunk writes are the most efficient writes performed by OnLine because they are performed as sorted writes. They are also performed when no other writes are allowed and thus can receive more CPU time.

Explanation of types of writes in `tbstat -F` output.

address	The memory address of the cleaner in the page cleaner table. Although the number of page cleaners is allocated according to the CLEANERS parameter in $TBCONFIG, the table will always have 32 slots, which is the maximum number of page cleaners.
flusher	The sequential ID number assigned to this page cleaner
snooze	The current sleep time for this cleaner. This value is set by the page cleaners based upon the amount of activity it is getting, but is a maximum of 60 seconds.

state	A code indicating what the page cleaner is doing at this instant:
	
	I Idle (sleeping)
	C Checkpoint (chunk) write in progress
	L LRU write in progress
	E Exiting. Either the system is shutting down or
	    the page cleaner timed out on its last run,
	    often due to a heavy workload. If it timed out,
	    you'll get a note in your online message logfile.

data	Used in conjunction with the state field above, this code is written in decimal, followed by an equals sign, then in hex:
	
	If state=C data is chunk number where buffers are
	             being written to
	If state=L data is LRU queue from which the page
	             cleaner is writing

Explanation of page cleaner data in tbstat -F output.

The `tbstat -F` command is often used in conjunction with `tbstat -R` to tune the page cleaner system. We'll get into more detail in the section on tuning in Chapter 8, but one point needs to be made now.

Different OnLine applications have different tuning needs and you have to be sensitive to what your system requires. This is one area where the DBA needs to make tradeoffs. Most of the early information on tuning OnLine emphasized the efficiency of `Chunk Writes` and a lot of effort was expended to cause systems to do most of their writes during checkpoints to maximize throughput.

The only problem with that technique is that users started screaming. Even though the throughput may have been much better, the users would have frequent interruptions because writes are prevented during checkpoints. The system would appear to freeze up every few minutes. This would be OK in a batch processing environment, but not in an OLTP (On Line Transaction Processing) environment. Here, the perceived utility of the system was enhanced by forcing the less efficient LRU writes to carry the page-cleaning load while minimizing interruptions to the users when the checkpoints were doing their admittedly more efficient but more intrusive work. The lesson: Know your system. Know your users. Don't follow rules slavishly.

`tbstat -l`

This option will give the DBA information about the physical and logical logging of the OnLine instance. There's a lot of information in this invocation, and it is used for both tuning and troubleshooting. We'll break it up into three sections. The first section contains physical logging statistics.

```
joe  62>tbstat -l
Physical Logging
Buffer bufused  bufsize  numpages numwrits pages/io
  P-1  69       128      713655   5901     120.94
       phybegin physize  phypos   phyused  %used
       117202   6000     2999     69       1.15
```

Buffer	Which of the two physical logs is being used, P-1 or P-2?
bufused	Number of buffer pages used
bufsize	Size of the buffer in pages
numpages	Number of pages written to the physical log
numwrits	Number of writes to the disk
pages/io	`numpages`/`numwrits`. This statistic is used to tune buffers.
phybegin	Page number of the beginning of the physical log file
physize	Size of the physical log in pages
phypos	Current offset into the physical log. Where the next page write will occur.
phyused	Number of pages used in the physical log
%used	Percentage of pages used (`phyused`/`physize`). This statistic is often used for tuning the size of the physical log buffers.

Explanation of `tbstat -l` (physical log section) output.

```
Logical Logging

Buffer bufused  bufsize   numrecs   numpages numwrits  recs/pages pages/io
   L-1  8         64       31030148 668262    21047     46.4        31.8
```

Buffer	Which of the 3 logical log buffers is used? L-1, L-2, L-3?
bufused	Number of pages in the buffer that have been used
bufsize	Size of the buffer in pages
numrecs	Number of records written to logical log files
numpages	Number of pages written to logical log files
numwrits	Number of disk writes to logical log files
recs/pages	`numrecs`/`numpages`. Dependent upon types of transactions logged.
pages/io	`numpages`/`numwrites`. Another tuning statistic. You can alter it by changing the LOGBUFF (buffer size).

Explanation of `tbstat -1` (logical logging section) output.

address	number	flags	uniqid	begin	size	used	%used
e06d26f0	1	F------	0	70f4f4	30000	0	0.00
e06d270c	2	F------	0	716a24	30000	0	0.00
e06d2744	3	U---C-L	2296	907533	30000	14897	49.65

address	Address of the log file descriptor
number	The log file number

flags	Status of each logfile:
	
	    F free, available for use
	    B backed up
	    C current logfile, now receiving transactions
	    U in use, still contains active transactions
	    A newly added. Will become available for
	        use after the next archive.
	    L contains last completed checkpoint

uniqid	The unique ID number of the logfile.
begin	Location of beginning page of the logfile
size	Size of the logfile in pages
used	Number of pages currently used
%used	used/size. How full is this logfile?

Explanation of `tbstat -l` (actual logfile status) output

The first two sections of this output see most use as a tuning tool. We'll go into more specifics in the section on tuning in Chapter 8, but basically the concept is to try to keep the pages per I/O statistics pretty close to the actual number of pages in the buffers, to insure that your writes are doing the most possible work each time they are done. This is logical, since the write will have to look at all of the data anyway. You may as well have the data it sees as full as possible to wring the most work out of each of your writes.

The last section will become one of your most familiar friends (or enemies) as a DBA. Since the logfiles are so important to recovery and since the consequences of filling them up are so disastrous, you need to keep a close eye on your logs. First , you need to have continuous backup going on your logs at all times. If you forget and don't turn it on, you'll have problems when they get full. Next, you're looking for incipient long transactions. If you see that you have many logfiles that show a B for backed up and do not show a F for free, you know that some sort of a transaction is still pending. If you have lots of logs, you can probably just let it go and wait for the transaction to complete. If you begin to get short of logs, you need to think about killing the runaway transaction. Do it early enough that you'll have ample logfiles to log all of the activities that accompany a rollback. If you allow the logfiles to reach the percentage full specified in the LTX_HWM parameter, the engine will lock all other users out of the system, causing their jobs to freeze up.

tbstat -p **and** tbstat -P

These two invocations of the tbstat utility provide the closest thing to a dashboard for the OnLine engine that Informix provides. It reports on statistics kept in shared memory that relate to the performance of the OnLine engine. This is probably the number one tuning and monitoring tool available to the DBA. The statistics are useful in evaluating the overall efficiency of your database system and in measuring the effects of changes in parameters upon your database operations.

The outputs for both the uppercase and lowercase invocations are the same except that the tbstat -P output includes an additional field, BIGReads as the first element in the report. Everything else is identical. The output is divided into four lines of data with headings above each line. We'll look at each line individually:

```
joe  63>tbstat -P

Profile

BIGReads dskreads pagreads bufreads %cached dskwrits pagwrits bufwrits %cache
    235 14970755 22166265 498552631 97.00   543747  2139408  49870693 98.91
```

BIGReads	In `tbstat -P` output only, the number of big buffer reads
dskreads	number of actual reads from disk
pagreads	number of pages read from disk
bufreads	number of reads from the buffer cache
%cached	percentage of reads cached 100*`(bufreads-dskreads)/bufreads` If this figure is above 95%, your system is performing very well.
dskwrits	number of actual physical writes to disk
pagwrits	number of pages written to disk
bufwrits	number of writes to the buffers
%cached	percentage of writes cached 100*`(bufwrits-dskwrits)/bufwrits` If this number is above about 85%, you're doing well.

Explanation of `tbstat -P` (buffer activity) output.

```
isamtot    open      start     read      write    rewrite  delete   commit rollbk
424714409 5813437   23348999 175473799 10989374 5499045   2603325  8699910  101
```

isamtot	Total number of ISAM calls. Does not necessarily correspond to queries, as a query may make many ISAM calls.
open	calls that open a tablespace
start	increments by one when positioning within an index
read	increments when the read function is called
write	increments when the write function is called
rewrite	increments when an update occurs
delete	increments when a row is deleted
commit	increments when a transaction is successfully committed
rollbk	increments when a transaction is rolled back

Explanation of `tbstat -p` (ISAM statistics section) output.

ovtbls	ovlock	ovuser	ovbuff	usercpu	syscpu	numckpts	flushes
0	0	0	0	387006.97	41611.33	294	587

ovtbls	Number of times the `tblspace` table has overflowed. In the `ovrXXXX` statistics that follow, a small number of occurrences is not necessarily critical. If the numbers are large or keep increasing, increase the parameter.
ovlock	Number of times attempted to exceed LOCKS parameter
ovuser	Number of times attempted to exceed USERS parameter
ovbuff	Number of times attempted to exceed BUFFERS parameter
usercpu	Cumulative total CPU time by OnLine processes, in seconds
syscpu	Total system CPU time (UNIX system calls)
numckpts	Number of checkpoints since last boot
flushes	Number of times the buffer pool has been flushed to disk

Explanation of `tbstat -p` (other statistics) output.

```
 bufwaits lokwaits lockreqs deadlks   dltouts   lchwaits ckpwaits compress
  21748     8046    476500421 9         0         1594907  1664      2220019
```

bufwaits	Increments when a process has to wait for a buffer
lokwaits	Increments when a process has to wait for a lock
lokreqs	Increments when a request for a lock occurs
deadlks	Increments when potential deadlock situation is automatically prevented by the engine. (It kills one of the processes.)
dltouts	Increments when a distributed deadlock timeout occurs
lchwaits	Increments when a process is forced to wait for a latch on a resource
chkpwaits	Increments when a process is forced to wait for a checkpoint
compress	Increments whenever a data page is compressed

Explanation of `tbstat -1` (wait states) output.

The first section concerning buffers and cache percentages is most useful in tuning your OnLine parameters for performance. You are looking mostly at the `%cached` fields for reading and writing. If these numbers are low, it is possible that you can increase your performance by tuning the buffer parameters. Be cautious about reading these figures immediately after starting the database. Until the database has "warmed up" and has representative data in the buffer pool, these `%cached` statistics will be low. One good method is to let the database run for a while, and then do a `tbstat -z` to zero out all of the statistics. The statistics gathered from then on will not be tainted by the initial loading of the caches that occur when the system is initially started up.

The second section will give you an idea of the types of activities that your system is performing. These statistics are only meaningful if you have something to compare them to. As you gather your performance statistics, you will begin to develop a feel for the patterns you can expect.

The `ovrXXXX` sections of the next line are an early warning of a need to increase the value of their respective parameters in `$TBCONFIG` file. For example, if you are getting high numbers for `ovlock`, increase the LOCKS parameter in your `$TBCONFIG` file. If you're regularly going over the parameters, your users are probably already complaining about jobs that don't complete.

The `lokwaits` and `lchwaits` statistics on the last line can tip you off to a need to increase the value of some of your `$TBCONFIG` parameters. They can also tip you off to poorly designed programs that may be hogging resources or causing contention between themselves and other programs.

The `status` script included in Chapter 6 makes extensive use of these statistics in preparing a more complete "dashboard" for monitoring the activity of your database engine.

`tbstat - r` **and stacking** `tbstat` **options**

The `tbstat` command can run with any combination of options. You can stack the options like:

```
tbstat -lsp
```

You can also use `tbstat -r` with an optional integer `number`. This option runs `tbstat` in a loop with a `number` second pause between loops. This can be quite useful if you are trying to establish trends or are just anxious to find out when something happens. With no `number`, it runs with a 5 second pause. For example, the following command runs the tables option every 15 seconds.

```
tbstat -tr 15
```

```
tbstat -a
```

The `tbstat -a` command gives you one output that includes the following options:

b	buffers
c	configuration
d	dbspaces
k	locks
l	logs
m	message file
p	profile
s	latches
t	tablespaces
u	users

```
tbstat -m
```

Runs the UNIX `tail` command on your online message log.

```
tbstat -c
```

Prints your `$TBCONFIG` file.

```
tbstat (no options)
```

Gives you a short combined output of:

u	users
p	profile

THE tbcheck UTILITY

The tbcheck utility is used to inspect the actual data on the disks. This is an important utility because this data is stored as binary data broken into pages. Short of writing specialized code to decode this binary data, tbcheck is the only way of accessing the actual data and index pages on the disk. In fact, in most UNIX installations, it is the only way to even *see* the data. This is because most UNIX installations will use *raw* disk devices to hold the OnLine chunks. Since these devices are not mounted in the UNIX file system, they never appear in most UNIX outputs. Even if the system were using UNIX *cooked* files for data storage, the data is stored in a binary format that cannot be viewed by normal UNIX commands.

UNIX commands such as dd can be used to relocate these chunks, but instances when this would be necessary are rare. Such instances could be the result of replacing a physical disk device. In such instances, the system needs to be down during the operations, as the UNIX commands have no concept of data integrity or consistency.

Commands such as od (octal dump) or hd (hex dump) could be used to inspect the data on the raw partitions, but these commands do not decipher the data layout of the OnLine chunks.

The Informix Customer Support engineers have access to additional tools to inspect and modify the data. They use an internal tool called tbdump to dump pages from disk and one called tbpatch to modify the pages. When the engineers call into your system to make repairs, they place these tools in the $INFORMIXDIR/astools directory. These tools are often left in the directory at the end of the service call.

The tbdump utility can provide some insights into the layout of the chunks if you have time to poke around in the chunks. The tbpatch utility can be very dangerous. Don't use it unless you are willing to risk losing all of your data.

If you ever get into a situation where things are totally bollixed up, check with Informix Technical Support. Some of their wizards may be able to twiddle the bits and get you back online.

One thing that they do quite often is change the online/offline bits that determine whether a chunk is usable or not. If you ever have a chunk that is down and you cannot get it to come back online, it's time to either restore from tape or call Informix Technical Support. Version 6.0 will allow you to bring a chunk back online yourself without assistance.

Many of the miracles that Informix Technical Support perform are brought about by some of the software tools that they have available to them. Short of having these specialized tools, tbcheck should be your tool of choice.

This utility can have serious side effects, though, and the DBA should be careful when using it. In many instances, tbcheck will place a shared lock on the tables it is addressing. This prevents others from updating the table during its use. This is most visible using the -pt and -pT options. Since these options look at every data (and index for -pT) page in the table, this shared lock can last for a long time. Use these options only during times when your users will not be bothered by your locking the tables. It's best to reserve these options for system downtime.

The other options that inspect data or index pages for specific tables may have similar effects. These include the -ci, -cI, -ck, -cK, -cL, and -cl options, along with their -p counterparts. Use them carefully.

Of the other useful options, -pe is one of the most useful. It does not have any harmful effects on the database and can be used freely without worrying about interfering with your users. The same command, with the check option -cc is also safe to use. The -pc and -cc options are also relatively innocuous. We'll note these side effects as we talk about each option.

The full invocation options of tbcheck are:

```
joe 26> thcheck --
TBCHECK
Usage:  tbcheck [-clist] [-plist] [-qny]
                [ { database[:[owner.]table] | TBLSpace number | Chunk numbe
}
                { rowid | page number } ]
-c      - check
    r   - reserved pages
    e   - TBLSpace extents and chunk extents
    c   - database catalogs
    i   - table indexes
    I   - table indexes and rowids in index
    d   - TBLSpace data rows including bitmaps
    D   - TBLSpace data rows including bitmaps, remainder pages and blobs
-p      - print
    r   - reserved pages (-cr)
    e   - extents report (-ce)
    c   - catalog report (-cc)
    k   - keys in index (-ci)
    K   - keys and rowids in index (-cI)
    l   - leaf node keys only (-ci)
    L   - leaf node keys and rowids (-cI)
    d   - TBLSpace data rows (-cd)
    D   - TBLSpace data rows including bitmaps,remainder pages and blobs (-c
    t   - TBLSpace report    (CAUTION:  Locks the table!)
    T   - TBLSpace disk utilization report  (CAUTION:  Locks the table!!)
    p   - dump page for the given [table and rowid | TBLSpace and page numbe
    P   - dump page for the given chunk number and page number
    B   - BLOBSpace utilization for given table(s) [database:[owner.]]table
-q      - quiet mode - print only error messages
-n      - answer NO to all questions
-y      - answer YES to all questions
--      - print this help text
```

**DANGEROUS OPTIONS: due to locking problems, be careful with the "i", "k",
                      "l" (ell), and "t" options, along with their capitalized
                      counterparts.**

We will only cover a few of the more commonly used options here. If you need further detail, go to the tbcheck sections of the Informix DBA manuals for more detail. We'll try to cover the options that you will use in normal operations here. The other options are usually used for debugging specific problems. If you are sophisticated enough to be doing this level of debugging, you can certainly handle the manual. The items that we will gloss over will be the sections that allow you to check and/or print specific data and index pages. If you're using these options, you are probably looking to correct specific data or index problems. Most of the time this is academic, because you'll have to restore or rebuild your data or indexes if your data is this corrupted.

tbcheck -ce **and** tbcheck -pe

These two options are options that can safely be used at any time to dump information about the extent usage of your OnLine databases. These options check the chunk free list and tablespace extents. The -ce option just does the checks. The -pe option checks the data and prints the extent and table information.

Both options first give you a check of any tablespaces that occupy more than eight extents. This number of extents is important. When a tablespace goes over eight extents, an additional disk access is needed to retrieve data. This is due to the sizing of the data structures that hold the disk access pointers. As a general rule, your tables should be sized such that they and all their related indexes occupy eight or fewer extents. This is not always possible, but it's a good thing to strive for. Oddly enough, some of the most common tables that you find with more than eight extents in larger databases are the system catalogue tables, notably systables, syscolumns and sysindexes. If you are expecting to deal with a large number of tables and indexes, it is advisable to increase the NEXT EXTENT parameter of the system tables before you begin to build the regular tables. This can be done with the following SQL statement:

```
ALTER TABLE systables MODIFY NEXT EXTENT 32;
```

The tablename and actual extent size will vary with your applications. You can alter the NEXT EXTENT, but not the initial extent.

The printing option (-pe) gives you a report in the following format:

```
WARNING:TBLSpace joe:informix.queries has more than 8 extents.
WARNING:TBLSpace joe:informix.performance has more than 8 extents.

DBSpace Usage Report:  rootdbs              Owner:  informix  Created:
06/24/92

      Chunk: 1   /dev/rootdbs3                       Size     Used     Free
                                                    135000    99713    35287

          Disk usage for Chunk 1                          Start    Length
          -----------------------------------------     --------- ---------
          ROOT DBSpace RESERVED Pages                        0       12
          CHUNK FREE LIST PAGE                              12        1
          PARTITION PARTITION                               13     2705
          dba:joe.test                                    2718        8
          dba:informix.syscolumns                         2726        8
          dba:joe.dummy                                   2734        8
          dba:informix.sysreferences                      2742        8
          dba:informix.extent_sizes                       2750       50
          FREE                                            2800   132200
```

This report will go on to cover every chunk, every extent, and every tablespace in your OnLine system, giving you useful information about the space utilization, fragmentation, and free space.

Practical uses for tbcheck -pe

Of all the information available from tbcheck, this report is the most useful. In addition to being safe to run no matter what users are doing, it runs relatively quickly and efficiently. It covers all data in the instance, spanning all databases.

One of the things that I do with my database is have the UNIX cron command run the following script every morning at 3:00 am:

```
tbcheck -pe >& /u2/informix/last_tbcheckpe
```

The output file `last_tbcheckpe` is useful for many things. First, it is a good reference to have around if you just want to locate data about a chunk or tablespace. This file can be compressed and saved in an archive on a regular basis to give you a sense of exactly how your databases are growing or changing.

A third very important use is to provide data for a table size tracking and reporting system. If you've looked at the data in the system tables, it is not always clear just exactly how much space is being taken up by a table's extents. Since the output of this daily report shows exactly how the extents are being used, it is worth the effort to massage the data a little more.

In Chapter 6, I'll show you a script that extracts pertinent data from this report, loads the data into OnLine tables, and generates useful reports from the data. This will be merged with data showing dbspace locations of the tables and will form the basis for a system to manage the size and proliferation of your database tables.

One of the more important things that the output of this command gives you is a picture of exactly how fragmented your tables have become. As a table grows in size, it attempts to allocate additional extents that are contiguous to the last extent. As you add tables, drop tables, add chunks, and generally fill up your dbspaces, it becomes harder for the OnLine engine to keep your extents contiguous. As the tables become more fragmented, the I/O system has to do more work to find all of the pieces of the tables.

This results in a generalized slowdown of access and increased cost in resources to do the work. If you begin to experience a general slowdown of operations, watch the fragmentation of the tables. It may be necessary to occasionally rebuild the tables in another dbspace to collect all of the extents and make them contiguous again. This shows up most emphatically when the engine needs to do long sequential scans of the data.

```
tbcheck -pt
```

This invocation of `tbcheck` generates a report that gives more detailed information about specific tables. It is invoked as:

```
tbcheck -pt admin:system

TBLSpace Report for admin:dba.system
        Physical Address                300220
        Creation date                   06/05/92 05:09:47
        TBLSpace Flags                  1            Page Locking
        Maximum row size                64
        Number of special columns       0
        Number of keys                  1
        Number of extents               3
        Current serial value            1
        First extent size               6
        Next extent size                4
        Number of pages allocated       18
        Number of pages used            17
        Number of data pages            15
        Number of data bytes            13952
        Number of rows                  218
        Extents
            Logical Page   Physical Page        Size
                      0         3030d4            6
        ......<several lines deleted>.......
```

In the output of this command the columns for number of pages used and number of data pages used represent maximums for the table as currently configured. It does not break down the number of pages into allocated versus currently used. Note that all of the numbers are in pages

```
tbcheck -pT
```

This command gives more detailed information about the use and allocation of extents for tablespaces and also includes information about index usage. It is invoked as:

```
tbcheck -pT admin:system

TBLSpace Report for admin:dba.system

        Physical Address                300220
        Creation date                   06/05/92 05:09:47
        TBLSpace Flags                  1               Page Locking
        Maximum row size                64
        Number of special columns       0
        Number of keys                  1
        Number of extents               3
        Current serial value            1
        First extent size               6
        Next extent size                4
        Number of pages allocated       18
        Number of pages used            17
        Number of data pages            15
        Number of data bytes            13952
        Number of rows                  218


        Extents
                Logical Page   Physical Page        Size
                        0          3030d4             6
                        6          303192             4

TBLSpace Usage Report for admin:dba.system

        Type              Pages      Empty   Semi-Full    Full  Very-Full
        ---------------  ---------- ---------- ---------- ---------- ----------
        Free                6
        Bit-Map             1
        Index               3
        Data (Home)         8
                         ----------
        Total Pages        18
```

```
Unused Space Summary

        Unused data slots                                    14
        Unused bytes per data page                           48
        Total unused bytes in data pages                    384

Index Usage Report for index system_ci on admin:dba.system

                     Average      Average
        Level   Total No. Keys Free Bytes
        ----- -------- -------- ----------
            1        1        2       2002
            2        2      109        930
        ----- -------- -------- ----------
        Total        3       73       1287
```

The output from the `tbcheck -pT` command contains all of the information that is in the `tbcheck -pt` command, with the additional information about unused space and index usage. Note that both the `tbcheck -pT` and `tbcheck -pt` place locks on the target tables, making it impossible for others to update, delete, or insert into these tables while the utilities are running.

This locking is unfortunate in that it limits the usability of `tbcheck` and makes it difficult to get detailed information about actual space utilization without locking tables. Some of the information can be gleaned from the innocuous options such as the `tbcheck -pe` option. None of the other options allows you to see what you need, which is the number of pages free in a tablespace. One way of working around this while the database is running is to compute some of the information from `tbstat -t`. This only works if the target table you want to check is currently open. The following script shows a way of opening the table and running a `tbstat` at the same time Create this script and name it `tstat`:

```
#!/bin/csh
(sleep 1; tbstat -t > tstat.out &
isql $1 << EOF
select * from $2;
EOF
```

In all of the scripts in this book, we are assuming that you are using isql as a data retrieval client. If you are using dbaccess rather than isql, simply change the isql to dbaccess in all of the scripts.

This script creates an output file called tstat.out. The program is invoked as:

```
tstat database_name table_name
```

(for this sample run, the invocation was:

```
tstat admin test_table

joe 61>  cat tstat.out

RSAM Version 5.00.UC2    -- On-Line -- Up 29 days 00:04:50 -- 12976 Kbytes

Tblspaces
```

n	address	flgs	ucnt	tblnum	physaddr	npages	nused	npdata	nrows	nextns
0	e00b85f4	1	1	1000001	10000e	5405	408	0	0	1
3	e00b8e40	1	1	4000001	500004	1355	2	0	0	1
4	e00b9104	1	11	3000002	300005	64	63	38	659	8
31	e00bdbb0	1	1	300021d	300220	18	17	15	218	3

```
4 active, 1100 total, 512 hash buckets
```

Looking at the tstat.out output file, we see that the last table is tblnum 300021d. By using the table script from Chapter 6, we can confirm that tblnum 300021d is indeed test_table.

The difference between the npages and the nused column is the pages free output of the tbcheck -pT program. The only problem with this script is that it outputs all of the target table's rows to standard output. If the table is large, this could take a while. You can run it for a second and then hit a CONTROL-C to exit and still get the output without danger of crashing the system. It's not as good as tbcheck, but it doesn't lock the tables.

`tbcheck - ci` **and** `tbcheck -cI`

The options for checking and repairing indexes with `tbcheck` are similar. The uppercase version is more complete and encompassing than the lowercase version. The `tbcheck -ci` utility just checks the key values of the indexes. The `tbcheck -cI` version adds to that a check of the `rowids` of the keys. If the indexes are consistent, there is no output. If there are problems they are reported.

Both of these options include the capability of attempting to repair the indexes. You will only be given these options if the system is quiescent when the `tbcheck` is run. You can give the `-y` or `-n` flags to indicate that you either do or don't want `tbcheck` to try to repair the indexes.

The option to repair the indexes looks good on paper, but it's really pretty useless. Repairing an index requires your system to be quiescent. It is much slower than simply dropping and recreating the index. As a bonus, dropping and recreating the index does not require you to bring down the instance. About the only time that there is an advantage to attempting an index repair is if the index is on a system table and you think that dropping the system table's index might hurt your performance or integrity. In that case, it might be worthwhile to attempt a repair.

`tbcheck -cc` **and** `tbcheck -pc`

These options will check and print the contents of the system catalogue tables. The `check` option will often complain about missing synonym and authorization records. I have yet to see any instances where these complaints are valid.

The printing options are somewhat useful in that they not only provide the same checks as does the `-cc` options, they also print extent information ala `tbcheck -pt`.

Again, on all of these options, watch for locking.

`tbcheck -pr database_name`

This option is another option that may be useful to the DBA. It provides the following output of data that is contained in the root dbspace reserved pages:

```
joe 71> tbcheck -pr
Validating INFORMIX-OnLine reserved pages - PAGE_PZERO
     Identity                      INFORMIX-OnLine
     Database system state         0
     Database system flags         0
     Page Size                     2048
     Date/Time created             06/04/92 13:24:33
     Version number of creator     2048
     Last modified time stamp      1
Validating INFORMIX-OnLine reserved pages - PAGE_CONFIG
     ROOTNAME                      rootdbs
     ROOTPATH                      /dev/root_dbs
     ROOTOFFSET                    128
     ROOTSIZE                      540000
     PHYSDBS                       rootdbs
     PHYSFILE                      4000
     LOGFILES                      3
     LOGSIZE                       60000
     MSGPATH                       /u2/informix/online.log
     CONSOLE                       /u2/informix/online.sys
     TAPEDEV                       /dev/rmt1
     TAPEBLK                       16
     TAPESIZE                      3950000
     LTAPEDEV                      /dev/null
     LTAPEBLK                      16
     LTAPESIZE                     13107200
     DBSERVERNAME                  robin
     SERVERNUM                     1
     DEADLOCK_TIMEOUT              60
     RESIDENT                      0
     USERS                         110
     LOCKS                         20000
     BUFFERS                       4750
     TBLSPACES                     1100
     CHUNKS                        27
     DBSPACES                      8
     PHYSBUFF                      128
     LOGBUFF                       128
     LOGSMAX                       35
     CLEANERS                      2
```

```
        BUFFSIZE                      2048
        CKPTINTVL                     1200
```

Validating INFORMIX-OnLine reserved pages - PAGE_1CKPT & PAGE_2CKPT
         Using check point page PAGE_1CKPT.

```
        Time stamp of checkpoint      528303532
        Time of checkpoint            01/13/94 17:47:12
        Physical log begin address    10152a
        Physical log size             2000
        Physical log position at Ckpt 208
        Logical log unique identifier 349
        Logical log position at Ckpt  1f9c760
        DBSpace descriptor page       100004
        Chunk descriptor page         100007
        Mirror chunk descriptor page  100009
        Log file number               1
        Log file flags                13        Log file in use
                                                Current log file
                                                Log written to archive tape

        Time stamp                    0
        Date/Time file filled         12/31/69 18:00:00
        Unique identifier             349
        Physical location             101cfa
        Log size                      30000
        Number pages used             8093


        Log file number               2
        Log file flags                0
        Time stamp                    521789106
        Date/Time file filled         11/18/93 15:06:51
        Unique identifier             0
        Physical location             10922a
        Log size                      30000
        Number pages used             0
```

Validating INFORMIX-OnLine reserved pages - PAGE_1DBSP & PAGE_2DBSP
         Using dbspace page PAGE_1DBSP.

```
DBSpace number              1
Flags                       1              No mirror chunks
First chunk                 1
Number of chunks            1
Date/Time created           06/04/92 13:24:33
DBSpace name                rootdbs
DBSpace owner               informix
DBSpace number              2
Flags                       1              No mirror chunks
First chunk                 2
Number of chunks            1
Date/Time created           06/04/92 13:31:44
DBSpace name                log_dbspace2
DBSpace owner               informix

DBSpace number              3
Flags                       1              No mirror chunks
First chunk                 3
Number of chunks            2
Date/Time created           06/04/92 13:32:42
DBSpace name                dbspace1
DBSpace owner               informix

DBSpace number              4
Flags                       1              No mirror chunks
First chunk                 5
Number of chunks            1
Date/Time created           06/04/92 13:33:42
DBSpace name                log_dbspace
DBSpace owner               informix
```

```
Validating INFORMIX-OnLine reserved pages - PAGE_1PCHUNK & PAGE_2PCHUNK
        Using primary chunk page PAGE_2PCHUNK.
    Chunk number                    1
    Next chunk in DBSpace           0
    Chunk offset                    64
    Chunk size                      270000
    Number of free pages            70645
    DBSpace number                  1
    Overhead                        0
    Flags                           2041        Chunk resides on RAW device
                                                Chunk is online
    Chunk name length               13
    Chunk path                      /dev/root_dbs


    Chunk number                    2
    Next chunk in DBSpace           0
    Chunk offset                    16
    Chunk size                      45000
    Number of free pages            14092
    DBSpace number                  2
    Overhead                        0
    Flags                           2041        Chunk resides on RAW device
                                                Chunk is online
    Chunk name length               10
    Chunk path                      /dev/logs2


    Chunk number                    3
    Next chunk in DBSpace           4
    Chunk offset                    16
    Chunk size                      500000
    Number of free pages            18527
    DBSpace number                  3
    Overhead                        0
    Flags                           2041        Chunk resides on RAW device
                                                Chunk is online
    Chunk name length               11
    Chunk path                      /dev/chunk2
```

```
Chunk number                4
Next chunk in DBSpace       0
Chunk offset                16
Chunk size                  500000
Number of free pages        88404
DBSpace number              3
Overhead                    0
Flags                       2041      Chunk resides on RAW device
                                      Chunk is online
Chunk name length           11
Chunk path                  /dev/chunk3


Chunk number                5
Next chunk in DBSpace       0
Chunk offset                16
Chunk size                  67500
Number of free pages        6142
DBSpace number              4
Overhead                    0
Flags                       2041      Chunk resides on RAW device
                                      Chunk is online
Chunk name length           9
Chunk path                  /dev/logs
```

```
Validating INFORMIX-OnLine reserved pages - PAGE_1MCHUNK & PAGE_2MCHUNK
        Using mirror chunk page PAGE_2MCHUNK.


Validating INFORMIX-OnLine reserved pages - PAGE_1ARCH & PAGE_2ARCH
        Using archive page PAGE_2ARCH.

    Archive Level               0
    Real Time Archive Began     01/12/94 09:18:23
    Time Stamp Archive Began    527989114
    Logical Log Unique Id       349
    Logical Log Position        a9c224
```

There's a lot of information available from the `tbcheck -pr` utility, and some of it is available nowhere else. It provides a good snapshot of the condition of your database at any particular time. It would be wise to occasionally run this option and save it off in an archive file. If this is accompanied by running `newschema` for the entire database, it would provide useful disaster recovery capabilities for the DBA. The `newschema` script is presented in Chapter 6. It allows you to generate a correct, detailed database schema that contains more detail than the Informix `dbschema` program.

The logfile and checkpoint information presented is also unique to this program. I know of no other way to get access to this data other than by using the `tbcheck` utility. Of course, all of this data can be massaged by UNIX scripts should the DBA have some more specific needs in mind.

DATA MOVEMENT UTILITIES

Before a database becomes useful for real work, it has to have data. Initially, this sounds like a really stupid statement, but it is really the place where we have to start in working with OnLine. The data does not just magically appear in the tables ready to be used in our applications. It has to be put there, most often by being imported from other non-OnLine sources.

Maybe your system is well established and the tables are already populated. You may be tempted to believe that data movement utilities are no longer of use to you. Wrong. You will have many instances in which these utilities will be used. You may need to upgrade your hardware to another machine. You may need to provide data dumps that can be read by another database system on another machine. Your users may want data that they can use in their PC programs. Maybe they want files that they can read into their spreadsheets or word processors. Maybe you need to move large tables from one instance to another or from one dbspace to another. Maybe you need to provide extra archive protection for a few tables. The data movement utilities are essential for all of these applications.

General concepts

There are some concepts that apply to moving data within OnLine or to and from other systems no matter what methods you choose to use. Data migration requires a knowledge of your particular OnLine setup and of the contents of your data tables. For the most part, unloading data from your OnLine system is fairly simple. It is when you need to load data from another source into OnLine that complications may arise. Choosing the proper tools for data migration depends upon several factors:

- Requirements of the other system
- Contents of the data
- Logging status of your OnLine system
- Indexing requirements
- Degree of consistency or concurrency required
- Time frame
- UNIX resources
- OnLine resources

Requirements of the other system

Whether the other system is providing data to OnLine or whether OnLine is providing data to the other system, they have to be aware of the other's needs. A basic need is that they both use the same character representations. If you output data in ASCII and the other system wants it in EBCDIC, you will need to use the proper UNIX utilities to translate the data.

Contents of the data

You need to know how the data is currently formatted and how it needs to be formatted for the other system. If the other system wants multiline records or is sending you multiline records, you will use different tools than you would if all records are single lines. For the methods that use ASCII dumps, you need to be able to choose a delimiter character. Your data will be junk if you try to use a UNIX pipe "|" symbol to separate your fields and your data actually contains the pipe symbol. Some of the means of unloading data are smart enough to watch out for this, but you need to double-check. For example, the UNLOAD TO xxxx SQL statement will escape a delimiter character if it finds one in a character field. You also need to be aware of how the each of the source and target systems handle null fields.

Logging status of your OnLine system

Logging status is one of the "gotcha's" of moving data to and from OnLine. This usually gives you trouble when you are loading data into an OnLine system. Some of the utilities require that the logging modes of the sending and receiving database (OnLine to OnLine) be the same. No matter what tools you're using, it is usually better to load into a database that has logging turned off. Of course, this is not practical if you are loading into a production system using logging and you can't or don't want to turn the logging off. It's tempting to try to get around this problem by loading data into a non-logging database and then either creating synonyms from a logging database into the new table or using INFORMIX-Star to load data from the new, non-logging table into your production system. This does not work, as OnLine enforces rules that require similarity of logging status on each side of synonyms and INFORMIX-Star links.

Indexing requirements

You should load into nonindexed tables and index the tables after the data is in place. If you are loading and indexing at the same time, you will have data pages interspersed with index pages in your tablespace. This causes the data to be fragmented and makes access to the data slower. This is especially noticeable with long, sequential, nonindexed reads of the data. If the data pages had all been contiguous, the reads would be quite efficient. The indexes would have also been more compact, as they would have been presorted. With data pages and index pages interspersed, the disk head has to jump around quite a lot to read the data. In addition, the entire process goes faster if the indexing is done later. Especially in versions later than 4.11, the engine supports parallel sorting via the PSORT environmental variable. If you have multiple processors, using this parallel sorting capability will make your sorts go much faster.

If you can, when you are unloading a table to a flat file for loading into another OnLine database, sort the output in the primary key order that is desired for the target table. That way, when the table is loaded, it is already clustered on the primary key. In addition, if a table is already in the proper sorted order, there is an environmental variable that you can set to tell the sort that the table is already sorted and that the engine does not need to perform a sort for this index. This variable is $NOSORTINDEX. Set it to 1 before creating the primary index for this table, and the sorting portion of your index build will go even faster.

Degree of logical consistency between tables

If you are dumping just one table or loading just one table, you usually don't have to worry too much about consistency, but it may bear some thought. If you are moving multiple tables that depend upon each other, you definitely need to consider whether you can unload them while database activity is occurring. First, you need to decide whether the data movement occurs when the database is online or when it is quiescent. Are others accessing or needing access to the tables? Does the table depend upon other tables for join information or lookup information? Can others access the table while the data movement is happening? Does the utility lock the table when unloading? All of these factors make a difference in deciding how you move data.

If you try to move two tables while the database is running, you could be facing some serious problems if changes were made to the first and second tables after the first had been unloaded and before the second had been unloaded. The tables could contain logically inconsistent data.

Time frame

How much time do you have to do this job? Do you need to have a table locked for hours? Do you need the database quiescent for hours? Just how long will it take to move a few million rows?

UNIX resources

If you're moving data to disk, do you have enough disk space? How much of load will the job place on your system?

OnLine resources

This is an important factor. First and foremost, will loading the data create a long transaction problem? If you're loading into a logging database, this could definitely be a problem. Make sure that you have enough logfiles and that other activities which generate heavy logging are not happening at the same time. Make sure that your LTXHWM and LTEHWM logfile high water marks are set lower than the defaults, as the defaults are too high for most real-world applications. Use at least 60 percent and 70 percent for the respective numbers. Make sure that you have enough locks in the system to handle the locking load. If you're loading using SQL into an existing or newly created table, lock the target table before beginning the load. That way, you'll use only one table lock instead of thousands of row or page locks.

We'll now look briefly at the tools for moving data. For full details on the operations of each of the utilities, look to your manuals. This is just an overview of the capabilities and applicability of each tool. We'll explore the tools from fastest to slowest.

`tbtape -s` **(archive and restore)**

This is by far your tool of choice if you are moving an entire instance. It will move everything: all databases, all indexes, all extent data, even all wasted space. If you want to move just one database from one machine to another, you can always move everything and drop the ones you don't want. You may even be able to use your normal backup archives as a medium of transferring data to the new computer without doing any extra work on your source machine.

Obviously, this only works from one OnLine system to another. Depending upon the differences between versions, it may work from one OnLine version to another. If the versions are close enough and if the machines have similar page sizes and similar ways of representing data, it may even work from one brand of computer to another. If you're upgrading to a bigger computer using the same operating system, the same OnLine version, and the same architecture, this may be the way to go.

At least with OnLine versions prior to Version 6.0, the host and target machines must have similar layouts. If you have a one gigabyte chunk on `/dev/chunk1` on the source machine, you must have a similar (or larger) size device on the target machine. The general rule is that the target machine must have everything that the host machine has. If you're working on a disaster recovery plan, make sure that your backup machine at least equals your source in disk space allocated to OnLine.

Along with the archives that are necessary for recovery, be sure that you have copied to a safe place any other information that would be necessary to recreate your system's layout. Keep a copy of the `tbconfig` file and a copy of the `tbstat -a` output. Also keep a copy of the output of the `tbcheck -pr` command.

If you can use `tbtape`'s archives and restores to move your data, you can expect to restart on the new system with it looking exactly like the old system with little or no effort.

`tbunload/tbload`

The `tbload` and `tbunload` utilities are a very fast means of moving tables and databases. They can work either on single tables or on entire databases. Like archive and restore, they work with binary pages of data and are very fast, similar in speed to the archive and restore utilities. Like archives and restores using `tbtape` they require compatible versions of OnLine, compatible page sizes and page format, and compatible integer representations. Unlike `tbtape` archives and restores, they do not require similar resources and identical chunk size and naming.

The `tbunload` and `tbload` programs also transfer index, extent, and other table information. One of the potential problems that can occur with the moving of indexes is the requirement that index names be unique over a database. You cannot have two indexes named `index_1` within a database even if they are on separate tables. The names must be unique. The `tbload` utility provides for this by providing a `-i` parameter that will allow you to rename indexes during the move to preserve the uniqueness of index names.

The `tbload` and `tbunload` utilities are designed to move data to and from tape. If you want to use a disk file instead, you should first create the file and make sure that it has proper ownership and permissions and then treat the file just like a tape device. Of course, you should be certain that you will have enough space on the device to hold all the data.

If you succeed in moving a table or a database using `tbunload/tbload`, always run the `tbcheck` utility on the resulting table or database. I have seen situations where the `tbload` completed with no problems, the tables showed up on the new system, and the data seemed to be there. However, when the `tbcheck` utility was run, there were internal problems with the data. Check it out carefully before putting your trust in it.

`dbexport/dbimport`

This utility pair moves entire databases between OnLine and/or INFORMIX-SE systems in the form of ASCII files. They transfer entire databases and cannot be used to add tables to existing databases. They create database schema files and database export files. The schema files and the export files can be individually directed either to disk or to tape. The schema files used by these utilities are basic and do not include information about extent sizes, locking modes, `dbspaces`, or logging modes.

These schemas are generalized so that they can be used to transfer data to and from both OnLine and INFORMIX-SE systems. If you are planning to send the data files to disk, be sure that you have enough disk space to hold your entire database.

Schema files can be edited if they are sent to disk, or they can be replaced with complete schema files such as those generated by the `newschema` program which is introduced in Chapter 6 of this book.

During operation of `dbexport`, the source database is locked in exclusive mode, so it is not suitable for operation while the database is in use.

`dbload`

The `dbload` utility does not have a reciprocal `dbunload` program. The `dbload` utility is used to insert ASCII formatted data into existing tables, with the loading parameters controlled by a command file. This utility is best suited for moving complex ASCII data into OnLine tables.

This utility is executed from the UNIX command line. It has many option flags that give you a lot of control over how the utility runs.

The `load` utility gives you detailed control over delimiters, frequency of commits to avoid long transaction problems, acceptable number of errors before abort, number of rows to skip at the beginning of a data file, and whether or not to lock the target table when loading.

The usage of the dbload utility is:

```
INFORMIX : 19> dbload

DBLOAD Load Utility              INFORMIX-SQL Version 5.00.UC2

Copyright (C) Informix Software, Inc., 1984-1991
Software Serial Number XYZ#C2999999

Usage:

dbload [-d dbname] [-c cfilname] [-l logfile] [-e errnum] [-n nnum]
       [-i inum] [-s] [-p] [-r]


       -d      database name
       -c      command file name
       -l      bad row(s) log file
       -e      bad row(s) # before abort
       -s      syntax error check only
       -n      # of row(s) before commit
       -p      prompt to commit or not on abort
       -i      # or row(s) to ignore before starting

       -r      loading without locking table
```

The command files can handle two main types of data: data that is delimited by a defined delimiter character and tabular data that is character-position dependent. This flexibility of input formats makes dbload a very powerful tool for loading ASCII files from sources other than an OnLine database. The dbload utility can be combined with other UNIX utilities to create flexible systems that takes a datafile or report from another source, massages it with UNIX utilities into a format that dbload understands, and finally loads the data into OnLine through dbload.

One of the main features of the dbload command is the -n parameter. It is possible that if you try to load a very large table into a tablespace you will run into problems with running out of locks or creating a long transaction. The -n parameter allows you to get around either of these problems, as the value of n tells dbload to perform a COMMIT WORK every n rows. These periodic commits prevent dbload from using all of your locks and from trying to do the entire load in one transaction, causing a long transaction and possibly filling up all your logfiles.

Another very useful capability of dbload is the -e parameter. Unless you are using dbload, if you attempt to load duplicate rows into a table with unique indexes or unique constraints, you will bomb out with an error message that tells you that you have duplicate data. This can become a real pain if you are trying to eliminate these duplicates. You can use the -e parameter to tell dbload to ignore bad rows and to place them in an error file (the name of which is determined by the -l parameter). The value of e is the total number of bad rows you will accept before allowing dbload to fail.

If you have a case where you have partially loaded a table, or if you have two tables that have duplicates, and you want to consolidate them, you can use dbload to create one table. Unload the first table into a flat file using the SQL UNLOAD TO command. Then do a dbload with a very large value for the -e parameter, loading the second table from the flat file that contains the first table's contents. The dbload command will complain about the duplicate rows, but it will load all of the nonduplicate rows into the second table.

Writing and debugging the command files for dbload is as much an exercise in programming as is writing SQL statements or writing C programs. If you need to use dbload to move data, sit down with the manuals and the examples and see how it is done. You may want to look at the *.unl files in the $INFORMIXDIR/demo file tree for examples of the use of this program.

The command file for dbload contains the name of the file from which the dbload program gets the data to load into the table. This does not necessarily have to be the name of a file. If your flavor of UNIX supports *named pipes* created by the mkfifo UNIX command, the data source can be a named pipe. You can use this to move data from table to table or from database to database without worrying about long transactions or running out of locks. Create the named pipe and start a SQL UNLOAD TO "named_pipe" command from your source table. From another terminal, run dbload with "named_pipe" as the source of your data. The data will be unloaded from the source table and inserted into the target table.

```
UNLOAD    TO    filename    select_statement    and  LOAD    FROM
filename insert_statement
```

This pair of SQL statements allows you to create delimited ASCII files from tables and to place the contents of delimited ASCII files into tables. They can be used either with `isql` or with `dbaccess`. The `select_statement` in the UNLOAD command can be any legal OnLine SELECT statement, so it is possible to create LOADS of partial tables or fragments of tables.

These commands are suitable for use on an operating production system provided you have covered the problems of insuring adequate resources and have adequately addressed the issues of logging and concurrency of access. The UNLOAD SQL statement is very seldom a problem in any manner, unless you don't have adequate disk space, but using LOAD can create long transactions or can cause you to run out of locks. In cases like this, the `dbload` program may be better for your use.

Reports to a File

ASCII files can be generated using a report writer. If you use `isql`, you can use the ACE report writer that is included with `isql`. These report files, if used with the default report format, will create character-position dependent ASCII output files suitable for use with `dbload`. By modifying the SELECT statement in the report, the report writer could create a delimited report.


```
OUTPUT TO   filename WITHOUT HEADINGS select_statement
```

This SQL statement is similar to UNLOAD except that it does not place delimiters in the output file. This makes it suitable for creating output files that are character-position dependent. It can also be run with the WITHOUT HEADINGS constraint that causes OnLine to omit the names of the fields. The OUTPUT TO or the UNLOAD TO SQL statements can create files that can be read by the `dbload` program.

An interesting and useful feature of the OUTPUT TO statement in SQL is the ability to use the PIPE TO statement in place of an output file. This statement takes the output of the SQL command and pipes it into a UNIX pipeline. Use of this construct is one way that you can cause a UNIX command to execute from within your SQL statements.

For example:

```
OUTPUT TO PIPE " > /dev/null; ls -la" select * from dummy
```

Since SQL does not have the equivalent of a `system` command, this trick can simulate a `system` command. The contents of the pipe command needs to do something with the standard output of the SQL statement.

If you just want to execute a system command and don't care about the output of the SQL command, just redirect its output to `/dev/null` as in the example.

Of course, this command is also very handy for its intended purpose, which is to pipe the output of the SQL to a UNIX command. This allows for further processing of the output by UNIX. This pipeline can be as complicated or as detailed as UNIX will allow.

If you wish, your SQL output can provide the starting point for extensive post-processing outside of the database. In some instances, this can be quite useful, as there are a lot of tasks that can be efficiently completed in UNIX but are difficult, expensive, or impractical to do within SQL.

In fact, it is possible to pipe the output to a long series of UNIX commands, massage the output, pipe the output into files, and then use one of the OnLine LOAD commands to retrieve the data back into the OnLine database. This gives you the capability of choosing your working tools based upon the job to be done instead of trying to attack everything using the OnLine tools.

isql **AND** dbaccess

For many users, the isql or dbaccess program is all they know of the OnLine system. This menu-based program is ubiquitous and is often taken for granted. There is a lot of utility in Informix's implementation of isql, and much of this utility is often overlooked. This seems to be especially true with users who have moved over from another database system to an OnLine system. Dbaccess is a stripped-down version of isql that is included with the 5.0 series of products. Dbaccess does not include the menu-creation and report-writing capabilities of isql.

Different database management programs all use extensions to ANSI SQL to achieve more functionality. Users coming from database management systems that add many extensions to their SQL products sometimes feel restricted when in the SQL query portion of OnLine. Such things as extensive string functions are not present as they are in the SQL's of programs such as Oracle. Heavy users of ESQL/C seem to feel this loss the most. They may use only the embedded SQL capabilities of OnLine and may miss out on some of the other functions available through isql.

The I-SQL program contains five major areas of functionality. For the SQL developer, the one that gets the most attention is the Query Language section. This system allows the user to create, modify, save, run, and redirect the output of SQL statements. A user who spends most of her time in the Query Language module may believe that some of the more sophisticated features of other database management systems are not present in OnLine.

Of course, this is not true. The isql module is a suite of packages. The main features are a form-based query and user-interface program, a report generator, the Query Language module, a user menu generator and runner, and a database and table status module. As an example, much of the character manipulation and string management functions are found in the report writer application. You can do things here that you cannot do in the query management module such as concatenation of strings, control of output format, and the like.

The forms module provides a very handy "quick and dirty" method of dealing with the data in the tables. You can generate, compile, and run complex, multipage screen forms quickly and easily. This forms module is not as comprehensive as the INFORMIX-4GL product, but it is a handy tool for rapid development and management of database systems.

The user menu module is also very useful in developing a user interface for various purposes. Using the user menu options, you can easily integrate Informix programs, scripts, UNIX utilities, and other executables into a seamless whole. It doesn't give you all the bells and whistles that custom development in C or Microsoft Windows™ will give you, but it doesn't take you months to do it either.

In my opinion, these tools are underrated and underused. As a working DBA, you will need to provide many services and rapid response to your user community. You will find yourself needing to develop and use many programs, scripts, and data management schemes to do your job. You can make the choice to develop your tools with lots of options and user-interface gadgets or to develop them quickly and simply. If you decide to go for the utility over the flash, you probably have all the tools you need using isql and INFORMIX-4GL.

The database world is changing, and things will be totally different tomorrow. Informix as a company is making a push to client/server computing and tools are becoming available which provide the rapid development capabilities and the bells and whistles. An example is the INFORMIX HyperScript Tools package that runs on client machines talking to databases over INFORMIX-Star or INFORMIX-Net. HyperScript Tools can also talk to a local INFORMIX-SE database. The world of client/server computing will add many more facets to the DBA's job. It will also allow the development of user programs which make the best use of the OnLine database and also utilize the sophisticated user-interface elements available in the Microsoft Windows™ environment.

This book will not go into detail about `isql`, INFORMIX-4GL, and the SQL query language. We are assuming that the DBA either has experience with, or can read the manuals for these programs. However, we will include examples of user tools developed with INFORMIX-4GL, forms built in the forms generator, and menu programs running under the menu module. All of these examples are of tools that will be helpful or informative to the DBA. As you are studying the examples, remain open to other things that you can do using these tools. I'm taking a typical UNIX approach to this. Show you the tools, show you how they can work together, and then turn you loose to develop your own variants.

If you develop some particularly interesting or useful variants, get on Internet and post them to the `comp.databases.informix newsgroups`. If they're handy for you, others can probably use them. Besides, it'll give you a moment or two of fame!

Chapter 6

How do I?

This chapter consists mostly of scripts, programs, and techniques for accomplishing specific tasks that often cause problems for DBAs.

While the individual scripts and programs should be useful in the day-to-day operations of your database, it is likely that you will have to massage and modify the programs for your own use. What you as a DBA should take from this chapter are concepts and approaches for how to use various tools to do your bidding. The goal here is to give you a place to start and to point you in the direction of creating your own database tools.

Just about every program will use the UNIX utilities to massage data. If you do not have a good background in UNIX, you need to get a few good books on UNIX and work at writing scripts. UNIX scriptwriters tend to develop intimate relations with several of the utilities at the expense of others. I am no exception. I use a lot of awk, grep, sed, and csh concepts. If you have other preferences, feel free to exercise your scriptwriting in the way you feel most comfortable.

With UNIX, there are usually several ways to accomplish a given task, from the most awkward to the most elegant approach. I make no claim as to the elegance of these DBA scripts. If you can modify them and make them prettier, faster, and more elegant, go to it.

All of these scripts and programs were developed "under the gun" as part of real business systems. Often, it is necessary to take shortcuts and to use brute force to accomplish jobs within a given time frame. These scripts are ample proof.

There, I think I've apologized enough for the inelegance.

RUN SQL FROM THE COMMAND LINE?

Although `isql` is a menu-driven program, it follows the standard UNIX I/O conventions. This allows input and output to and from I-SQL to be redirected and to come from or go to UNIX devices such as terminals and files. It is also possible to pass parameters to `isql` from the command line or from files or scripts.

Note that in all of the included scripts, we are assuming that you are using `isql` and not `dbaccess`. If you use `dbaccess` instead of `isql`, just replace all instances of `isql` with `dbaccess` and the programs should work the same.

As example, take the sample script `dbcat`:

```
#!/bin/csh
echo "select * from $2;" | $INFORMIXDIR/bin/isql $1
```

The syntax is `dbcat database_name table_name`. The `database_name` is passed as parameter `$1` and the `table_name` is passed as parameter `$2`. This concept can be extended in the C-Shell by using aliases to provide complete SQL services directly from the command line. To do this, place the following aliases in a file called `aliases.rc`.

```
alias alter  "echo 'alter \!:*;'  | $INFORMIXDIR/bin/isql $DB"
alias create "echo 'create \!:*;' | $INFORMIXDIR/bin/isql $DB"
alias delete "echo 'delete \!:*;' | $INFORMIXDIR/bin/isql $DB"
alias drop   "echo 'drop \!:*;'   | $INFORMIXDIR/bin/isql $DB"
alias grant  "echo 'grant \!:*;'  | $INFORMIXDIR/bin/isql $DB"
alias insert "echo 'insert \!:*;' | $INFORMIXDIR/bin/isql $DB"
alias rename "echo 'rename \!:*;' | $INFORMIXDIR/bin/isql $DB"
alias revoke "echo 'revoke \!:*;' | $INFORMIXDIR/bin/isql $DB"
alias select "echo 'select \!:*;' | $INFORMIXDIR/bin/isql $DB"
alias update "echo 'update \!:*;' | $INFORMIXDIR/bin/isql $DB"
alias info   "echo 'info \!:*;'   | $INFORMIXDIR/bin/isql $DB"
```

These aliases receive the name of the requested database through the $DB environmental variable. The aliases are defined when you run the command `source aliases.rc`. Each time this file is `sourced`, the aliases are redefined. To make these aliases point to another database, reset the $DB environmental variable and then run `source aliases.rc`. If you need to only access one database, or if you work predominantly with one database, you may want to set the $DB environmental variable in your `.cshrc` file and add the contents of `aliases.rc` to the end of your `.cshrc` file.

The thing that makes these aliases work is the `\!:*` in the first half of the aliases. It takes the first word of the command, either `alter`, `create`, `delete`, etc., and turns it into an alias. Whenever you type the first word, that is interpreted as an alias. The rest of the command line is indicated by the `\!:*` structure. It is passed to the `echo` statement that is sent to `isql` by the magic `\!:*` clause. This construct works only in the C-Shell.

Another way to pass parameters to a script running `isql` is to use a UNIX *here document*. This type of script instructs the shell to take the command and the input from the same source. For example, look at the sample script, `get_accounting_data`:

```
#!/bin/csh
$INFORMIXDIR/bin/isql $1 << EOF
SELECT   * from accounts_payable
WHERE   date = "$2" and
        code = "$3";
EOF
```

Running this script would allow you to pass a database name as $1 and `date` and `code` as $2 and $3. In the here document, the key is the << construct. This means that the shell is to use the code immediately following the << as a marker delimiting input to the script. Using "EOF" as a marker, the first "EOF" indicates the beginning of the input.

The entire select statement, up to the semicolon that immediately precedes the last "EOF" is then taken as input to the `isql` command. The handy part is that the shell first interprets any shell parameters before it evaluates the input. This is what allows you to pass the parameters.

Find out how much space is being used by tables?

Tbstat -d gives you an output that shows the raw information necessary to calculate the free space in your database, but it is not organized in a way that is easy to comprehend.

This script, a C-Shell script called dbdf does a much cleaner job:

```
#!/bin/csh
#dbdf
$INFORMIXDIR/bin/tbstat -d | grep / | grep -v bpages | sort +2 -3 -n |awk
'{printf("%s\t%s\t%s\t%s\n", $3,$5,$6,$8)}' > /tmp/c$$
$INFORMIXDIR/bin/tbstat -d | grep informix | awk '{print $2, $8}' > /tmp/s$$
join  /tmp/s$$ /tmp/c$$ > /tmp/j$$
awk '\
BEGIN {name=""} \
      {total[$2]+=$3; free[$2]+=$4} \
END { for (space in total) printf("%-12s is %.2f percent full and has %6d fr
pages \n", space, (1-free[space]/total[space])*100,free[space])}' /tmp/j$$ |
grep -v log

rm /tmp/c$$ /tmp/s$$ /tmp/j$$
```

This script uses tbstat -d and massages the output with grep and awk. It creates three temporary files in the /tmp directory that are erased at completion of the script. These files will be cXXXXX, sXXXXX, and jXXXXX where the XXXXX is the script's process id number (PID). This PID number is created by the $$ construct as used in rm /tmp/c$$ /tmp/m$$ /tmp/j$$. The second tbstat command makes one assumption. It assumes that the owner of all of the Informix chunks is user informix. If for some reason you have a custom installation that does not follow this convention, you will need to modify the grep informix. The last statement before the UNIX command rm /tmp/c$$ contains another section of code that you may want to modify. It uses a grep -v log to exclude any lines that contain the word log. All of my logs are in separate dbspaces that are called logSOMETHING. Since the space utilization of these logspaces does not vary (the logs are allocated and take up space whether they're full or not), I'm not interested in monitoring changes in the space utilization of these dbspaces. If you use similar conventions in naming your chunks and dbspaces, you may want to use a similar exclude statement.

Place the script in your $INFORMIXDIR/local_bin directory and chmod it to be executable by whomever you wish to give the right to run dbdf. This program does not understand multiple OnLine instances. If you want to make it do so, you'll have to pass it a parameter for the name of the $TBCONFIG file and have it set the $TBCONFIG environment variable to the passed value and then run the script.

FIND DUPLICATE VALUES IN A TABLE?

There are several reasons that you may want to find duplicate values in a table. The main reason is when you are attempting to build a unique index on a field and the index build crashes with a SQL duplicate value error. This error message does not go far enough in that it tells you it has a problem, but it does not tell you where the duplicate value occurs. All that you know is that you have a duplicate value somewhere.

There are several approaches to solving this problem, and one good method for avoiding it. If you initially build the table with a unique index on the field in question, you will avoid the duplicates in the first place. This requires planning ahead. You have to know in advance that you want field x to be unique.

Even if you know in advance that you need a unique field, it is often not possible to prebuild the index. This often happens when you are loading a table from outside sources. When doing this type of a load, you may wish to do it without indexes for performance reasons. When you try to build the index, you get the duplicate key error.

Assuming that you are loading from an outside data source, you have the option of using UNIX commands on the raw data files prior to trying the LOAD. You can use the UNIX sort -u command to presort the data.

If the data is already in a table, you can use SQL to identify the duplicate entries. Given the following table,

```
CREATE TABLE person ( ssn  char(11), name char(20));
```

assume that you are getting a duplicate key error on `ssn`. To identify the duplicate `ssn` entries, use the following SQL statement:

```
SELECT ssn FROM person
       GROUP BY ssn
       HAVING count(*) > 1;
```

The GROUP BY/HAVING combination allows you to pick out the duplicate values in the `ssn` field. A slightly more complex query will give you all of the data instead of just the `ssn`:

```
SELECT * FROM person
       WHERE ssn in
       ( SELECT ssn FROM person
               GROUP BY ssn
               HAVING count(*) > 1)
       )
```

CLEAN OUT TABLES?

There are two distinct parts to the problem of cleaning out tables. The first part is knowing that the tables need to be purged. The second part is the mechanical question of how to do it.

We'll cover the mechanical aspects here. Look to the sections on database monitoring and table proliferation for methods of discovering which tables need to be cleaned.

Assuming that you know that table x needs to be purged, how do you go about it? If you have determined that the table needs to be completely emptied, you may be tempted to use this SQL statement

```
DELETE FROM x;
```

to remove all of the rows. This is OK for a small table, but it can take a significant amount of time on larger tables. To completely empty a large table, it is easier to drop the table and recreate it. Use the dbschema utility to create SQL statements that will recreate the table:

```
dbschema -d dbname -t tabname mk_tabname.sql
```

Then go into isql and drop the table

```
DROP TABLE tabname;
```

Finally, recreate the table from the script you just created with dbschema

```
isql dbname < mk_tabname.sql
```

Note, however, that the dbschema utility does not preserve dbspace, extent, and locking information. If you use dbschema, be sure to modify the mk_tabname.sql script to include the proper dbspace, extent, and locking information.

A better solution to the problem of preserving this information is to use the newschema script included in the next section. The newschema script creates a more complete schema.

RECREATE A TABLE WITH THE SAME PARAMETERS AS THE ORIGINAL?

As mentioned above, the Informix dbschema program has some noted limitations. While it will create all of the SQL statements necessary to rebuild the table in its most basic form, some very valuable information is lost. This is the information regarding the extent sizes and the locking mode of the table.

As the DBA continues to tune the database, it becomes very important to keep the tables within the minimum number of extents. It is often necessary to adjust the extent sizes of a table to make sure that it uses its space most effectively and to make sure that its access speed is maximized. When rebuilding the table, much accumulated tuning work would be lost if the latest EXTENT SIZE and NEXT SIZE parameters were lost. The newschema script is designed to capture this otherwise lost information and to create a schema program that is truly useful.

Newschema is composed of two parts. The first is a report in the isql report-writer, ACE. The second part is a script that merges this information with the output of the OnLine dbschema program to provide the information needed.

The ACE report is called storage.ace. If you do not have the isql package containing ACE, the same report could be written in SQL.

```
database
    admin <--(*NOTE* Put your own database name here)
end
define
param [1] which_table char(50)
variable mode char(4)
end
output
top margin 0
bottom margin 0
left margin 0
end
select
        tabname,
        owner,
        locklevel,
        fextsize,
        nextsize
from systables where tabname = $which_table
end
format
   on every row
   if locklevel = "P" then
   begin
      let mode = "PAGE"
   end
   if locklevel = "R" then
   begin
      let mode = "ROW"
   end
   print "EXTENT SIZE ", fextsize using "######",1 space,"NEXT SIZE
",nextsize using "######",1 space,"LOCK MODE ", mode clipped
end
```

The above ACE program is compiled by using the isql Forms Compile option or by using the appropriate command line options to compile the program. The output program will be called storage.arc.

The following C-Shell script needs to be placed in the DBA's path (I suggest creating a $INFORMIXDIR/local_bin directory and placing all of the included DBA scripts and programs in it.) Set the $INFORMIXLOCALBIN = XXXXXXXX environmental variable to point to the location of this local directory. If you place all of your site-specific scripts in a local bin directory, this directory will be preserved with subsequent Informix installs and upgrades. If you have put your scripts in the $INFORMIXDIR/bin directory, you will someday need to decide which are your "local" scripts and which are the "real" Informix distribution programs. You might as well do it right the first time.

The actual script that makes use of the storage.arc report is newschema.

```
#!/bin/csh
#newschema
set INFORMIXLOCALBIN = $INFORMIXDIR/local_bin
$INFORMIXDIR/bin/dbschema -d $1 -t $2 /tmp/tempschema$$
set storage_option = `$INFORMIXDIR/bin/sacego -s -d $1 $INFORMIXLOCALBIN/storage
$2`
cat /tmp/tempschema$$ | sed "s/ );/ ) $storage_option ;/" > /tmp/tempschema2$$
cat /tmp/tempschema2$$ >> $3
rm /tmp/tempschema$$ /tmp/tempschema2$$
```

The newschema program is similar in concept to the Informix dbschema program with the exception that it works for one table at a time. Invocation is as follows:

```
newschema   database_name   table_name   destination_file_name
```

This script will append its schema to the destination_file_name, which makes it usable in creating schemas for multiple tables. This is done by using one of my most-often-used UNIX tricks, taking input from a file. Suppose you wanted to do a newschema for all tables in database admin. The first job would be to create a UNIX file of the tables in the subject database. The SQL commands for this would be:

```
DATABASE admin;
SELECT tabname FROM systables WHERE tabid > 99;
```

These SQL statements take advantage of the fact that all of the internal tables that OnLine creates for a database will have a `tabid` in the `systables` system table of less than 99. Anything greater than 99 must be a user table. Place the output of this script into a file called `targets` (or whatever else you want to name it). This can be by using the `isql` query language and using the Query-Language menu option followed by the Output option to place the output in a new file, `target`. If you are using the SELECT alias under C-Shell, it would be nice if you could simply type from the UNIX prompt:

```
SELECT tabname FROM systables WHERE tabid > 99 > target
```

Unfortunately, the shell will not understand this construct in conjunction with an alias. If you are using C-Shell with the history mechanism, you can get around it by using the following series of commands:

```
SELECT tabname FROM systables WHERE tabid > 99
```

You then get an output to your screen. Then you type:

```
!! > target
```

The `!!` (bang bang) command repeats the last command and puts the output in `target`. The next step is to clean out everything but the tablenames from the file `target`. This is easily done using a word processor. If you're after a system that can be run without human intervention or if you simply want to make the script more elegant, you could populate the `target` file by using an ACE report instead of `isql`. The report writer gives you a lot more flexibility in formatting and layout than `isql`. For this case, `isql` works fine, because we're just doing this to show you the techniques.

Okay, you now have a file called `target` that contains only the names of the tables you want to include in your schema. Now comes time for the UNIX wizardry that makes the job work. You want to tell UNIX to run `newschema` on every table in `target` and put the output in the file called `mk_admin.sql`. Write a C-Shell script called `newschema_alldb` that looks like this:

```
#!/bin/csh
foreach table (`cat target`)
$INFORMIXLOCALBIN/newschema  admin  $table  mk_admin.sql
end
```

When you run this script, it does a newschema on each table in the target file and appends it to mk_admin.sql. You can then recreate the database by running the SQL script from within isql. This method of massaging an output file and then running multiple jobs against it is a most handy tool, especially for all of those "quick and dirty" jobs that you want to do. The same type of approach can be taken with either the Bourne or Korn shells. However, I'm a C-Shell bigot, so I'll leave it to you to translate the scripts if you care to use any of the lesser shells.

CLEAN SELECTED DATA OUT OF A TABLE?

The above methods are workable if you want to delete all rows from a table. What about when you need to delete only some of the rows? Or you need to move some of the rows out of the table and archive them in another table. This is a common task in database management, and it is one that seems to be forgotten many times in the design of applications.

Programmers seem to spend a lot of time figuring out how to put data into tables, but they often do not spend quite as much time devising methods to remove obsolete data. In many ways, the database is a black hole to developers. They tend to think that they can continue to add data to it forever. But the DBA knows different. We have to clean these things up!

As a DBA, you should be a strong advocate for an entire life-cycle approach to designing your applications. Every time a developer approaches you with a request for a new table, you should inquire about how the data gets into the table and how it goes away. Get the developers to thinking about means of keeping the data current and getting rid of the trash. Data does not have to be kept online forever.

There are also significant technical problems with deleting specific rows from a table, especially a large, frequently-used table. The I-SQL delete statement will place locks on the table being deleted from. The level of locking will be the lock level as established for the table unless an explicit table lock is placed on the table. If the locking granularity is either row or page, it is possible that a long delete will overflow your lock table. Such a delete is also considered a transaction and could possibly throw you into a long transaction situation with regard to your logfiles. The same problems apply to updates to tables and to saving rows to history tables. The history table problem can be broken down into two parts, inserting the row into a history table, and deleting the row from the old table.

The major problem here is that the deletes, updates, or movements of data are done in one big transaction. Solving the problem requires that the tasks be broken into smaller manageable units.

The following 4GL program is called `sample.4gl` and it utilizes a concept I have called *flutter locks*. Flutter locks are locks that are placed and released on small units of data. As such, they are much less intrusive in day-to-day operations. When using programs similar to `sample.4gl`, you can have archiving and table cleanup programs that will peacefully coexist with an active user community.

Programs using flutter locks should pay careful attention to the concept of a *transaction*. A transaction is a group of statements that should be completed as a unit. If any of the parts are not completed, none of the statements are executed. For most deleting and archiving situations, these transaction units can be made at the row level. Either a row needs to be deleted or it doesn't. In an archive situation, the transaction should consist of two parts. First, copy the row to the new table. Second, delete the row from the old table. Most of the time you really don't need the very broad transaction units utilized by the DELETE or UPDATE SQL statements. These statements interpret the transaction as, "DELETE all of the rows covered by the WHERE clause or ROLLBACK all of the rows." If your application requirements really require such an all-or-nothing level of transactions, using a flutter lock program will not solve the problem. Such instances are rare, however.

In the case of an archive program in which you are moving rows based upon certain criteria, the world will not fall in if you miss a row or two. They'll get archived next time the program runs. One very important implication of using a flutter lock program for deleting or row archiving is that the jobs can be easily interrupted. Try interrupting a long SQL DELETE statement after it's worked for an hour, and you'll see about an hour of rollback. Even worse, imagine what happens if you've had a DELETE or UPDATE SQL statement going on for several hours and your system crashes. Your fast recovery on restart will be anything but fast. Your system will probably be down for hours recovering.

Using flutter locks allows you to perform this "transaction chopping" and to completely avoid most of these problems. I have chosen to demonstrate this in I-4GL rather than in ESQL/C. The same programming concepts are available in both tools.

The general concept of the program is to first open a cursor in which you select the rows on which you wish to operate. You may then wish to DELETE the data, archive the data to another table, or perform other SQL operations on the data. The key thing to note is that this outer cursor is opened using the parameter WITH HOLD. This causes the program to maintain its position within the list of rows that need to be acted upon.

For each row in the outer cursor, the program goes into the table, does its BEGIN WORK, locking the rows, does its DELETE or UPDATE statement, and does its COMMIT WORK. Then it goes out to the outer cursor again and picks its next row, etc. Without the hold cursor, each time it went out to the outer cursor, the SQL statement would have to be reevaluated and a new SELECT done.

When you get your rows from the cursor, you can do any amount of work you wish in the inner sections. An archive requires an INSERT into another table and a DELETE from the old table, but you can perform much more complicated tasks within the inner loop.

Just remember to think about keeping the actual work within the transaction to an absolute minimum. Also, it is necessary for you to closely monitor the success or failure of the jobs done within the transaction. If the status indicates that the work failed, you need to be sure to roll back the entire transaction explicitly.

A couple of things to note about the `sample.4gl` program. First, don't worry about trying to work through the `outer_count` and `quitflag` variables. They are in there so that you can group the transactions into bigger transactions, maybe committing after every 100 or 200 executions. There are cases in which the overhead cost of doing a BEGIN WORK/COMMIT WORK for every single row in the outer cursor would be prohibitive.

Rather than COMMITTING after every single, *atomic transaction*, this code allows you to group several hundred such atomic transactions together. Either they all succeed or they all fail. If you need the capability, it is available. I've found that committing after every atomic transaction does not create a problem with resources in most cases. Also, note that the 4GL program follows the PASCAL conventions of including comments within pairs of curly braces. `{ this is a comment }`.

```
joe 58>  cat sample.4gl

DATABASE admin

GLOBALS
DEFINE s_order RECORD like order.*
DEFINE s_order_tran RECORD like order_tran.*
DEFINE counter INTEGER
DEFINE outer_count INTEGER
DEFINE quitflag INTEGER
DEFINE total INTEGER
END GLOBALS

MAIN

CALL startlog("d_order.errors")

ALTER TABLE order LOCK MODE (row)
     IF status < 0 THEN
             WHILE status < 0
                   SLEEP 2
                   ALTER TABLE order LOCK MODE (row)
             END WHILE
     END IF

{ comment:  all of this status checking is to be sure that the lock }
{           mode really gets changed. The row locking makes the program
}
{           even less intrusive to users.   }
{ NOTE:  this will cause short lockouts during operations.  Make sure
that }
{           this short lockout will not crash other users }
ALTER TABLE order_tran LOCK MODE (row)
     IF status < 0 THEN
             WHILE status < 0
                   SLEEP 2
                   ALTER TABLE order_tran LOCK MODE (row)
             END WHILE
     END IF
```

```
DECLARE drop_order CURSOR WITH HOLD FOR
select * from  order where
              due_date < current - 3 units month
          AND
          start_date < current - 3 units month
FOR UPDATE

{  comment:  this is the outer cursor.  The "with hold" is critical }
{            the "for update" is what allows you to do a delete inside }
{            the loop with a "current of cursor" clause  }

DECLARE copy_order CURSOR WITH HOLD FOR
   INSERT INTO order_hist VALUES (s_order.*)
{ doesn't always need to have "with hold" }

LET outer_count = 0
LET quitflag = 0
OPEN drop_order
OPEN copy_order
WHILE TRUE
LET counter = 0

WHILE counter < 1

{comment:  if you wanted to change your number of transactions per }
{          commit, change the 1 to however many rows you want to work }
{          between transactions.  }

BEGIN WORK
{   this is the beginning of the transaction.  Keep the transactions
short }
FETCH drop_order into s_order.*

IF status = NOTFOUND
    THEN COMMIT WORK
    LET quitflag = 1
    EXIT WHILE
END IF
{ always check to see that the statement completes properly }
```

```
PUT copy_order
{ first, insert into the history table }

IF status < 0 THEN
    ROLLBACK WORK
    CALL errorlog("ERROR........SKIPPING")
    EXIT WHILE
END IF

INSERT INTO order_tran_hist SELECT *
                    FROM order_tran
                    WHERE order_number = s_order.order_number
                    AND   order_type   = s_order.order_type
{ do a little more work with another table while we're in the loop }

IF status < 0 THEN
    ROLLBACK WORK
    CALL errorlog("ERROR........SKIPPING")
    EXIT WHILE
END IF

DELETE from order_tran
              WHERE order_number = s_order.order_number
              AND   order_type   = s_order.order_type

{delete from the other table}

DELETE from order
              WHERE current of drop_order
{delete the current row in the outer cursor table }

LET counter = counter + 1
COMMIT WORK
LET total = outer_count + counter
DISPLAY total

{ provide a heartbeat to the standard out to let us know the program' }
{ still alive and where it's working.  You can direct the standard out }
{ of the compiled program by invoking the program as : }
{     sample.4ge >! sample_log &     }
```

```
END WHILE

IF quitflag = 1
    THEN EXIT WHILE
END IF

LET outer_count=outer_count + 1
END WHILE

ALTER TABLE order LOCK MODE (page)
    IF status < 0 THEN
            WHILE status < 0
                    SLEEP 2
                    ALTER TABLE order LOCK MODE (page)
            END WHILE
    END IF
{ put the tables back in their old lock mode }

ALTER TABLE order_tran LOCK MODE (page)
    IF status < 0 THEN
            WHILE status < 0
                    SLEEP 2
                    ALTER TABLE order_tran LOCK MODE (page)
            END WHILE
    END IF

END MAIN
```

The `sample.4gl` program is compiled within the INFORMIX-4GL program or directly with a command-line interface. It can be run from a command-line interface or it can be put into your `cron` file to run automatically.

KNOW IF ONLINE IS RUNNING?

Occasionally, the DBA needs to be reassured that the database has not aborted and is still running. This need for reassurance often occurs after the DBA mistakenly kills a `sqlturbo` backend or does something else stupid.

The DBA wants a quick check to see if he needs to start making excuses about why he crashed the database.

This information is also useful in writing scripts and programs that execute across the network on multiple machines. There are many reasons that a script would benefit by being aware whether or not OnLine was running on machine B.

I find the `ok` script handy in cases like this:

```
INFORMIX 23>  cat ok

#!/bin/csh
if ( `$INFORMIXDIR/bin/tbstat - |grep RSAM |awk '{print $5}'` == On-Line
) then
    echo "  ....'saaaaaaawwwwwright......"
else
    echo "Mucked Again"
endif
```

Feel free to change the `echo` statements to give you any cute and/or nasty comments that you wish to display. Run the script with no parameters.

CONVERT TABLE NUMBERS TO TABLE NAMES?

All of the `tbstat` outputs refer to tables by `tblnum`, which is a hex number. In true, user-friendly fashion, OnLine uses an integer number to identify the tables in the `systables` system table. To convert between the two, you need to use the following SQL conversion:

```
SELECT tabname, hex(partnum) FROM systables;
```

This will give you a list of table names and `tblnums` (as used in `tbstat`) for all of your tables. The OnLine manual recommends that you keep a hard copy of this list available to use for debugging.

A somewhat better approach is to create the following script, `table` in your `$INFORMIXLOCALBIN` directory:

```
joe 67> cat table

#!/bin/csh
set search = $2
set SEARCH = `echo $2 | tr "[a-f]" "[A-F]" `
$INFORMIXDIR/bin/isql $1 << EOF
OUTPUT TO PIPE cat WITHOUT HEADINGS SELECT "$1" as database,tabname ,
hex(partnum) as tablenumber from systables WHERE hex(partnum) MATCHES
"*$SEARCH*" or tabname MATCHES "*$search*";
EOF
```

The `table` program is invoked as :

```
table database_name tblnum_fragment or
table database_name table_name_fragment or
table database_name
```

The `tblnum` as used in the `tbstat` outputs is a seven-digit hex number, and it's sometimes possible to make an error in entering it. That's why the `table` script does a

MATCH and not an equals. If you see a `tblnum` of `300021e`, you can just enter the fragment `21e` and you'll get a listing of all matching tables. You can also enter either the complete table name or a fragment of the name and receive all matching table names and their `tblnum` equivalent IDs.

FIND DATABASE NAMES FROM A SCRIPT?

The DBA sometimes needs to be able to run scripts or programs that will take an action on every database in an OnLine instance. An example would be if the DBA wanted to do some reports of space utilization by database. Another example would be running an UPDATE STATISTICS command in SQL for all databases. OnLine does not make it easy to do this. The information is readily available, since `isql` asks you to choose a database before you do any work from the menu, but there is no simple and straightforward way I know to do this from a script.

In this case, we need to take the brute force approach. This information is available in the `tbcheck -pe` output as part of the fully qualified table names. The following script, named `find_db_names`, will output the names of your databases:

```
$INFORMIXDIR/bin/tbcheck -pe |grep systables |grep -v WARNING | tr ":" "
" | awk '{print $1}' | sort -u
```

This script is pretty slow, and it's certainly an awkward approach, but it works. Since it uses `tbcheck -pe`, it does not lock up any tables and can be run with no danger to an operating Informix system.

FIND DATABASE NAMES FROM AN ESQL/C PROGRAM?

If you have access to ESQL/C, there is a somewhat more elegant approach to determining the names of databases. The following program utilizes an undocumented function in ESQL/C. As such, the function is subject to change at any time by Informix. As a general rule, Informix does not recommend that users use undocumented functions and they take no responsibility for any problems that you may have in the use of undocumented functions.

Just remember that Informix may change this at any time. Until then, this program is much faster than the `find_db_names` shell script.

This program is called `find_db_names.ec`

```
main()
{
#define MAXSPACES 256#define MAXSTRINGS (15 * MAXSPACES)
char *name[MAXSPACES];
char space[MAXSTRINGS];
int basecount=0;
int answer=sqgetdbs(&basecount, name, MAXSPACES,
space, MAXSTRINGS);

if (answer==0 && basecount >0)
        {
            int i;
            for (i = 0; i < basecount; ++i)
            printf("%s\n", name[i]);

        }
)
```

To compile this program, compile it with ESQL/C using the following command line:

```
esql -o find_db_names find_db_names.ec
```

When this successfully compiles, you will have an executable program called `find_db_names`. If you use this compiled version of `find_db_names`, you can either overwrite or rename the script version presented above. Either one can be used with the other scripts in this book. If you do not have ESQL/C, it may be worth your while to try to find someone else who is running your version of UNIX who does have ESQL/C. If you can get a compiled version of this program you will find that it is definitely an improvement over the script version.

Maintain a current UPDATE STATISTICS?

The operations of the OnLine optimizer depend upon the data that is collected from runs of the SQL UPDATE STATISTICS command. This command looks at the distribution of data in the tables and indexes and stores it internally. Based upon this information, the optimizer decides the best way to execute your SQL statements. If the statistics information is stale or nonexistent, you could get SQL statements that perform poorly.

Get your users and developers into the habit of running an UPDATE STATISTICS FOR TABLE `tablename` every time they create a new table, create a new index, or significantly modify the distribution of data within a table. If you already have your users trained in the use of the SET EXPLAIN ON command in SQL and they are optimizing their own queries, be sure that they run the UPDATE STATISTICS before they do the SET EXPLAIN ON.

It is also a good procedure to have UPDATE STATISTICS in your UNIX `cron` file to be run occasionally. Once a night is not too much. Since UPDATE STATISTICS when invoked without a FOR TABLE clause works on a database level, you first need to feed the program the information about the names of your existing databases. This script is named `update_statistics`:

```
#!/bin/csh
echo "Please wait.........."
foreach db (`$INFORMIXLOCALBIN/find_db_names`)
echo "TIME: `date`   UPDATING STATISTICS FOR DATABASE:   $db"
$INFORMIXDIR/bin/isql $db << EOF
update statistics
EOF
end
```

This script includes an `echo` statement that can be removed if you want it to operate silently. I usually prefer to run the script with a redirection of the output to a logfile so that I can verify when the last updates were done. This information is not easily available unless you keep track of it yourself.

GET TABLE INFORMATION?

It is advantageous for the DBA to be able to make ad hoc inquiries about database elements such as tables, columns, indexes and rows. Users always seem to be asking about table structure, existing indexes, and the like. It is very handy to have a command-line program that will allow these types of questions to be answered from the UNIX command line.

The section above on running `isql` from the command line contains a C-Shell alias called `info` that pipes information to `isql`. The same could be done with a standard shell script if you are not a `csh` user. The `csh` alias is:

```
alias info    "echo 'info \!:*;'   | $INFORMIXDIR/bin/isql your_database"
```

This alias is invoked in several ways, depending upon the information that the DBA wants to locate. This alias uses one of the more obscure SQL commands called INFO. The command does not seem to be used very often by SQL users. They are missing a very useful tool. It just goes to show that you should go through the reference manuals occasionally just to see if there is something there that you don't usually use.   Several possible ways to call this alias are:

```
INFORMIX 3>info tables
Table name

"dba".a31save        "dba".a_ab091993   "dba".a_ap091993
"dba".a_di091993     "dba".a_ia081993   "dba".a_ia091993
"dba".a_io091993     "dba".a_it091993   "dba".a_model_type
"dba".access_6       "dba".access_60    "dba".access_61
"dba".access_64      "dba".access_65    "dba".access_67
"dba".is_system      "dba".isboxes     "dba".ka_calendar
"dba".key_acct       "dba".key_acct_mem "dba".key_acct_code
```

```
INFORMIX 4>info columns for sample_table
Column name          Type                              Nulls

system_num           smallint                          no
sys_code             char(5)                           yes
name                 char(30)                          yes
phy_city_loc         char(3)                           yes
system_type          smallint                          no
access_meth          smallint                          no
start_date           datetime year to second           no
end_date             datetime year to second           no
change_num           integer                           no


INFORMIX 5>info status for sample_table
Table Name           system
Owner                dba
Row Size             64
Number of Rows       216
Number of Columns    9
Date Created         06/24/1992

INFORMIX 6>info indexes for sample_table
Index name           Owner     Type     Cluster   Columns

sample_ci            dba       dupls    Yes       system_num

INFORMIX 10>info access for sample_table
User         Select           Update        Insert   Delete  Index  Alter

bull         All              All           Yes      Yes     No     No
chris        All              All           Yes      Yes     No     No
danny        All              All           Yes      Yes     No     No
```

MAKE A FAST RECOVERY GO FASTER?

This is a trick question. It can't be done. If your system comes down ungracefully, either because of a crash or because you initiated an immediate shutdown, you will be forced to go into recovery mode when you restart the database system. The length of time for fast recovery depends upon how much work has been done since the last checkpoint. If you absolutely have to bring the system down ungracefully, try to do a checkpoint before the shutdown. It will help speed up the recovery process. This is one thing to consider when establishing the frequency of your checkpoints. Spacing your checkpoints further apart may make the interruptions that they cause to processing less intrusive, but you'll take the risk of longer recovery times. You need to decide upon a balance between performance and speed of recovery.

As part of the recovery, the system will roll back any transactions that were working at the time of the shutdown and that were not yet committed. If you have a very long transaction working at the time of shutdown, your recovery time will be much longer. You can get a feel for how long it will take to recover by looking at how much logfile data you have. Recovery, especially in cases caused by long transactions, can take hours. Remember this when you're designing applications. This is another reason to keep your transactions short. You can alleviate these types of problems to a large extent by using programs with flutter locks that keep transactions as short as possible.

You will sometimes need to decide whether or not to bring the database down ungracefully. At least you have a choice here. In a crash, you have no choices at all. When making this decision, you must think about what is going on in your system and how long it will take for the recovery to take place. You may save some time by bringing the database down to stop a rogue process, but doing so may increase your recovery time. It's sort of a case of "pay me now or pay me later." Either way, it will take some time. You need to watch these things, especially if you are running a production database and your users need to have it working all the time.

You will eventually be faced with a fast recovery time that seems to go on forever. Maybe someone crashed the system while a long job was going on. Maybe someone brought the database down without checking for active transactions. Anyway, your database, which usually takes about 15 seconds for fast recovery on a restart, has already been cranking away for 15 minutes and the users are beginning to call, wondering when the database will be back up. You need to know how long it will take to recover.

First, run `tbstat -l` to check the status of your logfiles. If you've followed my suggestions, you've monitored your recovery times and have a rule of thumb for how long it takes to recover per logfile. This number is a very rough estimate. Sometimes it can be off by several factors of ten. During recovery, you cannot access the database. This means that the system tables are not available to you. However, the `tbstat` utility will run during recovery. Usually, what takes a lot of time during fast recovery is the rollback of transactions that were not committed when the system went down. You can do a `tbstat -u` and see which daemons are running during the recovery. This will be a very simplified output. All that will show up are the daemons for fast recovery and rollforward. Nobody else can be in the system.

A common cause of long recovery times is bringing the database down in the middle of long inserts into a table or deletes from a table. If you know, for example, that a table was being built from scratch, that is, it had no rows in it (or if you knew how many rows it initially had), you can get a very good estimate of your rollback time. Do a `tbstat -t` command and look at the number of rows in any table whose `tblnum` does not end in `00001`. This will be the table that is being rolled back. Then run several `tbstat -t` commands and note whether this number of rows is increasing or decreasing. If it is a scratch-built table, your recovery will go on until the number of rows equals zero. You can run several `tbstat -t` commands and calculate the rate at which the rows are being deleted. Extrapolate that number and you'll have an estimate of the rollback time. If it's a delete, and if you know how many rows were originally in the table, the number of rows will be increasing. You can perform the same extrapolation in the opposite direction to get an approximate rollback time.

None of this will make the recovery go any faster, but it'll help you make decisions about what to tell your users. If nothing else, having an accurate estimate and an explanation of why the rollback is occurring will make you look somewhat more in control of the situation.

KNOW WHAT A CERTAIN USER IS DOING?

Database administrators spend a lot of time monitoring the database, looking for things that could cause problems. After a while, it is usually possible to identify several of your peers that need to be looked in upon occasionally. After about a thousand repetitions of "DBA, I've got a job I want to kill, would you do it?" I developed the following scripts:

The first is called `seeuser` and it tells you what a certain user is doing in the database. Since I get tired of deciphering the `flag` codes in the `tbstat` output, I also put a legend at the bottom of the output telling me what each code means:

```
JOE 71>  cat seeuser

#!/bin/csh
if ( $#argv == 0 ) then
    echo -n "Enter the USER NAME you want to check on ( . for all) :  "
    set target = $<
  else
    set target = $1
endif

echo Looking at INFORMIX jobs for $target
echo "\
Users \
address  flags  pid    user    tty      wait     tout locks nreads nwrites"
echo " "
$INFORMIXDIR/bin/tbstat -u | grep $target | grep -v grep

echo "\
          ^ ^ ^ ^  \
          | | | | \
POSITION  1 2 3 4 \
\
1 WAITING ON: B(uffer) C(heckpoint) L(ock) S(latch) X(rollback) G(log)\
2 TRANSACTIONS: B(egin work)  T(in a transaction)  R(ollback)  A(rchive)\
3 STATUS:    R(eading)    X(inside a write, checkpoints frozen)\
4 PROCESS:   M(Monitor)   D(aemon)  C(Dead, awaiting cleanup) F(PageFlusher)"
```

You can invoke `seeuser` with or without parameters. If you use no parameters, the script will prompt you to enter the name of a user to check on, or to enter a period to check on all users. You can also invoke the program with a user name as a parameter. In either case, user could be anything that shows up in a `tbstat -u` output. For example, you could type a `seeuser L` and it would show you any users who were waiting for a lock to release (has an L in the first field of the flag field). Of course, it would also show you anything that user Lincoln or firewaLL was doing, too, but you wouldn't use capital letters in a user name, would you?

There's another variant of the `seeuser` script called `checkon`. This gives you all that `seeuser` does, but also includes any UNIX processes owned by the user. Here is the `checkon` script:

```
INFORMIX 83> cat checkon
#!/bin/csh
echo LISTING ALL jobs for $1
echo " "
ps -fu $1
echo " "
echo Looking at INFORMIX jobs for $1
echo " "
echo "\
address  flags   pid    user     tty     wait      tout locks nreads nwrites
$INFORMIXDIR/bin/tbstat -u | grep $1 | grep -v grep
echo "\
          ^ ^ ^ ^    \
          | | | |  \
POSITION  1 2 3 4 \
1 WAITING ON: B(uffer) C(heckpoint) L(ock) S(latch) X(rollback) G(log)\
2 TRANSACTIONS: B(egin work)  T(in a transaction)   R(ollback)  A(rchive)\
3 STATUS:    R(eading)    X(inside a write, checkpoints frozen)\
4 PROCESS:   M(Monitor)   D(aemon)    C(Dead,awaiting cleanup) F(PageFlusher)
```

This script is a little more particular with input that the `seeuser` script is. This is because of the UNIX `ps` command in the third line. Depending on your UNIX flavor, you may need to modify this line anyway, because different versions of UNIX have some differences in the `ps` command. Here, `ps` is looking for a complete user name. If your user name does not match, the script will fail on the `ps` command but will give you the `tbstat` output anyway. You could change the command to a simple `ps` command piped into `grep` something like this.

ps -aux | grep $1

instead of the `ps  -fu  $1` and this would allow you to use a partial username.

TRANSLATE A UNIX USER ID TO A REAL NAME?

This short script is helpful when you're looking at the OnLine logfile trying to find out why something strange has happened. In the logfile, OnLine will tell you that a certain PID (process identifier) owned by a certain user has caused a problem. For example, the following two lines appeared in a logfile just before the database aborted and crashed:

```
11:42:24  Process Aborted Abnormally: pid=26630 user=129 us=e0002bf0 flags=1
11:42:24  Process Aborted Abnormally (latch): pid=26630 user=129 flags=1
```

Here, a backend, process ID #26630, was killed by user #129 at 11:42 while holding a latch, causing the system to abort. To find the name of user 129, run the following script, called `username`.

```
INFORMIX  73> cat username

grep $1 /usr/passwd | awk -F: '{printf("The culprit is %s, aka: %s\n",$1,$5))}'
```

Feel free to change the "culprit....etc." to your favorite pejorative comments. The script is invoked as `username user_number`, for example, `username 129`.

RUN AN ARCHIVE IN THE BACKGROUND AND MONITOR IT?

The OnLine archiving programs assume that there will be a user sitting at a terminal monitoring the archiving process. Many times this is not a realistic option due to staffing problems. If you have large capacity tapes, you can place the archiving and automatic backup of logfiles in the background and monitor them through log files. These techniques will only work if you are *absolutely sure* that you will not need to change tapes in the middle of an archive. Another reason to buy big DAT tape drives!

Refer to the chapter on "Understanding the Concepts" for a more detailed discussion on archives and the limitations of the OnLine archiving system. In that chapter we presented the following script, called `do_level_1_archive`.

```
INFORMIX 73> cat do_level_1_archive

#!/bin/csh
date
$INFORMIXDIR/bin/tbtape -s << EOF
     {note, this line is a control-m, or carriage return.  don't type
note}
1
EOF
```

Running the do_level_1_archive script will send the output of the tbtape command to the standard output, your current screen. For running in the background, this is not what we want. I use a script to drive the do_level_1_archive script and redirect the output. This script is called run_level_1_archives.

```
INFORMIX 74: cat run_level_1_archives

#!/bin/csh
$INFORMIXDIR/local_bin/do_level_1_archive >& $INFORMIXDIR/archive.log &
```

This script provides us with several useful features. First, it lets the archive run in the background, and second, it gives us a log file to check to see how far along the archive has progressed. The tbtape program uses the UNIX curses screen I/O functions and is designed to provide screen output, not file output. As such, the output looks like one long character string to UNIX. The tbtape command does provide a running count of the percentage complete on the archive. To return a percentage complete string out of the archive.log file, use the peek_arc script.

```
tail -30c $INFORMIXDIR/archive.log
```

You'll see peek_arc used in the status script later that pulls many of these one-liner and other scripts together into a dashboard to look at the performance of the OnLine engine.

LOCATE AREAS OF HIGH DISK ACTIVITY?

As you do such activities as archiving, you often want to get a feel not only for what percentage of the job is done, but also for exactly where in the database the program is now working. This is helpful in being able to predict how long something is going to take to complete as well as for getting a feeling for the performance of your system. As disk I/O is the slowest thing that your computer system does, you need to know where your disk input and output is occurring. We've shown a simple script called hotspot in the tbtape -D utility explanation earlier. Let's gussy it up a little and make it a little more useful. The new script is called watch_hot.

```
INFORMIX 75> cat watch_hot

#!/bin/csh
while ( 1 == 1)

$INFORMIXDIR/bin/tbstat -z
sleep 5
$INFORMIXDIR/bin/tbstat -D | grep /
end
```

There are not many changes from hotspot, but this script continues until you press BREAK or CONTROL-C, zeroes the statistics between each run, and shows you only the relevant chunk information. You can change the sleep period to whatever you like if you want to use watch_hot for a while and monitor your disk activity. As in the hotspot script, remember that the tbstat -z command will zero out the performance statistics each time it is run (every five seconds in this case).

If you have some programs that are monitoring the statistics, this will no doubt interfere with them. Don't confuse the statistics maintained to monitor performance with the statistics maintained in the UPDATE STATISTICS command in SQL. They are two entirely separate sets of statistics.

TELL IF CONTINUOUS BACKUP OF LOGFILES IS RUNNING?

For many applications, it is wise to have the added security of continuous backup of logfiles to tape. If you're running a database with logging, it is very important to stay on top of freeing up logfiles. The best way to do this is to have `tbtape -s` running as much as possible. Even if you are using mirrored devices to hold your chunks, you need to think in terms of avoiding a single point of exposure to failure. This means running archives to tape regularly and it means backing up your logfiles to tape regularly. It also means physically separating the tapes from the computer. All of the redundancy and fault tolerance in the world won't save you if your computer room catches fire and everything in it burns.

If you have two tape devices available, it is possible to have continuous backup of logfiles running at all times. Note that I said possible, not recommended. Even with large tape backup devices, it is risky to backup your logfiles until the device fills. If you have a catastrophic tape error, it is possible that you could destroy hundreds of logs if you have a very large tape drive and had been running the logfile backup for a while. Why take the chance? Tape is cheap.

If you have only one tape drive available, you're forced to be conservative. You have to shut down continuous backup of logfiles to run your database archives. When you complete your archives, you have to put a log tape in the tape drive and restart the logging. This more or less forces you to swap log tapes at least once a day as a part of the archive/log cycle. Even if you have two tape drives, this is a good habit to get into. Plan on swapping out your log tapes at least daily, maybe more often if you have a very busy database. This also cuts down your exposure to massive data loss due to a bad tape. Once logfile data has been backed up to tape, it's lost to you. You can't undo it without restoring the database and reapplying logfiles. If you have backed up some logfiles to tape and find that the backup is questionable, do an archive immediately. It's the only way that you can insure recovery.

If you are starting and stopping logfile backup or alternating archiving and logfile backup, you have the danger of human error. Someone may forget to start the logfile backup. Another point of exposure is errors on your tape device. If your tape device goes offline while continuous backup of logfiles is running, you will not always get notification in your online logfile. Here's where a script comes in handy to check to see if logging is still on. This script is called `logging`.

```
INFORMIX 94> cat logging


#/bin/csh
ps -efa  | grep "tbtape -c" | grep -v grep > /dev/null
if ($status == 0) then
    set CONTINUOUS = "ON"
else
    set CONTINUOUS = "OFF"
endif
echo $CONTINUOUS
```

The `logging` script is run with no parameters and returns either ON or OFF. You'll see it in the `status` dashboard script later. Closely kin to this is the `archiving` script that tells you whether or not an archive is running.

```
INFORMIX 95> cat archiving

#!/bin/csh
ps -efa  | grep "tbtape -s" | grep -v grep > /dev/null
if ($status == 0) then
    set ARCHIVING == "ON"
else
    set ARCHIVING == "OFF"
endif
echo $ARCHIVING
```

You'll find this script called in the `status` program also, in conjunction with the `peek_arc` script.

KILL A BACKEND?

Informix OnLine versions earlier than 6.0 maintain a two-process architecture. Whenever a tool such as I-SQL or ESQL/C or I-4GL makes a request of the database, the tool is considered a client process. This client process spawns a server process that does the actual access to the database. This server process is called a "backend" process.

OnLine takes great pains to insure the consistency of the data in the database. Whenever something occurs that could potentially destroy this consistency, OnLine will immediately abort. When the database is restarted, the fast recovery process will roll back any processes that are not completed and would therefore cause the inconsistency.

One of the major actions that can cause the database to become inconsistent is the premature death of a backend process. If a backend is killed before it has the chance to insure the consistency of the database, it can abort the entire database and cause a database crash. There are two specific instances in which a prematurely killed backend can cause an abort:

- The backend dies while in a critical section (writing to the database)
- The backend dies while holding a latch.

You can't depend on being able to look at a `tbstat` output to see whether or not these circumstances apply. By the time you try to kill the process, the circumstances may have changed.

This means that you should ***never, never, never use a kill -9 on a backend***!

Did I make my point? Sometimes you can get away with it. There may even be occasions where you go ahead and break this rule, hoping that you'll dodge a bullet and be able to kill the backend without aborting the database. If you do ignore it, be prepared for crashing the system. Use the `kill  -9` command only as a last resort.

Why would you want to kill a backend? Many times, a user has started a query and then realizes that she is joining every table in your database with every other one and the query should generate a few billion rows. Or, someone has started an update that was wrong and will destroy your biggest database table. Maybe someone's killed a client process and the server process is still running. There are many reasons why you may be tempted to kill a query. Sometimes it's best just to let the query continue to run if it will not destroy a table or eat up a lot of system resources. If the query is running from within `isql`, it is usually possible to press the BREAK or CONTROL-C key and gracefully stop the query. That's usually the user's first option.

Assuming that you've determined that a query should be terminated, how do you kill a backend properly? The recommended method is with the following command:

```
tbmode -z PID_OF_THE_BACKEND_PROCESS
```

The `tbmode -z` command usually succeeds in killing the process. After running the `tbmode -z` command , run `tbstat -u`. The entry for the process should be gone or should have an R in the second position of the `flags` field. This indicates that the process is being rolled back. If this is not the case, try the `tbmode` command several times. If the query is still cranking away, it's time for a few more desperate measures. Try:

```
kill -15 PID_OF_THE_BACKEND_PROCESS
kill -13 PID_OF_THE_BACKEND_PROCESS
```

These UNIX `kills` are caught properly by the engine and are safe, posing no danger to your database. Like the `tbmode` command, try them several times if needed. You may need to change user to `root` to get the appropriate permissions to kill the backends. Again, check the `tbstat -u` output to see if the processes are dead or in rollback.

There are some processes that seem to be unkillable. Anything that is creating an index will be unkillable. UPDATE STATISTICS commands seem to be unkillable. Many of these unkillable processes are so deep into their programming loops that they are not checking their global `killflags` that the signal sets in the backend. Be patient in trying to kill with a `kill -15` or a `kill -13`. The processes may not go away immediately.

There's one final method of killing a `sqlturbo` process. This is definitely a last-ditch effort. When you do it, be ready to crash the system because it is definitely dangerous. Informix Technical Support doesn't even acknowledge the existence of the technique. They certainly don't recommend it. I don't even recommend it. But, if you're faced with having to bring down a production database to kill a job and you've tried everything else short of a `kill -9`, what do you have to lose?

This method depends upon your flavor of UNIX's having some kind of process control. Do a man on `kill` and look for some sort of kill that will halt a process in the same way that the CONTROL-Z key halts it for process control. If you can't find it in the man page, try running a `kill -1` to list the options. Also, look for the reciprocal command that restarts the stopped job. On my Pyramid, the stop command is `kill -STOP PID` and the restart command is `kill -CONT PID` where `PID` is the UNIX process ID of the process you want to kill.

The problem with trying to use `tbstat` information to decide whether or not you can safely kill a process is that `tbstat` is instantaneous and that your process may either acquire a latch or enter a critical phase in the time it takes you to read the `tbstat` output and execute your `kill` statement. To do this safely, you have to stop the process completely, check it with `tbstat` while it is stopped, and then either do your `kill` or restart the process and stop it again, checking each time to see if the stopped process is safe to kill.

Run the `kill - STOP` command and continue running `ps` until the process is getting no more processor time. Then do a `tbstat -u`. Look to see if the third position of the flag field is anything but an `X`, which indicates that the job is not in a critical section, writing to the database. Note the value of the first column which is the address of the user process. Now look at the last column of the `tbstat -s` output which tells you the owner of any latches. Does your offending process own a latch? If it doesn't, and if it's not in a critical section in the `tbstat -u` output, and if the process really is stopped, kill the process with a `kill -9`. If it is in a critical section or if it's holding a latch, run the `kill -CONT` or whatever command restarts the process, let it run a while, and repeat the process. If you can stop the process when it's in a safe status, you have a decent chance of killing it without harm.

Remember, this is a last-ditch measure. Although I have used it for several years without harm to the database, I've seen stranger things happen to databases. I would only use this if I were prepared not only to have to restart the database from a crash but also to be forced to recover from an archive. About the only thing that would justify it is if a process is destroying a table that, if the table were gone, I would have to recover from tape anyway.

IDENTIFY TEMPORARY TABLES?

Temporary tables are created in the OnLine system either explicitly or implicitly. Explicit temporary tables are created with the CREATE TEMP TABLE or the SELECT ... INTO TEMP ... command variants in SQL. Implicit temporary tables are created by the engine in the process of executing certain queries. None of these temporary tables ever receives an entry in any of the system tables and thus it is difficult to see exactly what is going on with temporary tables.

These temporary tables are stored in the rootdbs dbspace unless they have been explicitly created in another dbspace. The rootdbs is always the first dbspace in an OnLine system, and its dbspace number is 1. Since the high order bit of the tblnum output in tbstat -t represents the number of the dbspace, all default temporary tables will have a tblnum beginning with 1.

For versions of OnLine greater than 3.3, sorting is no longer done in the rootdbs. In these later versions, sorting is done in the directory identified by the $DBTEMP variable, in /tmp if $DBTEMP is not set, or in the directories specified in $PSORT_DBTEMP if you are using the parallel sorting option, PSORT. The only table that should normally reside in the rootdbs is the tablespace tablespace, which is identified with a final 1 in the tblnum. Thus 1000001 identifies the only non-temp table in the rootdbs in the default installation. Any other tables beginning with 1 should be temporary tables.

This is assuming that you are not placing ordinary databases and tables in the rootdbs. For maximum flexibility you should not be placing data in the rootdbs. The rootdbs is the only dbspace that cannot be dropped. If you have your databases located other than in rootdbs, you can always rebuild the dbspace on a larger device should your needs change. If you have tables in rootdbs, you lose this flexibility. As long as you have your initial three logfiles in rootdbs and as long as your physical logfile is in rootdbs, you probably don't want to add to the I/O load there anyway.

OnLine Version 6.0 will allow you to designate the location for your temporary files. In many cases, it will make sense to place your temporary files in a separate dbspace custom designed to hold the temporary tables. Again, for flexibility, having them in anywhere but rootdbs will give you more options. If you are not yet on 6.0, you may want to go ahead and set up a dbspace for temporary files and build your explicit temporary files with the IN DBSPACE option to place them in the correct dbspace. This will allow you to have a somewhat easier transition to 6.0.

Temporary tables are deleted when the SQL statement that has created them is finished or when the database initializes. When a system crash occurs, the SQL statements do not complete and temporary tables can remain. It is possible to initialize OnLine with a tbinit -r command that tells the engine not to bother removing temporary tables. This may make the database initialization somewhat faster, but it runs the risk of leaving temporary tables lying around when they are not in use. I know of no way to actually use the data that's in these zombie tables.

KNOW WHEN I'M IN A CHECKPOINT?

Checkpoints can be disruptive to your users in that some user processing is halted during a checkpoint. Depending upon how long the checkpoint takes, users may experience a temporary "freeze" in their activities. Often, these users will call the DBA with a complaint that "the database is down" as soon as one of their queries gets delayed. It's handy for the DBA to have a quick script that lets her know the checkpoint status. This script is called checkpoint.

```
INFORMIX 37>  cat checkpoint
#!/bin/csh
$INFORMIXDIR/bin/tbstat -
echo Current time is: `date`
grep Checkpoint `grep MSGPATH ${INFORMIXDIR}/etc/${TBCONFIG} |
    awk '{print $2}' ` | tail -5
```

This script is also useful in monitoring the frequency of your checkpoints. If you find that your checkpoints are coming too close together, you should consider retuning the database to provide longer times between checkpoints.

Actually, any of the tbstat invocations will include the header that gives the checkpoint status, but the simple minus option gives only the header. The grep statement in line 3 is a little more complicated than usual because we are picking up the value of $TBCONFIG and getting the message file name from the $TBCONFIG file rather than hard-coding it into the script. This makes it possible to report on various OnLine instances just by making sure that the $TBCONFIG is set for the proper instance.

This technique of getting data from the $TBCONFIG file rather than hard-coding it into the script is a useful programming technique if you are running multiple instances of OnLine.

MONITOR AND REPORT ON TABLE SIZES?

Tables in an OnLine database seem to take on a life of their own, especially in a heavily used system with many developers. It is a twofold problem. First, there's the problem of proliferation of tables. This will be addressed later in a table warehouse program.

The second part of the space problem concerns the growth of existing tables. In other sections, we have seen various programs for performing data archiving and table cleaning, but to do any of these, the DBA needs to know where the problem lics. We need a way to track the size and space utilization of tables.

At first glance, this seems to be an easy task. Just write a report that looks at the system catalogs. There are a couple of problems to this, the main one being that the data in systables is not always accurate. The system catalogue systables has a field called npdata that nominally contains the number of pages used by the table. However, this table is only updated when the SQL statement UPDATE STATISTICS is run. On top of that, even when update statistics is run, the number in npdata is not always accurate. It seems to be an approximation.

There are only two reliable ways to get the accurate data that actually represents the real utilization of the disk. This involves using the OnLine utilities tbstat or tbcheck.

The tbstat -t output contains a column called npages. This is an accurate number and represents the actual number of pages on the disk that are currently allocated to the table and to all of its indexes. Some of these pages may be empty, but it doesn't matter. The table still has these pages allocated. The data about a table only shows up in tbstat -t if the table is in use when the utility is run. One way to do this is to do an isql retrieve from the menu on one terminal while running a tbstat on another. This is fine for one-time checks but is not practical for compiling reports.

Another source of accurate data is tbcheck -pt. The output from this utility has a row called Number of pages allocated that gives an accurate page count.

However, this utility has two drawbacks. The first is that it places a lock on the target table and prevents users from updating the table. This is even more disruptive because the report for a table of significant size can take a while to complete, keeping it locked for a longer period of time. This can be overcome, but not without manual intervention. The information that you want appears quickly after the utility is started. As soon as you see the data you want, you can break out of the utility by pressing CONTROL-C. You will not keep the table locked for long. The main problem, however, is the same as with the tbstat command. It doesn't lend itself well to creating reports.

The solution for running reports lies in the tbcheck -pe utility. This utility does not lock tables, so it can be run at any time without disrupting access to the database. It does have a few drawbacks, but they can be handled. The first drawback is that the output from tbcheck -pe uses a significant amount of space. The second drawback is that the data is arranged in the form of an extent-by-extent report and does not provide summary data for tables. If you've read this far, you can probably expect that the next thing we see will be a script that massages the data.

Actually, we'll be doing something a little more complicated here. Since the extent data can be useful, we'll create our own system table and keep the extent data there. First, create a database called dba (or whatever you want to call it, or even keep it in rootdbs if you insist). Place the following table extent_sizes, in the database:

```
create table extent_sizes
   (
     database char(8),
     owner char(8),
     tabname char(20) not null,
     extents decimal(7,1),
     dbspace char(12)
   );
revoke all on extent_sizes from "public";

create index ext_tabname on extent_sizes (tabname);
```

The program that runs the tbcheck, massages the data, and then loads it back into the extent_sizes table is called last_table_sizes.

```
INFORMIX 92> cat last_table_sizes

#
$INFORMIXDIR/bin/tbcheck -pe  >! $INFORMIXDIR/last_tbcheckpe

cat $INFORMIXDIR/last_tbcheckpe | /bin/grep : | /bin/grep -v Chunk: |
/bin/grep -v WARNING | /bin/grep -v SAM | /bin/awk '\
BEGIN     {FS = " "} \
/DBSpace/ {dbspace = $4;next} \
         {printf("%s  %s\n",$0,dbspace)} ' \
| awk '{print $1,$3,$4}' | /usr/bin/tr ":" "|" | /usr/bin/tr "." "|" |
tr -s " "   " " | tr " " "|" > $INFORMIXDIR/tempsizes

$INFORMIXDIR/bin/isql dba << EOF
DELETE FROM dba:extent_sizes;
LOAD FROM "tempsizes" INSERT INTO dba:extent_sizes;
SELECT database,owner[1,3],tabname,dbspace, count(*) as extents,
sum(extents) as pages FROM extent_sizes GROUP BY
database,owner[1,3],tabname,dbspace ORDER BY pages desc;
EOF
/bin/rm $INFORMIXDIR/tempsizes
```

A few notes about the `last_table_sizes` script are in order. The second section beginning with `cat $INFORMIXDIR/last_tbcheckpe` is one long pipeline. Where it hits an end-of-line, use the backslash (\ ) to continue the line. None of the punctuation here is a backtick (`). This script uses just single and double quotes.

The final section is an `isql` command that first cleans out all of the rows of `extent_sizes` and then repopulates the table using a `load` from the destination of the long pipeline above. The report goes to standard output. If you wish, you can put the script in your `cron` file to run every night. If so, use a command like this:

```
$INFORMIXLOCALBIN/last_table_sizes > $INFORMIXDIR/last_table_sizes &
```

The resulting report looks like this.

```
database owner tabname        dbspace          extents           pages
admin    dba   loader_data    slowdbspace         17         210795.0
admin    dba   vmx_config     dbspace1            12         135349.0
admin    dba   person_addr    dbspace1            28         127767.0
admin    dba   mem_grp_code   dbspace1            14          82542.0
admin    dba   ticket_desc    dbspace1            41          71839.0
admin    dba   access_pre     dbspace1             6          67556.0
```

If you wish, you can then delete the `last_tbcheckpe` file, but if you can afford the space, leave it around. This file, if updated daily, can provide much valuable information about the general layout of your system. You can get valuable space utilization data as well as table fragmentation information by looking at the file.

Another good thing to do in your `cron` file is to move the `last_table_sizes` file into an archive directory before creating the new one. You can then do a UNIX `zip` or a `compress` on the old file if you wish. Keeping the `last_table_sizes` data around for a while can let you track and report on table and extent growth over a period of time. This sort of data is most helpful when you are trying to forecast future database needs. I keep the data around for a year and have written INFORMIX-WingZ programs to extract the data and draw impressive charts and graphs of table size growth. This is great when you're going to management requesting more hardware!

While the `last_table_sizes` report gives you useful information in terms of absolute number of extents and number of pages, it is often good to get this information in percentages. This lets you answer questions such as "What percentage of my database does table XXX occupy?" Since we have now gone to the trouble of building and populating a table with extent sizes in it, and updating it nightly, why not get a little more mileage out of the data?

The `last_percentage` script is very similar to `last_table_sizes`, with the exception that this scripts that the `extent_sizes` table is already populated.

```
INFORMIX 99> cat last_percentage
#
$INFORMIXDIR/bin/isql dba << EOF
SELECT database, owner, tabname,dbspace[1,8], count(*) as extents ,
sum(extents)/26165  as percent
FROM dba:extent_sizes
GROUP BY database, owner, tabname,dbspace[1,8]
ORDER BY percent desc
EOF
```

This script gives you the following report:

database	owner	tabname	dbspace	extents	percent
admin	dba	loader_data	slowdbsp	17	8.06
admin	dba	vmx_config	dbspace1	12	5.17
admin	dba	person_addr	dbspace1	28	4.88
admin	dba	mem_grp_code	dbspace1	14	3.15
admin	dba	ticket_desc	dbspace1	41	2.75

You will need to make one change in the script to customize it to your environment, or change the script to handle this automatically. The SELECT statement divides the sum(extents) by 26165 in my sample. Your number will be different. Do a tbstat -d and look at the chunk data. Add up all of the size columns for chunks that you want to consider as the total available. Divide this number by 100 and use the result instead of 26165. You may want to exclude your rootdbs and logfile chunks as not being available for use. You may also want to play a little with the figures to give you some "fluff factor." Users are going to scarf up any amount of space you have. You might want to keep a little bit hidden.

Sometimes, you want information similar to that from the table script, only with information about the actual space utilization. The following tabuse script simply runs the UNIX grep command against the last_tbcheckpe file:

```
INFORMIX 43>  cat tabuse
#
#tabuse

echo " "
echo "ACTUAL DISK USAGE REPORT FOR TABLES IN ALL DATABASES"
echo This data is as of:  `ls -la $INFORMIXDIR/last_table_sizes | cut -c
32-44`  based on the $INFORMIXDIR/last_table_size file
echo " \
database owner tabname              dbspace         extents         2K
pages"
echo "name                                                  used
used"
echo \
"======================================================================="
echo " "
grep $1 $INFORMIXDIR/last_table_sizes
```

The spacing of the echo statements may need to be adjusted if you are typing the program into your system. Just put in or take out some spaces to make it line up correctly on your terminal. Depending on your UNIX version, you may also need to alter the `cut` statement. Adjust the columns until the `cut` returns only the date.

This script does not provide real-time data. If you have your `last_table_sizes` script running in `cron,` tell your users to look at the top line of the `tabuse` output to see when the `last_tbcheckpe` file was generated.

Since we're using a `grep` statement, you can invoke the script by typing the command `tabuse any_fragment` where `any_fragment` is any text that can be found on a line in the `last_tbcheckpe` file. Thus, you could query by table name, table name fragment, database, owner, or dbspace.

This can be a useful utility. It's an example of a general method of doing things that would otherwise be very difficult or take a lot of time. In cases where real-time data is not absolutely critical, generate a workfile for the data during a slow period and query the workfile during heavy use periods.

FIGHT TABLE PROLIFERATION?

If your users and developers have resource privileges on the database, you will find that you are constantly having to play "table janitor." It's funny how tables named `temp_XXX` are never really temporary and how tables that were going to hang around for "just a coupla' days" become institutionalized as part of your database.

What we need is a tool that will allow the DBA to monitor the tables in a database, know what should be there and what shouldn't be there, and notify the DBA when certain tables should be removed.

This is a situation that is quite common to UNIX system administrators. Any time that you have a community of users who are utilizing common resources, you have to deal with resource hogs. While many users are quite diligent about taking out their trash, there are many others who are packrats. "I never saw a table I didn't like," seems to be their motto. Whether or not you are able to enforce some level of control over this situation depends on how much actual leeway you have in removing other people's tables.

You can send e-mail harassing and whining to the users about removing old tables and you'll probably get fairly decent results. Nobody's out there just to fill up your database. The only problem is that you will be forced to be the policeman, and frankly, you have better things to do.

The UNIX system administrators solve this problem by having "file eater" daemons that automatically delete old files. The users know that these file eaters are there and they know how to protect their important files, but they have to take affirmative action to do it. The responsibility is on the users, not on the administrator. Here is a method of doing the same thing with OnLine tables.

The basis of this "table warehouse" is a database table that establishes ownership and longevity for all tables in your database. This table is called `auth_tables` and is in your `dba` database. It is designed to join with the various `systables` in each of your users' databases, with the join being on two fields, `tabname` and `owner`. These fields should be unique within each database and will uniquely identify tables. Create the `auth_tables` table using this SQL script:

```
INFORMIX 1>cat mk_auth.sql

create table auth_tables
    (
       tabname char(18),
       owner char(8),
       database char(8),
       good_til datetime year to day,
       user char(10),
       application char(10)
    );
revoke all on auth_tables from "public";
create index auth_tables_x1 on auth_tables(tabname,owner);
```

The `tabname` and `owner` fields are identical to their counterparts in `systables`. This is where the tables join. The `good_til` column is a "drop dead date" for a particular table. When a user creates a table that should remain in the database, the user must register the table information with you. The user field should be the person who takes responsibility for the table, not necessarily the owner in `systables`. The application should be the name of the application or module that uses the table. If the table is temporary, the user should give you a `good_til` date at which time the table can be removed. Tables that are permanent should have a date far out in the future, like `3000-12-31`. Users should be taught that any table that is not registered in the `auth_tables` table is subject to immediate deletion after one publication of its table name in a warning e-mail message to everyone.

You may wish to be a little more lenient with unregistered tables. If you can identify the owner of an unregistered table, you may wish to modify the scripts to send them an e-mail message. If a table is not registered, you will not have a `good_til`, a `user`, or an `application` field since you don't have an entry in the `auth_tables` database. If the table is not registered, you will have to make do with the `owner` name in `systables`. If your system does not enforce individual table ownership, the only way that you can notify an anonymous owner or user of a table is by an e-mail posting to all users.

There are several ways that you can initially populate your `auth_tables` database. If you are just beginning with OnLine, you can develop a system in which all tables that go into the database must be manually registered with you. If you have an existing application, put together a group and do a thorough cleaning of your database, getting rid of all the junk. Then go into the individual systables tables in each database and insert the tabname, owner, and database name into auth_tables. You may have to make several tries at it, but try to get all of the "legal" core tables identified as fully as possible with user, application, and good_til entries as appropriate. The following ACE form oktables should be helpful. Note that this is just a default form on auth_tables with headings added.

```
INFORMIX 3>cat oktables.per
database dba
screen size 24 by 80
{

                    Authorized Tables in the Database

tabname              [f000                    ]
owner                [f001     ]
database             [f002     ]
good_til             [f003       ]
user                 [f004       ]
application          [f005       ]

}
end
tables
auth_tables
attributes
f000 = auth_tables.tabname;
f001 = auth_tables.owner;
f002 = auth_tables.database;
f003 = auth_tables.good_til;
f004 = auth_tables.user;
f005 = auth_tables.application;
end
```

Compile this form and use it to get all of your legitimate forms registered in your auth_tables table. Now, the task is to create reports that show you which tables are candidates for execution. Since we are going to kill these tables, I've chosen a good Texas term for them, "outlaws." That's the name of the report script.

```
INFORMIX 4>cat outlaws

#
if ( $#argv == 0 ) then
    set database = "admin"   <------You need to change this to your default
endif

if ( $#argv == 1 ) then
    set database = ${1}
endif

$INFORMIXDIR/bin/isql $database << EOF

SELECT
        systables.tabname,
        systables.owner,
        systables.created,
        systables.nrows,
        systables.npused * 2048 as bytes

FROM    systables, OUTER dba:auth_tables

WHERE   systables.tabname = dba:auth_tables.tabname AND
        systables.owner   = dba:auth_tables.owner    AND
                        systables.tabid > 99     AND
                        systables.tabtype = "T" AND
                        systables.tabname not in (select tabname from
                        dba:auth_tables where good_til > current)

                        and systables.tabname not matches "rev_*"
                        and systables.tabname not matches "access*"
                        and systables.tabname not matches "usage*"
                        and systables.tabname not matches "a_*"
                        and systables.tabname not matches "tmp_*"
                        and systables.tabname not matches "crev*"
ORDER by bytes desc
EOF
```

This script has a few things that are specifically designed for my database applications that you will need to change to fit your needs. First, you can invoke the script with or without a database name. If it is invoked without a database name, it defaults to my main database, admin. Of course, you'll need to change this. Based upon some of our earlier scripts, you may remember that the npages field in systables is not necessarily an accurate count of real size, but it is close enough. I just want to be able to tell the users in a general way how much space this table takes up. I have this number multiplied by 2048 for a 2K page size. If your system uses 4K, change the script. All of the SQL statements that are connected by AND are required. At the end, you see several statements that are connected by "and." These are optional and are local to my system. In my system, we have many tables that are legitimate but can be identified by the first characters in the name. The rest of the name is dependent upon the process ID that created the tables. These last SQL clauses cause these "wild card" table names to be accepted as legitimate tables. If you want to get fancy, you could put these names in a table and do the exceptions from fragments of names from the table. It's easier the way I did it. The outlaws script gives you a report similar to this:

```
INFORMIX 50>outlaws
tabname            owner    created       nrows          bytes

ry_invoice_def     rodney   10/06/1993    24600          3149824
zip_xref           dba      03/28/1993    43635          2078720
djcmv3             support  01/08/1994     2474           362496
conn11024          chris    01/17/1994     2024           188416
```

One of the drawbacks (or features, depending on whether you wrote it or I wrote it) to outlaws is that it must be run for each database. If you wanted to run it once for all of your databases, you could use our old friend find_db_names. Write a short script called find_all_outlaws and run it with no parameters. The reports will be placed in files called XXXXX.outlaws where XXXXX is the name of each of your databases.

```
INFORMIX 200> cat find_all_outlaws
foreach database (`$INFORMIXLOCALBIN/find_db_names`)
echo "`date`:  OUTLAWS REPORT for database: $database" >! ${database}.outlaws
$INFORMIXDIRLOCALBIN/outlaws $database >> ${database}.outlaws
end
```

THE status SCRIPT

In this chapter, we've seen a lot of individual scripts and programs that enable the DBA to deal with different parts of the database. Now, it's time to pull them together and create a "dashboard" for the OnLine system.

Of all the tools that come with OnLine, there is nothing that provides a quick, one-page peek into the engine. Various invocations of tbstat will allow you to look at individual items, but nothing gives you a quick status report. If the OnLine system is a database engine, certainly there should be a dashboard. Like a dashboard, the status script gives you or your users one place to look for indications of current problems or problems to come.

This script depends upon having other scripts located in your $INFORMIXDIR/local_bin directory. It requires the following scripts:

- logging
- archiving
- thislog
- dbdf

Here is the code for the status script:

```
INFORMIX 103>  cat status

#!/bin/csh
clear
set INFORMIXLOCALBIN = "$INFORMIXDIR/local_bin"
echo "Please wait....."
set list = ( `$INFORMIXDIR/bin/tbstat -p | fgrep -v e` )
set dskreads = $list[1]
set pagreads = $list[2]
set bufreads = $list[3]
set readcache = $list[4]
set dskwrits = $list[5]
set pagwrits = $list[6]
```

```
set bufwrits = $list[7]
set writecache = $list[8]
set isamtot = $list[9]
set open = $list[10]
set start = $list[11]
set read = $list[12]
set write = $list[13]
set rewrite = $list[14]
set delete = $list[15]
set commit = $list[16]
set rollbk = $list[17]
set ovtbls = $list[18]
set ovlock = $list[19]
set ovuser = $list[20]
set ovbuff = $list[21]
set usercpu = $list[22]
set syscpu = $list[23]
set numckpts = $list[24]
set flushes = $list[25]
set bufwaits = $list[26]
set lokwaits = $list[27]
set lokreqs = $list[28]
set deadlks = $list[29]
set dltouts = $list[30]
set lchwaits = $list[31]
set ckpwaits = $list[32]
set compress = $list[33]


if ( $lokwaits > 0 ) then
     @ lokhold  =  ( $lokwaits * 100  ) / $lokreqs
     @ lokfigure = 100 - $lokhold
else
     @ lokfigure = 100
endif
if ( $lchwaits > 0 ) then
     @ lchhold =  ( $lchwaits * 100 ) / $isamtot
     @ lchfigure = 100 - $lchhold
else
     @ lchfigure = 100
endif
```

```
fgrep Checkpoint $INFORMIXDIR/online.log | tail -6 >! ~/temp_stat
#ps - efa > ~/tempjobs
ps -a > ~/tempjobs
@ NUMBERFULL = `$INFORMIXDIR/bin/tbstat -l | grep -v RSAM | grep U | wc -l`
endif
@ cpunum = `echo $syscpu | awk -F. '{print $1}'`
@ usernum = `echo $usercpu | awk -F. '{print $1}'`
if ( $cpunum == 0 ) then
   @ cpunum = 1
endif
@ ratio = $usernum / $cpunum
echo "\
INFORMIX STATUS:COMPUTER NAME:    TIME: `date` \
`$INFORMIXDIR/bin/tbstat -` \
CPU UTILIZATION: \
 `uptime` \
\
RATIOS: READ CACHE    WRITE CACHE    LOCK HIT%    LATCH HIT%    USER/SYSTEM\
     $readcache           $writecache          $lokfigure          $lchfigure
     ${ratio}-1 \
WAITS: CHECKPOINTS    BUFFERS         DEADLOCKS      \
         $ckpwaits             $bufwaits              $deadlks "
echo "\
LOGS:  There are now ${NUMBERFULL} log(s) in use.  This includes the current
log:\
`$INFORMIXLOCALBIN/thislog`"
echo "\
\
CHECKPOINTS:  The last six checkpoints occurred as follows:\
`cat ~/temp_stat | sed 's/Checkpoint Completed/  /g'`"
echo \
===========================================================================
echo -n "  CONTINUOUS BACKUP OF LOG FILES: `$INFORMIXLOCALBIN/logging`
ARCHIVE: `$INFORMIXLOCALBIN/archiving` "
echo   " "
sh $INFORMIXLOCALBIN/dbdf

$INFORMIXDIR/bin/tbstat -d  >! ~/temphold99
fgrep PD ~/temphold99 > /dev/null
```

```
if ($status == 0) then
   echo "CAUTION:  A CHUNK IS DOWN"
endif

rm ~/temp_stat* ~/temphold* ~/tempjobs*
echo " "
```

This script is designed to be relatively portable across systems. I've avoided hard-coding anything into the system, with the exception of some of the code in the dbdf script that excludes page usage in my logspaces. Since the logfiles are preallocated, the space usage does not vary. You may or may not want to see the data.

The screen output looks like this:

```
Please wait.....

INFORMIX STATUS:COMPUTER NAME: batman  TIME: Fri Jan 21 15:40:11 CST 1994
RSAM Version 4.10.UD4   -- On-Line -- Up 3 days 17:41:18 -- 18704 Kbytes
CPU UTILIZATION:
   3:40pm  up 3 days, 17:46,  79 users,  load average: 12.94, 13.50, 13.27


RATIOS: READ CACHE   WRITE CACHE    LOCK HIT%   LATCH HIT%   USER/SYSTEM
           98.39         97.10          100         100         9-1
WAITS: CHECKPOINTS   BUFFERS              DEADLOCKS
           125          9941                  5


LOGS:  There are now 2 log(s) in use.  This includes the current log:
e06d26f0 11      U---C-L  3214     70f4f4      30000      13435     44.78


CHECKPOINTS:  The last six checkpoints occurred as follows:
12:59:42    13:31:53    14:04:41    14:22:41    14:56:41    15:33:37
============================================================================
  CONTINUOUS BACKUP OF LOG FILES: OFF    ARCHIVE: OFF
rootdbs      is 37.34 percent full and has 167305 free pages
dbspace2     is 23.56 percent full and has 206379 free pages
dbspace1     is 89.84 percent full and has 166120 free pages
slowdbspace  is 92.90 percent full and has  61061 free pages
  (Chunk down warning appears here if applicable)
```

The screen does tend to get a bit crowded. In fact, if you have more than four or five dbspaces in your system that are reported by the dbdf script, your report may scroll off the page. If this is the case, you could either reformat the screen output, taking out some of the blank lines that I put in for readability, or you could pipe the result through the UNIX more utility, which would allow the user to page through the output.

Understanding the status screen

The first four lines of the screen give you basic status and identifying information about the system. It includes the computer name (from the UNIX hostname utility, some UNIX versions may not have this utility,) and the status date on the first line. The second line is the header from tbstat and tells you the RSAM version of OnLine, its status (online, offline, checkpoints), its uptime, and the size of its shared memory segment. The fourth line gives you the output from your UNIX uptime utility so that you can get a feel for the load on your system.

The RATIOS section gives you the read cache and write cache figures from tbstat -p. A well-tuned system will have 95+ % for read and 85+% for write cache hit rates. The next two numbers are derived from tbstat -p output. The LOCK HIT % entry gives you the percentage of time that requests for locks were successful. It is calculated by this formula:

```
lock hit %  =   100   -   ( lock waits  x  100) /(lock requests)
```

This number should be close to 100% at all times. If this number begins to drop, it means that jobs are having to wait for locks to be released. Look for applications that are holding locks for too long or for problems with long transactions.

The LATCH HIT % statistic is similar to the LOCK HIT % statistic and shows you the number of times that latch requests were successful. There is no statistic available for the number of latch requests issued by the engine, so we used the statistics for the total number of ISAM calls. This gives a count of the number of database primitives that were executed. The formula for this calculation is:

```
latch hit % =  100 -  ( latch waits x 100)/ (number of isam calls)
```

This number should also remain at 100%. If it starts to go down, look at contention for resources such as buffers, logfiles, etc.

The WAITS line tells you the actual number of times that processes had to wait for checkpoints to complete and for buffers to get free. Use this in conjunction with the LATCH HIT and LOCK HIT percentages if you begin to see slowdowns. The DEADLOCKS number gives the number of times that the engine has taken action to avoid a deadlock situation. This is not the number of times the engine has been deadlocked. Theoretically, a deadlock cannot happen. If your DEADLOCKS count is large, look to your applications. Jobs are failing and are being rolled back because of these potential deadlocks. You have a design error somewhere.

The LOGS lines give you a count of the number of logs that are not yet freed by being backed up to tape. This count also counts the number of logs that have been backed up but have not been released because they hold information regarding uncommitted transactions. Watch the number of logs carefully. If it gets close to your total number of logfiles, you could be looking at a long transaction rollback. Check this screen to be sure that you have continuous backup of logfiles running. If it is running and if you have many logs in use, run a tbstat -u and look for transactions that have a lot of reads or writes. They are probably the long ones. The second LOGS line shows you the information about the CURRENT logfile. It is in the same format as the tbstat -l output.

The CHECKPOINTS lines show you the times of the last six checkpoints. If these checkpoints are closer together than you usually see, look for some jobs running that are causing a lot of logging. Long inserts and long deletes are a common culprit here. Unless you begin to get into logfile problems, there's not a lot that you can do. If you find the checkpoints occur too frequently, you may need to tune the database.

The line immediately after the double lines gives you a quick status of your logging and archiving processes. If you are doing archives using the scripts in this section, you will be piping the output to the archive.log file. If so, when you are doing an archive, the percentage complete will appear after ARCHIVE. If not, it will just read ON or OFF. Continuous backup of logs will be a simple ON/OFF display.

The final section gives you dbspace by dbspace figures of percentage used and free pages. The final section will give you a warning about chunks that are offline if you have any. Note that this script does not consider mirroring chunks. If you are using Informix mirroring, you may wish to modify the script to show the mirror chunk data.

Chapter 7

Common DBA Tasks

INSTALLING AND SETTING UP ONLINE

At some point, you will need to be able to install and set up an OnLine system. This will occur during an initial OnLine installation, during an installation on or upgrade to a new computer system, or during an upgrade to your existing system. As installations go, the Informix install process is usually relatively painless, but of course there are exceptions.

There seems to be a rule that software companies spend twenty quadrillion man years developing their products and about ten minutes writing the install programs. Be very wary of all install programs, not only for OnLine, but for all computer software. The rule seems to be uniform. If you have a chance, look at scripts before you run them, just to be sure that they don't do something stupid. Do this especially for upgrades. Install programs often are unclear about the extents they go to to preserve your existing data and environments. The better ones will warn you and ask your permission before making any modifications to anything critical. The worst ones will merrily blow away your data, configuration files, user files, and the like and not even bother to let you know what they've done.

Luckily, Informix has a fairly robust set of install routines. In most cases, an upgrade will try to preserve existing data and environments. If the documentation does not make it clear, call Informix Technical Support. They may not, and probably will not, immediately know the answer, but they will research it for you.

In all cases, make a complete backup of your system before trying any type of installation procedure or upgrade. Back up your UNIX file system, making sure that you get all of your critical files. Do a complete, level 0 archive of your database, and back up all logfiles to tape. Don't scrimp or try to save time by not doing the backups. There's no such thing as a "safe" upgrade.

Maintaining a logbook

A basic need common to all computer administration is the need to document and track the system configuration. Installation of software, changes to tuning parameters, changes or upgrades of the operating system, system crashes, and calls to support all need to be written down somewhere for future reference. Too often, the DBA gets so involved in solving the immediate problems that the job of documenting the problem gets a very low priority. A common train of thought is "Of course I'll remember what changes I'm making."

For the same reason that software must be rigorously documented, all of the primary and side issues of administering the database should be documented. Software that you install today may need to be reinstalled next year. You'll need the serial numbers, installation manuals, and software protection codes later. When you've discovered that something unusual has happened to your data two months ago and you're just now finding out about it, you'll want to know what types of tuning or database changes you made then. Some day you'll want to take a couple of weeks of vacation and let your assistant handle the database while you're gone. This person won't remember all of the things that you did. For all these reasons, you need to keep a logbook.

Computer people seem to want to try to do everything on the computer. That's why software developers can sell thousands of copies of home budget, recipe tracking, and videotape tracking programs that get used once or twice at the most. It's tempting to want to keep track of your database management activities using (surprise, surprise) the database. Avoid this. Take the simple, low-tech approach. Use a physical logbook that you write in with a pen. (Try it, I'm sure it'll come back to you. It's the way you did it in elementary school.)

Make a big thing out of the logbook. Get a nice, bound book. Make it look good. You want something that gives you an incentive to use it and to keep it up. If you use some plain, ordinary notebook, you'll find yourself tearing pages out of it when you need to write down the plumber's phone number. The logbook is something you want to keep. Besides, if you make a production out of it, it'll be more convincing if you need to pull it out to convince a manager or a vendor that you know what you're talking about. True, it's a little thing, but little things count.

What should you keep in the logbook?   At the very minimum, you need to have:

Telephone numbers	hardware and software vendors service vendors important staff members facilities people (A/C, electrical, etc.) modem numbers for your incoming lines
Serial numbers	hardware software (with key codes, too) O/S versions and revision levels version numbers of all installed software
Configuration data	disk layout documentation mirroring and striping information sample `.profile` or `.cshrc` files scripts that set environment variables
Written procedures	startup and shutdown procedures archive plan logging procedures emergency procedures shutdown and startup procedures for applications support policies documentation for local utilities location of full Informix manual set

Site-specific data	contents of your `tbconfig` file
	`tbstat -a` output
	`tbcheck -pe` output
	`dbschema` output

For the most part, most of the items listed above are one-shot items. Sure, there's a lot of information to put together, but after it's done you'll only have to change it occasionally.

Other items need a running log that is more or less a system diary. These sections need to be added to as events happen. They need to be logged with a date and time:

Tuning changes	What parameters did you change? What were you trying to do? What was the result of the change? Is this a permanent change?
User complaints	What was the problem? Was it fixed? How? Is it a training issue?
System crashes	When did the system go down? Was there any data lost? What was the problem? How was it fixed?
Downtime	Was this scheduled or unscheduled downtime? Who was affected? How long was the system down? Who started it back up? Was there preventative maintenance done?

Support calls	Date and time of call to Informix Technical Support. Who did you talk to? What was the case number they gave you? What did they recommend? Did it work? Is this a continuing problem? What was their response time?
Software changes	Full information about any new software installed. Information on any upgrades made.

This list is just the beginnings of an outline, but you should get the general idea. This may be a pain to do right now, but when you find yourself with Informix licenses for twenty computers trying to figure out which versions are where and how to upgrade everyone to the same version, you'll be glad you took the time.

The installation procedure

Before you attempt an install or an upgrade, look through the documentation included with the software. Informix usually includes a booklet that details install procedures for the entire release set. These booklets are done by overall version of the product. Thus if you have a 5.01 install, you may be installing a 5.01 engine and earlier, possibly 4.11 tools. There should be separate install booklets for the 5.01 and the 4.11 software. They'll probably say the same thing, but read through them to see if anything's different. You'll also get lots of registration forms and license forms. Put them aside and handle the paperwork later. You will, however, receive an envelope with the software serial number and installation key codes with each set of disks or tapes that make up one product. Be sure and keep track of which codes go with which products. I always try to write the serial number and key codes on the installation media. If you do this, be sure to maintain tight physical control over the media.

The booklets and distribution media will contain commands for loading the media. Take these with a grain of salt. The actual commands are probably right, as are the flags to the commands, but you'll probably have to do some interpretation of the device names.

Just know the device names for your tape drives and/or floppy devices, and you'll get through it with no trouble.

It is very important that you have created the `informix` user and group properly. Check the installation booklet carefully to see if there are any restrictions on proper user or group numbers for `informix`. The instructions will tell you to place certain environmental variables such as `$INFORMIXDIR` into your environment. It's best to create the `informix` login first, then re-login as `informix`. You can check that you have the proper variables in place by using the UNIX `echo` command as in `echo $INFORMIXDIR`. If the outputs are correct, you have the variables set correctly for your login. The actual installs are done as user `root`.

The actual installations usually follow a similar sequence of events.

1. Load the software as `root` in the `$INFORMIXDIR` directory.
2. Run the install script named `./installXXXX` (XXXX is the product name).

Running the install script usually consists of entering the software serial number and key code and then watching the install script move things into the proper places. Part of the process is *branding* the code, which is Informix's means of protecting its software from pirates. If for some reason the install doesn't go properly, it is usually better to re-install from the installation medium. If something got branded improperly or didn't get done at all, you'll have problems in the near future.

The order of installation is important in installing OnLine products. Usually, the order is:

1. Install tools first (earliest versions first)
2. Install the OnLine engine
3. Install communications products like INFORMIX-Star and INFORMIX-Net.

A good mnemonic for remembering the order is: TEN, for Tools, Engine, and Network.

Be sure to completely install one product before you copy the media from the next product. The process should be: copy media, run `install`, copy media, run `install`, etc.

After all of the products are on the disk and have been installed properly, you need to initialize the database. Refer to the installation booklets for this, but I'll give you a few suggestions covering items that may not be clear in the documentation.

First, plan your install. Know which devices you are going to use for disk chunks. Make sure that all of these devices are owned by the `informix` user and that they have the proper access permissions. OnLine is very picky about permissions, and the error messages are not always clear that they're complaining about permissions. In fact, if anything doesn't work correctly in the installation process, look at your permissions. If one of the install scripts did not complete properly, it may not have changed the permissions of the software correctly. If you already have a running engine, run a directory of all of the OnLine code for future reference. There may be a time that you'll want to come back and compare your permissions with a known good system.

Also, be prepared to relink your kernel several times to get OnLine to run properly. One common problem is with shared memory and semaphore limits. Have your UNIX system administrator (or the system administration manual) handy. It is a good idea to check the release notes after all of the software is installed but before you try to initialize the engine. These release notes are in the `$INFORMIXDIR/release` directory. If your machine's release requires any special kernel parameters, they will be found in a file called `*ONLINE*`. Go through everything in the release notes directory. It'll save you a lot of time down the line.

DESIGNING THE DATABASE

Once your OnLine system is correctly installed and running properly, the job becomes one of deciding how to structure and organize the data. Decisions made at this time can have lasting impact upon the performance and usability of the database.

Depending upon the scope of the duties assigned to you as DBA, you may or may not have responsibilities in the actual design of the database. Even if you do not actually design the database, you need to be aware of the factors relating to the design decisions. You need to be able to provide Informix-specific information relating to performance and design decisions.

This task requires an understanding of the database structure, an understanding of the needs of your users, and an understanding of the resources and capabilities available to your system.

Understanding your database structure

It is important to differentiate between knowledge of the structure of the database and knowledge of the contents. It is possible for the DBA to administer a large, complex database with little or no knowledge of what the actual data looks like. In a smaller, simpler system, the DBA may wear DBA, developer, and even user hats. As a system grows larger and more complex, the users, developers, and DBA's develop more stratified views of the system. Each views the database from his or her own level of abstraction. The users don't care about the structure but understand the data. The developers understand part of the structure and part of the data. Finally, the DBA understands how pieces fit together but doesn't necessarily understand what the pieces are.

This stratification of knowledge can be a help or a hindrance. In any case, the DBA must deal with the highest levels of abstraction, for it is only here that the overall operations of the system can be maximized. If you can work with and understand the lower levels of abstraction, by all means do so, but start from the top.

Normalization of the database

If you are inheriting an existing database system you will probably be more or less stuck with the database design. It becomes more and more difficult to make wholesale changes in the structure of a database with time. As more applications are developed that access the database, you tend to get more and more locked into the structure dictated by the original designers. Remember this if you are in the enviable position of starting at the beginning. Either you or your successors will have to live with your design decisions for a long time.

We're not going to get into a long discussion on normalization. There are books devoted to the subject and there is an entire calculus devoted to the theory of database design. Besides, it's probably academic if you are dealing with a legacy database. There's not much you can do to change it anyway. Instead, we will look at the extremes of not normalized versus fully normalized databases.

Most databases have had at least some attempt at normalization. With relational databases such as Informix, some degree of normalization is expected, if only from the fact that it is a buzzword that lots of people know and few people understand. A totally non-normalized database would essentially be a flat file. All data items would be in one table. This environment would be extremely wasteful of space and would be a poor performer, but it would have some advantages. It would be easy to understand. Users could do ad hoc queries without having a detailed knowledge of the structure of the database.

The fully normalized database will have the data elements spread out in many tables that can be joined to extract needed data. A database in the fourth normal form is usually more efficient in the use of disk storage and computer resources. It can also be more difficult to understand both for the end users and for the DBA. Often, a highly normalized database can suffer a performance penalty because of the amount of joining that is needed to access data. In these instances, some denormalization of the database can help improve performance. For example, your application may access information in two tables very often using a particular join. In this case it might be advisable to denormalize and put the data together in a single table to eliminate the constant joining. Even though the normalized version may actually be more efficient in use of overall resources, the perceived speed of access to your users may be more important than milking the absolute maximum efficiency from the database.

Even in databases that begin as a normalized database, we often see a "creeping denormalization." Sometimes this de-normalization is intentional, but more often it is the result of expediency. Developers may add redundant tables "just this once" or for a "temporary project." The lesson here is that normalization of the database is a constant process. If you have a normalized database, you have to enforce normalization throughout the development process, not just in the initial design phase.

Don't be enslaved by the theoretical arguments for or against various normal forms. While it may be interesting to decide how many angels will fit on the head of a pin, the answer will probably change tomorrow. Look at the overall balance between database efficiency and usability. Don't be afraid to denormalize when there are good reasons.

TABLE MANAGEMENT

The tables are the reason for the existence for the database system. Using the "black box" theory of databases, users tend to believe that once they have created a table, everything is automatically taken care of and handled by the omnipotent and omniscient database management system. For the user, it is often enough to allow his understanding to stop at this point. Ask a user where his data resides, and you'll probably get "in a table" as an answer.

One of the most important DBA functions is the arrangement and management of the tables and indexes in the database system. Unless the basic requirements of efficient table and index layout are achieved, the entire system starts off at a disadvantage and optimum performance becomes an illusive dream. Once the system is initially set up properly, the DBA must continuously monitor these aspects of the database system. It will always be evolving, and the DBA needs to be able to at least stay abreast of the changes. To effectively set up and maintain a database system, the DBA needs to have a deeper understanding of the physical layout of tables and indexes. This understanding must start with the sizing and physical storage of tables within databases.

Sizing and physical storage

INFORMIX-OnLine's database tables are stored either in dedicated UNIX files or on raw devices. Raw device storage is more efficient and much more common than UNIX file system storage. Since tables are not stored in individual files that are visible to UNIX, the DBA has to use OnLine utilities to view table data.

Much useful information is contained in the OnLine table `systables`. Every database managed by OnLine will have a separate set of system tables. These tables can be inspected either by the `isql` utility, by the `dbaccess` utility, by INFORMIX-4GL or other client programs, or by embedded ESQL code.

Data about physical storage locations on disk is available only through use of the `tbcheck` utility. This utility is very useful and is one of the few ways that the DBA can see how the physical data is actually stored and arranged.

When an OnLine table is first created, a typical SQL statement to create the table might be:

```
CREATE TABLE test_table
(
 field1  SMALLINT,
 field2  SMALLINT
)IN dbspacename EXTENT SIZE XXX NEXT SIZE YYY
```

From a physical storage standpoint there are three interesting areas of this SQL statement. They are discussed in the next three sections.

IN DBSPACENAME

Here, DBSPACENAME would be replaced with the name of one of your system's dbspaces. At table creation time, this is just about the only way that you can specify where to put the table. Physical table location is most important when trying to place active tables in preferred locations on the disk. If you have some tables that are very active, you may wish to create dbspaces that are made up of chunks from your fastest disk devices. You may also wish to create dbspaces composed of chunks on different devices or controlled by different disk controllers to separate two tables that often get accessed together. Such a scheme would allow simultaneous access of both tables without the disk thrashing that would be caused if both tables were on the same disk and accessed by the same read head.

EXTENT SIZE

This is the size in kilobytes of the first extent of the table. Whether the table has one row or hundreds, it will still occupy this amount of space in the database. This space is reserved at table creation time and is only released if the table is recreated. Due to the internal layout of OnLine, it is better if an entire table will fit within a total of eight extents. If the number of extents goes above eight, OnLine has to access another page from disk each time the table is accessed. It is best to try to build your tables so that the first extent will contain all the data and indexes. Putting the majority of data into the first extent ensures that most of the data will be located in a contiguous area of disk, with resulting performance gains in long sequential reads.

NEXT SIZE

When the first extent is filled, OnLine automatically allocates an additional extent of NEXT size in kilobytes. As these extents are filled, more are allocated. Once an extent is allocated, it is not released unless the table is rebuilt. This means that when left alone, tables will grow in size or remain the same in size. They never decrease in size without manual intervention.

There are some cases in which the OnLine engine modifies the NEXT SIZE. There is an internal limit to the number of extents that OnLine can physically assign to a tablespace. This limit varies with the OnLine version. For example, in Version 4.XX the limit is approximately 200 extents. If a table is created using the default EXTENT SIZE and NEXT SIZE, it is possible for the table to grow to its maximum number of extents, preventing it from growing any further.

To partially alleviate this limitation, OnLine does several things to minimize the number of extents used. In the first case, when OnLine is allocating a NEXT extent, it will try to allocate it contiguous to the previous extent. If it is possible to do this, it considers the added extent space to simply be an enlargement of the last extent and does not call it a separate extent. This can sometimes cause confusion to the DBA when she is looking at `tbcheck -pe` outputs. Although the CREATE TABLE statement for the table may specify a NEXT SIZE the real extents may vary in size from that specified.

Another approach the engine takes to reduce extent usage is called *extent doubling*. Whenever the number of extents in a table reaches a multiple of 64, the NEXT SIZE parameter is automatically doubled. For example, in a table created using the default eight pages of EXTENT and NEXT sizes (16 K on 2K page machines), the 64th extent will be 16K in size. The 65th extent will be 32K in size.

At any time during the life and growth of a table, you can alter the NEXT SIZE parameter by using the ALTER TABLE SQL statement. This will not affect existing extents in use, but the next extent to be allocated will be given the new size. This allows a certain amount of tuning to be done to table allocation schemas after the table is created.

Finally, if a dbspace begins to get full, the NEXT SIZE parameter will be limited to the actual available space in the dbspace. For example, suppose your NEXT size is 64K and when it comes time to allocate another extent to the tablespace, there is only 40K left in the tablespace. The final extent will be 40K, not 64K. This will allow all of the space in the dbspace to be used.

Correct use of EXTENT SIZE and NEXT SIZE can allow creation of extremely large tables without choking the OnLine engine. There is one case, however, that can cause a problem. It involves the creation of implicit temporary tables. You will remember that these implicit temporary tables are created by the engine for various internal uses. These tables are created with default extents and they are not under user control. It is possible for these implicit temporary tables to reach their maximum number of extents at about 8 megabytes due to the limitations on the number of extents.

Reclaiming space

The only way to recover the extents allocated to a table is by dropping and recreating the table. This can be done explicitly with commands to drop and recreate the table or implicitly as part of a command that recreates the table as a side effect of doing something else.

Dropping and recreating the table

This is the most flexible method of recovering space that is no longer needed by a table. The DBA simply creates a dummy table in the correct dbspace, copies the data from the original table into the new table, drops the original table, and then renames the new table the same as the old. Since the DBA is recreating the table totally, the new table can be in whichever dbspace is needed, with whatever FIRST SIZE and NEXT SIZE is desired.

Implicitly recreating the table

There are several SQL commands that recreate a table as a side effect of doing another job. In general, any *Data Definition Language* (DDL) statement can cause a table to be rebuilt. For example, the following command causes the table `sample` to be rebuilt.

```
ALTER TABLE sample  ADD newfield integer
```

The table must be rebuilt because of the addition of the new column, `newfield`. Any such DDL command can cause the table to be rebuilt. Statements which create cluster indexes also force a physical rebuild of the table.

```
ALTER INDEX xxxxxxx TO CLUSTER;
CREATE CLUSTER INDEX  yyyyyyy (colname);
```

Both these SQL statements make use of the main property of clustered indexes, i.e., a clustered index rearranges the physical layout of the table. It essentially creates a new table with the rows rearranged in the order of the cluster index. This has the by-product of freeing up unused NEXT extents. It does not allow placing the table in another dbspace or altering the FIRST EXTENT or NEXT EXTENT numbers. It simply releases any extents that are not used.

When a new cluster index is created, or when an existing index is altered to cluster, the engine creates a temporary copy of the table that is dropped when the index is completed. If the table is very large, this could result in space problems during this process. Be sure that you have enough space available in your system to create the large temporary table needed. This table will be the same size as the existing table.

AVOIDING AND CURING TABLE FRAGMENTATION

There are several practices that you can follow to eliminate and cure table fragmentation. In the first place, estimate the anticipated size of your tables and create them with proper FIRST and NEXT SIZE parameters. Doing this means that the engine will create larger, contiguous extents for the data and indexes to occupy. If you have created tables with a large enough FIRST extent parameter, you can be sure that the data will be compact and relatively easy for the engine to get to without forcing it to jump all over the disk.

It is also possible to reduce table fragmentation by intelligent use of the bulk loading utilities. As a general rule, it is preferable to do your loading into tables that have no indexes, creating them after the load. This has the advantage of being faster, especially in versions of OnLine newer than 5.0 that have improved indexing algorithms. The second advantage is that your data pages and index pages become contiguous. All of the data pages are together and all of your index pages are together. When you do your bulk loads with the indexes already built, your extents will have a few data pages followed by a few index pages, followed by more data pages, etc. Rather than having data and index pages alternate randomly within an extent When you do your load with no indexes in place and create the indexes later, the data pages are grouped together, followed by the index pages. If you create your indexes one at a time after the data is loaded, the index pages will become even more effectively located, with pages for one index being together followed by pages from the next index, etc. Having these pages located contiguously makes it easier for the engine to access them without thrashing all over the disk. This also allows the use of *big buffer reads*, which uses more efficient reading mechanisms if the data is located contiguously.

You can cure fragmented tables in the same way that you drop unused extents from tables by recreating the tables or by altering indexes to cluster. Actually, any DDL command that alters the table, such as adding a column or changing the structure of the table will cause a rebuild of the table, but altering to cluster is probably the most innocuous approach.

The benefits of defragmenting tables begin to go away as the table is used and modified. If you begin to notice a slow degradation of access time and performance, look at table fragmentation. It often occurs so slowly that you don't notice it.

INDEX MANAGEMENT

The indexes in your database are absolutely the single most important determinant in the performance of the database. An awful database design that has a good index structure will almost always out-perform a wonderful design that is indexed poorly. The importance of indexes becomes more important as the table sizes get larger.

Indexes seem to be even more of a "black box" than tables. DBA's often do not understand the actual layout of the indexes. Books have been written about different methods of indexing, so the area can be somewhat intimidating. For our purposes, a simple explanation of the indexing mechanism should suffice.

B+tree indexes

INFORMIX-OnLine indexes use the b+tree method of indexing. Basically, this is a method that stores the key values and pointers to the `rowids` of the rows containing that key value. These key/pointer pairs can be searched to retrieve the `rowids` of matching rows. Using the indexes means that a search has to inspect far fewer pages to find the needed rows than would be necessary if a sequential scan of the entire table were to be needed.

The key/pointer information is stored in fixed-size data structures called nodes. The first node is called the *root node*. When the table is small, an index could possibly be no larger than this root node. Accompanying the key value will be a pointer that points directly to the `rowid` of the rows. As the table grows larger and more and more key values need to be indexed, the root node may fill up. At this time, additional nodes may be added.   This is known as adding a level to the tree. When a level is added to the tree, the root level no longer contains pointers to the actual `rowids`. Each entry in the root node now points to a new node in the tree.

At the lowest level of the tree, the pointer will point to an actual `rowid`. The nodes that actually point to the `rowids` are known as *leaf nodes*. They are the end point of the search.   As additional levels and additional nodes are added to the tree, the index becomes larger and more complex.

Since an index must accommodate change in the table's data, it is possible that some of the nodes will fill up and some will become too empty. The engine attempts to balance and prune the b+tree to maximize the usability of the index. To do so, it occasionally merges adjacent nodes into one, splits full nodes into two, or shuffles key/pointer pairs from one index to another. For the most part, these activities are completely invisible, even to the DBA. However, their tracks can be seen by inspecting the logfiles using the `tblog` utility. (Be careful with `tblog`. This utility will freeze your database while you're looking at logs in use. If you must inspect logs, look at logs on tape, where they're harmless.)

How indexes are stored

Pages containing index data are stored within the dbspace that contains the tablespace. Index pages contain nothing but index data and miscellaneous overhead items relating to the index. Each page of index data is a b+tree node.

These pages are not allocated in any particular order. Thus, a dbspace may be composed of random index and data pages. To further complicate matters, the dbspace may contain data from multiple tables and multiple indexes, all thrown into one big pot.

If the data and index pages for a particular table become strewn across the disk, table fragmentation can occur. This fragmentation means that the engine has to work a lot harder to get to the data it wants. As a general rule, it is best to work to avoid this type of fragmentation.

MEETING USERS' NEEDS

No two database systems are the same. Some may be composed of data that is accessed only through canned programs that are fully optimized. Others may be decision support applications that see a lot of nonstructured, ad hoc query activity. Others may have data that remains in the system for years. Still others may move data through the system in a day and then throw it away. These different modes of use and purpose must be understood by the BD if he is to manage the entire system.

The purpose of the database is to make the information contained in the database tables accessible in some form to the users. The most controlled access is a system of structured access in which all data flows through well-defined programs. This is the typical form of access in most current database applications designed for end users. Essentially an extension of the "big iron" philosophy, it stresses centralized control over the data resources.

At the other end of the spectrum is a more free-form type of access in which users execute many ad hoc queries. As users become more empowered by the client/server paradigm, DBAs can expect to field more requests for this type of access, with the opportunities and pitfalls that accompany it.

Additionally, different types of users may view a database management system in completely different ways. The DBA has to understand all of their uses and needs.

Understanding the needs of your users

Different levels of database users can expect to view the database in different ways: users at different levels need different information about what is going on inside the system. Of course, the lines between different types of users is fuzzy at best. It's fun to generalize, but it's also impossible. You are dealing with people, and they will tend to distribute themselves all over the spectrum. I'm certain you will recognize most of your users somewhere in this list.

End users

The database is usually invisible to the end user. They simply do not see the database: they see the applications. In most cases, the end users do not even know that the application is based upon a database. For them, the whole system, from hardware to application programs, is known simply as "the computer." They do not make the differentiation between hardware, software, and applications.

The end user mostly runs "canned" programs. These programs were either bought from others or developed by other users, the programmers.   End users want results, answers, numbers. Give results to the end users and they'll be happy.

End users also want fast response times. The system is not only important to them, often it is the major tool that they use to do their job. If a query that has been coming back in three seconds starts to take six seconds, expect to hear from the users. They are your first line of alert to problems.

Advanced users

Advanced users are at a point somewhere between end users and programmers. They still get their information from the existing applications, but they have discovered that much more information exists.   They will try to get to it either by having programmers write them hundreds of reports or by pushing for client/server tools that let them use the database's data from within their comfortable, PC-based tools.   In the absence of client/server orientation, these advanced users may be intercepting print spool files from the print queue or requesting that their reports be formulated to fit their spreadsheets. These advanced users still probably have little or no knowledge of the underlying database.

Advanced users in client/server environments usually learn SQL because their spreadsheets or other client programs (e.g., INFORMIX-WingZ) accept SQL commands. These users learn a subset of the database's structure and often use tools such as advanced 4GLs and data import/export tools to integrate their PC's with the database. These advanced users often use third-party tools as well.

Programmers

Programmers can run the gamut from inexperienced to very sophisticated. Either type can make incredible demands upon the DBA. Given exposure to the database, the novice programmers usually learn the system quickly. Using programmatic interfaces like ESQL/C, programmers soon begin to view the database as just another function call. As long as they can get the results they are seeking, they do not care much about the inner workings of the database. They tend to view the database as yet another "black box."

The sophisticated programmers often know as much about what's going on "under the hood" as the DBA does. At least, they can seem to know as much. If their knowledge transfers to the overall workings of the database system, these gurus can become quite a resource. Often, however, their in-depth knowledge is restricted in breadth. Many times, they will be generalizing from other databases or from generic experience and will engage you for hours in esoteric discussion of paging algorithms. They can easily suffer from a typical DBA problem, that is, focusing too narrowly in one area. It is possible to write tight, high-performance code that pushes the database to its absolute limits of performance. It's also possible that this same code can bring the system to its knees if the developer has neglected to see how the code interacts with other programs.

Executives

Executives have their own set of needs in understanding the database. Dealing with executives requires the best technical expertise that the DBA can bring to bear, but it also requires at least an awareness of the politics of the situation.

Depending upon the background of the executive, their needs can be met from anything from a confidently delivered "I've got it handled" to a detailed technical explanation. Know which to use and when.

Remember that executives have the same goals you have. They want to accomplish a task efficiently and with the least effort and expenditure. If you can communicate your needs and requests to them in such a way that they can relate it to the overall needs of the organization, you will receive more satisfactory responses.

The quality movement is currently very big in corporate environments. It's been my experience that once companies get on the total quality bandwagon, you can use the jargon and techniques of your particular quality dialect to your advantage. If you phrase your requests and suggestions using the approved quality dialect you'll find that most executives will be more receptive. If you're asking for additional disk space to make your administration job easier, you may or may not be listened to. If you need the same disk space to improve the process of retaining information and making it available to your internal customers on a more timely basis, you'll have a lot better chance of getting your disks. You've requested the same disks in both cases, but in the second you phrased the request in such a way that only opponents of quality could refuse.

DBAs

The DBA needs to be able to understand the mechanics at the lowest level of database operations. DBAs also need to have an overall picture of the operation of the system as a synergistic whole. Knowledge of the low-level operations are critical when debugging the system, as problems often seem to revolve around just one item that refuses to work properly. This in-depth knowledge of the architecture also helps the DBA deal with his own system gurus and with the Informix helpline personnel.

If nothing else, the DBA needs to maintain professional control over database operations. The ability to explain, argue fine points, and to solve unusual problems can do nothing but enhance the DBA's professional stature.

Being able to see the overall picture is at least as important. In many organizations, database design, applications programming, and providing ad hoc data to advanced users is spread across several departments and across many individuals. The DBA has to be able to integrate the different pieces and make them work together in an efficient whole.

Often, there is nobody else with a sufficiently broad job description to handle this most important task.

DESIGNING DATABASE SYSTEMS

This section will be applicable to you only if you have the luxury of building your database system from scratch. If you are starting with a blank sheet of paper, an empty computer room, and a bottomless bank account you can build a nearly ideal system.

Of course, an ideal system designed to spec today, delivered by the vendors in three months, and operable in nine to twelve months will never be ideal when it goes into production. At current rates of hardware and software development, something new and better seems to come along every three to four months. So, the ideal system is just that, an ideal. System vendors themselves never have ideal systems, so why should you expect it for yourself?

In real life, you are probably inheriting an existing system. You have time and budget constraints, you have to maintain production (whatever that means in your environment), and you have a backlog. Welcome to the real world.

Still, the design issues that you would face in building a state-of-the-art system from scratch are applicable to you even if you have an existing system. As your system grows and matures, you will probably have opportunities to upgrade your system, add peripherals, upgrade the software, and modify your applications. Who knows, your company may land a big contract and the CEO might come into your office some day with a blank check.

So, what is a state-of-the-art system? The answer, of course, is highly time-dependent. What is hot and new as I am writing this chapter will be old news in a year. You'll find the latest and greatest in current magazines. Maybe you'll see it from your hardware vendors, but in my experience if you don't ask for it, you'll never find out from vendors. An amazing attitude from people who make a living selling you things!

Your hardware decisions will mainly concern choice of equipment manufacturers, processor layout, and peripheral layout. We'll stay away from questions of who makes the best hardware, because there is no correct answer. Your best manufacturer is the one who makes something you feel comfortable with and from whom you can get the best service. I've always found that the service component is much more important than the hardware end. If you have a company that gives you A+ hardware and B- service you'll probably be much less pleased than with a company giving you B+ hardware and A+

service. Hardware is something that you agonize over while making the original choices and then find ways to live with for the rest of the life cycle. As long as it works and performs adequately, you'll probably be happy. Service is something that you have to live with daily. When you need support or service, odds are you're in a bind and you need it NOW. You probably have users screaming at you and you cannot put up with lackadaisical support or service. Go for the service! With luck, you can get both good hardware and good support, but don't hold your breath.

Hardware

Computer systems continually evolve. A decade ago, proprietary systems were the way to go. You would get all of your hardware and software from one source and that one source would hold your hand forever and handle all of your needs. The end result of this commitment to proprietary systems was that the user became locked into one vendor. Purchasers of systems began to realize that this limited their flexibility and their bargaining power with their system vendor.

Systems are now evolving towards the concept of open systems. Rather than being locked into one "big iron" vendor, you pick the best pieces from best vendors and somehow make them all work together. The glue that ties it all together is the UNIX operating system and the evolving standards that are being adopted by vendors. These standards include UNIX for the operating system, TCP/IP for networking, X-Window for graphical displays, C and C++ as programming languages, and SQL for the database language. Informix is a major player in the open systems movement, with database engines that run on everything from PCs to mainframes. Personal computers, even those not running UNIX or UNIX-derivatives, also play in the open systems arena. Microsoft Windows™, Microsoft Windows NT™, and OS/2® systems are increasingly finding themselves used in connection with UNIX servers. These personal computers often serve multiple purposes, ranging from acting as terminals talking to UNIX boxes over the network to serving as X-Window displays using the PC's intelligence to emulate an X-Window terminal. Personal computers are also serving as full-fledged clients in distributed applications, with the PCs handling the input/output and the graphics and the UNIX servers handling the database management.

A big advantage of the open systems concept is scalability. By choosing to remain compliant to standards, a system can grow and evolve as your needs change. Applications running on an SCO® UNIX server on a 486 personal computer can easily be ported to larger minicomputers or even mainframes as long as the basic database and language tools are available. This flexibility also extends to your choice of vendors. You are no longer married for life to a hardware or software manufacturer. If you find that you've made a bad choice or two, or if the vendor is no longer providing you with what you need, you no longer have to scrap everything and begin anew. The vendors realize this and are beginning to behave in a more competitive manner. They now see that users and purchasers have choices. This will give users much more leverage with vendors.

Processor decisions

In today's market, the rising stars in the hardware arena are the multi-processor or parallel-processing systems. We are discovering that several less powerful processors that can cooperate inside one box can often outperform one super-fast processor. By breaking tasks up into pieces that can be farmed out to multiple processors, the central processing unit can often get much more work done and provide a higher level of throughput.

In some systems, the multiprocessing or parallel-processing paradigm can also allow for more tolerance for failure, as the processors can fill in for each other should one fail. This is by no means universal. In fact, in some multiprocessing arrangements, failure of any one processor will bring the system down, giving you a higher probability of failure.

The OnLine product provides for various levels of support for multiple and parallel processors. This is version-dependent. Beginning with OnLine 4.1, Informix provided the `psort` capability that will farm out sorts to multiple processors if your system has them. This was enhanced in Version 5.0. Version 6.0 provides more utilization for multiple processors in the areas of sorting, indexing, archiving, and database access. Version 7.0 will provide support for fully parallel architectures and should provide outstanding performance.

Disk storage systems

Much of the work that the OnLine system does revolves around taking information that is stored on a hard disk drive and making it available for user processes. On most computer systems, the slowest thing that happens is transferring data to and from a hard disk. It's obvious that if a product depends so heavily on something that is relatively slow, management of the slow resource takes on a critical role.

This is the case with OnLine. Many of the setup and tuning strategies the DBA employs to extract the best performance from the system have to do with reducing the amount of time the system spends accessing the disks. Thus we have a large emphasis on caching data items in the shared memory where access is many times faster than from disk. A lot of time can be spent in trying to physically place tables in areas of optimum ease of access on the disk. The aim is to cache the data in shared memory if you can, but if you have to go to the disk, go there with as little relative motion of the disk drive heads as possible. When you have to move data from the disk to shared memory the data movement should be as fast as possible and involve the least possible movement of the disk heads.

From these requirements, it is obvious that you should have the fastest disk storage system that you can obtain if you are looking for peak performance. Since the disk system is such a common bottleneck to high performance, improvements in this area can often pay impressive performance dividends.

In the area of disk layout, there are four main areas that you need to consider: actual disk configuration, disk striping, mirroring, and *RAIDs* (Redundant Arrays of Inexpensive Disks).

Physical disk configuration:

No matter what your disk system type, you need to carefully consider how you use it to get the best performance. The choices that you make regarding placement of the `rootdbs`, your logfile placement, the placement of your physical logs, and where you place your most active tables can make a big difference in performance.

If you have multiple disks, it is usually better to place the database components on different physical drives from the UNIX filesystems used by your applications. This way, movement of the disk heads caused by UNIX jobs do not interfere with those belonging to Informix. If you can place these areas on separate controllers, so much the better.

I'm assuming that you are using raw devices for your OnLine data areas. They will show a uniform improvement over UNIX filesystems for the simple reason that the work that UNIX would do to maintain a filesystem is redundant for an OnLine chunk.

Informix is running its own routines to manage its chunks and there's no need to duplicate them.

If you have multiple raw disks available for OnLine, you have to decide how to divide up the space. Often, an inexperienced DBA will simply create one large `rootdbs` and place everything there. This is not usually a good idea for several reasons. The `rootdbs` can never be dropped. To get rid of it, you have to reinitialize your database and restore the data from tape or other sources. As such, space that you devote to `rootdbs` in OnLine is space that you can never get back. If you need to make changes or allocate resources, you have to rebuild.

On the other hand, if you have a reasonably-sized `rootdbs` with separate `dbspaces` for various tables or databases, you maintain some flexibility in dealing with change. You can move databases or tables from dbspace to dbspace a lot easier than by recreating everything from scratch. These convenience and flexibility items are in addition to the performance issues that can be addressed by having separate `dbspaces` for different database components.

You may have some disks that perform better than others. If so, this is where you want your most active tables. You can put them there by creating `dbspaces` on the fast devices and using the IN DBSPACE clause of your table creation statements. You'll find that some tables and some portions of the database system will get a lot more writing activity than others. Put these on the faster devices. Good candidates for placement on faster devices are your physical and logical log files.

Disk striping

Disk striping is a method of creating logical disks that are actually composed of several physical disk devices. Striping is supported on many UNIX machines and is often beneficial to OnLine performance. With striping, a logical disk is composed of data tracks that are interleaved across several devices. Thus, you can give a command calling for accesses to the disk and have the heads of several devices move at once to retrieve the data. In some cases, this can improve performance. It makes actual physical placement of tables and `dbspaces` on disk less critical, as the striped volume is distributing the read load across many spindles. It also cuts down on the possibility of contention, or forcing a disk head to make large jumps from disk request to disk request.

Striping is an operating system function. OnLine does not know or care about how the volume is laid out. As long as OnLine can execute calls to the logical volume and receive data, it does not matter whether the underlying device is a physical device or a logical device.

Striping is a powerful tool in your search for performance. If you have it available to you, it is almost always better to use it than not to. If you have an efficient, reliable striping method, it will mean that you do not really have to worry about the physical location of tablespaces and dbspaces in your system. This can drastically cut down on your possibility of error and on the amount of time you spend fiddling with disk layout. With striping, you can do it once and let UNIX take care of it in the future.

Disk mirroring

Both striping and mirroring are actually subsets of the RAID concept, each being a different RAID level. There are two choices for mirroring with OnLine. You can either let UNIX handle the mirroring or you can let OnLine handle it.

If you enable UNIX mirroring, UNIX handles it much like a striped device. When one side of the mirror device has a data change, the UNIX drivers automatically make the change on the other side. Mirroring is not really a positive performance issue. It is more of a redundancy issue. Using mirrored devices allows you to survive a failure of a physical drive and to continue running on the other device. Mirroring actually slows performance down somewhat, but the added fault-tolerance makes it often worth the cost.

The other approach to mirroring is to let Informix handle the mirroring. Whenever you create a chunk, you can tell OnLine that you want to mirror it. To do so, you must have twice the space normally required on your drives. Thus, to mirror a 1-gigabyte chunk, you would need to have two 1-gigabyte chunks available, a primary chunk and a mirror chunk. OnLine will automatically apply changes from the primary chunk to the mirror chunk. OnLine mirroring is somewhat slower than UNIX mirroring, especially if your UNIX mirroring is built into your hardware.

The natural question is "Which one is better?" I generally tend towards taking the UNIX mirroring over the Informix mirroring. Mirroring which is integrated into either your hardware or your UNIX operating system can be more highly optimized for your specific environment. OnLine mirroring is a fairly generic product. It works the same for all environments, while the native mirroring is often more highly tuned. From an operations standpoint, they both seem to provide the same level of security.

RAIDS

Both mirroring and striping are considered to be low level RAID implementations. RAIDs utilize several physical disks that are addressed as one logical disk. Various levels of RAID systems lay out the disks in ways that can provide performance gains as well as increase reliability.

A good RAID implementation can provide several advantages to a state-of-the-art system. First, the individual disks that comprise a RAID system are usually less expensive than traditional disks used with larger UNIX systems. These disk drives are often 1-gigabyte drives designed to be used with personal computers. These disks are priced more for the PC market than for the UNIX market and are relatively inexpensive compared to those sold strictly for the UNIX market.

Second, RAIDs provide a level of redundancy and can survive the failure of one or more of the individual disks. Some of the better implementations also allow a *hot swap* capability in which a bad disk can be replaced without taking the system offline. After the bad disk is replaced, the RAID will begin the process of resynchronizing the disks so that the redundancy is restored.

Not only can you get better performance due to the striping capability of RAIDS, you can also get a level of tunable performance. Some systems can allow different levels of RAID redundancy in different parts of the file system.

As an example, some areas such as physical and logical logs in OnLine see a lot of write activity and little or no reads. If these areas can be put in an area that is tuned for writing, not for random reading, the overall performance will improve.

Avoiding Mistakes in the Development Process

The concept of distributed databases is a most attractive one to the modern corporation. Coupled with the flashy, icon-driven front ends that are becoming more and more available in the marketplace, this concept is almost too attractive to resist. What could possibly be wrong with downsizing applications from mainframes to minicomputers and even desktop PCs? What could possibly be the problem with allowing data to be owned where it originates? What could be the drawbacks of allowing end-users to step up from dull, dumb terminals to the modern-looking interfaces as typified by the Microsoft Windows environment.

The answer is, there's nothing intrinsically wrong with the concept. True, the technology is still in its infancy and there are bugs that need to be worked out. Modern-day PCs capable of running Windows are as powerful as the minicomputers of several years ago. Desktop PCs can now have more than 32 megabytes of memory and can have several gigabytes of hard disk storage. Modern network operating systems are approaching the flexibility and performance of mainframe and minicomputer operating systems such as UNIX. Even more powerful desktop machines are on the way. Even better operating systems and application software is being released on an almost daily basis. Costs seem to be going down, making downsizing look better and better every day.

So, where's the drawback? Is there a drawback? Are we really living in computer heaven? Can you really get something for next to nothing? An example taken from the real world may shed some light on some of the things that can go wrong.

The OSCAR syndrome

Several years ago a medium-sized corporation had a legacy software package that had been running for years on a mainframe. The application was a database that managed several gigabytes of data. This was the main application for the firm, mission critical in the truest sense of the word. The firm could not live without it.

The problem with the old legacy system was that the ongoing costs, which included rental of time on another firm's mainframe, came to about $500,000 a year. The director of Information Services saw that downsizing the application to a network of UNIX machines could save the company millions. So, without the approval or knowledge of the CEO, he began a secret project to begin to port the legacy application to UNIX. He hired a programmer out of his regular budget and put that programmer to work with an Oracle database. This went on for several months until the programmer completed a demo application.

The director of Information Services then presented the demo to the officers of the company. The demo was a smash hit. The old green-screen CRT's of the legacy system were replaced with color PC's with pop-up windows. Whenever a data item crossed a threshold of criticality, the data was shown in blinking red. Users who saw the demo were thrilled with it. Management saw visions of cost savings. The PR people saw a showcase application that would certainly impress new customers. This company was going to become a technology leader! After much wrangling and ego bashing, the new program was called OSCAR and funds were allocated.

Now the project began to pick up steam. Five outside consultants were hired to develop the entire system. The team was given carte blanche. They were given their own offices, away from the rest of the developers so that they could concentrate on OSCAR alone. They began an exhaustive series of Joint Application Development (JAD) meetings with users, soliciting their input and trying to design a user interface that the users would love. Everything was done to empower the end users, knowing that their approval and participation in the project would ensure its success.

Eventually, plans were made for the actual implementation of OSCAR, Phase I. Remote locations were wired for the UNIX terminals. PCs were bought to serve as terminals. Several mid-range UNIX machines were purchased. Beta testing went off without a hitch. Life was wonderful. A few weeks before the scheduled implementation there was only one little hitch.

Phase I was not going to totally replace the legacy system. It was going to offload a few of the processing modules and remove some of the load from the mainframe. The mainframe database was to feed data to the UNIX machines, the UNIX boxes would do some processing, and eventually give the data back to the mainframe. Finally, someone asked the critical question, how were they going to keep the databases in sync? What happened if data on the mainframe was changed while the UNIX box was working on the same data? Nobody had given serious thought to the problems of data concurrency.

The interface was wonderful. Users were excited. But OSCAR would never work. The department was eventually outsourced after blowing $6 or $7 million.

So, what's the lesson learned from OSCAR? Everyone involved fell into a trap that is very easy to fall into. Data concurrency was only the executioner's blade. If it had not been concurrency, it would have been something else. The project was doomed to failure from the start.

The emphasis was on the front end. The interface. The GUI. This was the sexy part of the project. It was flashy, attractive, a wonderful tool for selling the project to the users. It was also the last thing that should have been done. The prototype turned into the project. As an afterthought, the team turned to the underlying architecture. By then, they had committed themselves too deeply. The architecture would never work.

Readers may say this was an incredibly stupid mistake. It was. They may say that nobody is that stupid anymore. They're wrong.

In their rush to please their internal customers, data processing shops are giving users unprecedented input into the projects being written for them. Users see a flashy demo running on a minimal database and think that this is the real application. They think that the job is finished when it has not even started.

There are several lessons to be learned from the OSCAR Syndrome. First, a prototype should never take more than a few weeks to develop. If you need to muster the political and executive support, go ahead and build a flashy interface with circles and arrows and a paragraph on the back of each one. Don't spend a lot of time worrying about which tools to use. Don't spend endless months benchmarking different products, at least not yet. Once you've gotten approval for the project, go right to work on the underlying architecture. Move data around. Update it. Insert it. Get the data flows and the data accessibility right. Once you are sure you can move the data into the right places, then concentrate on the flashy screens. Choose your tools. Bring the users in and let them become your partners in building the interface. Just don't do it until the underlying structure is tested and proven.

GUIs and flashy screens are downright seductive. The excitement of seeing your applications almost magically change from a green and white terminal to a brilliant color monitor is almost too much for anyone to resist. Sure, get excited about the interface. Just don't confuse it with the real application.

MONITORING AND TROUBLESHOOTING

The most common cause of database crashes

In an environment with many programmers who are familiar with UNIX, your most common problem will occur when somebody kills an engine process. Informix does not take lightly to the untimely death of a `sqlturbo` engine. This often causes the database to abort, necessitating a restart and recovery that can take anywhere from minutes to hours. In general, if a `sqlturbo` process is killed with a `kill -9` command while it is in a critical section of code or when it is holding a latch, the engine will abort.

This problem can best be solved by enforcing a prohibition that no one but the DBA can `kill -9` a `sqlturbo` process. It's safe for anyone to `kill -15` a process. The problem here is that if a UNIX user gives a `kill -15` command, the process will not necessarily die immediately. If the `sqlturbo` process goes into a rollback status because it received the command in the middle of a transaction, the process will remain around until the rollback completes. An impatient user may try a few `kill -15` commands and finally try for a sure kill with `kill -9`. If the system is in rollback, OnLine will probably crash. If the process was holding any locks or if it was in a critical write process, the OnLine system will crash. The Informix command `tbmode -z` command works in the same way. The job doesn't immediately disappear.

Both `kill -15` and `tbmode -z` are safe to use any time, as long as the user is prepared to be patient. It's usually best to have the users check with the DBA if the jobs don't die within about 15 minutes.

Processes that take longer than about 15 minutes can pose a quandary even to the DBA. It's possible that the query is a disjoint query and that the system is trying to process millions of rows. You could be in a long transaction on the verge of either going into forced rollback or filling up all your logs, causing a crash. If the DBA can't identify exactly what's happening, it is usually best to let the process finish its job, unless this will cause other problems in the database such as filling up the logs. If the runaway job begins to affect performance or response time, the DBA usually needs to kill it.

By the time the DBA sees the typical rogue `sqlturbo` process, the user has probably already tried to kill it with `kill -15` or `tbmode -z`. It's probably in rollback. Rollback can be identified by the flags `--R--X--` in the `tbstat -u` output. Using the UNIX `ps` command will tell the DBA whether the `sqlturbo` process is getting any time. If so, your rollback is in process. No matter what you do, the rollback has to complete. It'll either complete with the system online or it'll complete during the recovery stage of database startup. Online is usually best.

The worst case for the DBA is the process that was written in ESQL/C or one that has other reasons why the process only recognizes a `kill -9`. Here, if you absolutely have to stop the process, a `kill -9` command is your last resort. If your UNIX operating system has process control (do you have a `bg` command to put a job in the background?), read the next paragraph before doing a `kill -9`. Otherwise, do it and cross your fingers.

Some UNIX operating systems that support placing jobs in the foreground or background have another option to the `kill` command that could possibly give you an out in the above situation. These versions of UNIX often have options to the `kill` command that allow you to stop execution of a process and restart it. On a Pyramid these options are `kill -STOP` and `kill -CONT`. These options are not universal and they are not uniform between versions of UNIX. Check your manpage with `man kill` to see if you have these options. If you can stop the process by process control or by using your version of the `kill -STOP` command, you may see that the UNIX `ps` command shows that the process eventually is getting no time and is in a sleeping state. You can then use `tbstat -u` and check the flags for the `sqlturbo` you want to kill. If the flags don't show an X indicating that the process is not in a *critical state*, you have a chance. If it is in a critical state, use your equivalent of the `kill -CONT` command to restart the process. Keep stopping and starting it until it gets no time according to `ps` and doesn't have an `X flag in the tbstat -u output`, meaning that it is not in a critical section of code. Note the `address` column of the `tbstat -u` output for the `sqlturbo` process that you are trying to kill. Run a `tbstat -s` command and look for that address in the `address` column of the output. If the `address` is there, your process is holding a latch and doing the `kill -9` will abort the engine. If the process is not holding a latch, you are safe in doing a `kill -9`. If it doesn't work and you really needed to kill the process, you haven't lost anything. You would have had to run the `kill -9` command anyway.

No matter what you do, no matter how careful you are, you will crash like this sometimes. If the consequences are bad enough, the users usually learn to make the DBA kill the tough jobs.

Thawing out a frozen system

One of the true tests of the DBA's understanding of the system occurs when everything just suddenly freezes up. Nothing is getting done. Users find their screens just sitting there, Jobs either fail or disappear into the ether. The calls start coming in and the DBA has to go to work.

After learning that there is a problem, the first thing to do is to isolate it. Is the operating system up? If you are getting no screen response to your keystrokes, the problem is probably somewhere upstream of OnLine. Either the OS is down or there is some sort of communication problem between the terminals and the system. How about the network? Call the system administrator and/or the network guru.

Assuming that you can actually communicate with the computer, run the Informix `tbstat -u` command. If it comes back with a shared memory error, your OnLine engine is down. Go into your `online.log` (or whatever you are naming it in your `$TBCONFIG` file) and look at the bottom of the file. Look for lines with the word "abort" in them.

If you can identify the job that caused the abort, you will probably need to chase down the culprit and string him up by his thumbs. The `username` script is useful here.

Other than as a post-mortem investigation, there's nothing else you can do. If the system has crashed, use `tbmonitor` or `tbmode` to bring it back up and hope that you aren't facing a long recovery period.

If you do not get a shared memory error when running `tbstat -u`, take a look at the `flags` column of the output. If you haven't committed all the flags to memory, run the `seeuser` script to look at the output with the added "training wheels" of informative column headings. The first character of the flag field will usually indicate the problem. If many or most of the processes show a "C," an "S," a "G," or an "L" in the first field, these jobs are waiting for something to happen. Usually, you can correlate this information with the information in the `tbstat` header and figure out why the engine is waiting.

If you are still in the dark about the situation, go back to the `online log`. Look towards the end, or at the approximate time of the initial problem report. Look for any kind of error message that you aren't used to seeing. This implies that you have to know what is normal and what is odd. That's why you should always be monitoring your `online.log`. Any time you shut the system down or start it up, take a peek at the `online.log` file and verify that all is OK. Look for anything out of the ordinary.

If you don't find anything by looking at the `online.log`, run a few `tbstat` commands. Run a `tbstat -p` and see if anything is out of place. You may find high numbers in the `deadlocks` section or you may find high numbers in the `ovlock`, `ovuser` or other resource limitations sections. Run the `status` program. It will help you spot anything that looks out of place.

If you're still frozen up, run a `tbstat -l` command. Are your logfiles full? Shame on you. You probably haven't backed up your logs, or you've failed to turn on continuous backup of logfiles. Go in and do a manual backup of your logfiles and you'll be moving again.

Still lost? Try running a few iterations of `watch_hot` and see if your system is getting any disk activity. If it is, something's going on. Do you know what it is? Maybe it's a backend run amok or a disjoint query. Run your `ps` UNIX command. Do you see any `sqlturbo` processes with lots of time on them? They may be the culprits.

If you see some backends that are running wild, trace them down using `ps`. If all of your jobs are run as individual users, the job will be easier. Who owns the `sqlturbo`? What else is she doing? One frequent cause of `sqlturbos` running amok often occurs when you are running INFORMIX-4GL. This product sometimes leaves the `sqlturbos` running if the 4GL process is either killed or orphaned. There is no known cure for this other than a DBA (or a script) that watches for processes that are running with no frontends attached.

If all of your jobs are run as a particular user, it may be more difficult to track down the particular job causing a problem. Look at the PID (process id) and PPID (parent process id) of the offending backends. Trace the ownership of the offender. The offender's PPID will be the PID of the job that started it. You may have to trace it back through several levels, but eventually you'll come up with some job that started the problem.

Or maybe you won't. Oftentimes a job that starts a series of processes will either be killed when the user realized that it was doing the wrong thing or will simply die of its own accord or when it begins to consume so many UNIX resources that the kernel kills the job. These "orphan" or "zombie" processes often cause problems with Informix, as the child processes can continue to run even if the parent is no longer viable. In these cases, you often have to take a chance on killing the process or just letting it run until UNIX finally gets around to killing it.

Jobs that just fail

Sometimes you will need to troubleshoot problems that are less drastic than the wholesale freezing up of your system. Maybe a program is not behaving as planned or maybe a job being run by one of your users fails for no apparent reason.

The approach is essentially the same as listed above except that you are often under less pressure to solve it because everyone else is still running normally. Avoid the temptation to put the troubleshooting job off until later. Usually when something like this comes up, it is a warning about other potential problems that are just lurking around and waiting for a chance to grab you.

In solving problems with specific jobs, it is most important that you get a full report of the symptoms and error messages from the user. Have them write down any error messages they get, or better yet, tell them not to touch the terminal until you have a chance to come see it. Don't ever assume that just because a user tells you something that it is either correct, complete, or relevant. Users often think they are doing one thing while they are really doing something completely different.

You still follow the logical progression of identifying and isolating the symptoms, checking the logs and utilities, forming a theory about the problem, and acting on the theory. Make lots of use of your logfiles. If the user's job has methods of logging errors or tracing execution, use them.

Many, if not most of your jobs that fail are caused by inconsiderate or uninformed user activity. This is defined as a user who is not following the general rules of courtesy and sanity in a multiuser database environment.

Some of the rules that are often broken are:

- Careless use of transactions

- Failure to promptly commit or roll back a transaction

- Creation of long transactions

- Trying to update or delete from a large, heavily-used table while the system is busy

- Careless query formulation

- Creation of disjoint queries that return billions of rows

- Failure to lock a table in exclusive mode while doing mass inserts into it or deletes from it. This causes the system to exceed the allowed number of locks.

If you find that the job that is failing is a long one or one that acts upon many rows, suspect either locking problems or long transaction problems. Either one should show up in the `online.log` as well as in specific error messages returned by the failing job.

If all else fails, consider whether your problem is really in the OnLine engine at all. Could you be reaching some sort of resource limits in UNIX? Could it be a terminal problem or a glitch on the line?

Above all, try not to be too dogmatic in your approach to troubleshooting. Try to be skeptical and flexible. Some of the worst troubleshooting problems are caused by red herrings. All the evidence seems to be pointing to one particular area. You've recently been having problems in just that area, and now, here it is again! Don't be too quick to make that assumption. It often seems that system problems come in clumps with complex failures of multiple systems at once. Unless you keep an open mind and look at each problem as an individual entity, you'll find yourself, like Alice, "chasing rabbits."

Chapter 8

Tuning the Database System

It's often said that you can't be too skinny or too rich. To that sweeping generality I will add that your queries can never return too quickly, your reports can never finish too early, and you can never have too much disk space. Some things are universal.

The search for increased system performance will occupy a lot of your time as a DBA. Watch your users some time when the system is running slower than normal. You'll see users tapping their fingers, talking to their terminals, alternately threatening and cajoling the system to complete their jobs. Now remember, these jobs are tasks that once took the users an hour to do manually. Now it takes five seconds, and if it stretches out to ten seconds, the users are impatient and irritable. It's a case of expectations. As the entire system gets more responsive, the users begin to expect more from the system. It's up to the DBA to provide the guidance and insight that allows your database system to continuously improve in performance.

ONLINE SYSTEM TUNING: THE PROCESS

Tuning a database system is a discipline and a process. There are few hard and fast rules. There is usually no set time to tune your system. It's not like you will have a schedule and will be able to work on tuning from twelve to five on alternate Tuesdays. You must continuously observe the operations of your system and always be receptive to ideas and input from your users. They are usually much closer to the performance than you are, and they often have very definite and worthwhile suggestions for improvements.

There are several goals for tuning OnLine systems. Often they will have conflicting or opposing aims. The most familiar is tuning for execution speed. This is what most people think of when you talk about tuning a database system. In some cases, making it go faster is the ultimate goal. But it's not the only goal of tuning.

An equally important tuning objective is to cure problems or impediments that prevent the proper operations of the entire system. An example here would be increasing the number of users or the number of locks to make the application behave as desired.

Another possible objective for database tuning may be to optimize the use of resources available to the system. There are instances in which a system could be tuned to reduce disk usage or to function with a smaller amount of shared memory to accommodate other processes on the computer system.

Tuning is not a simple, cut-and-dried task. You have to know where you stand, where you want to go, and how you want to get there. In between times, you have to be sure that you don't blow the entire system into the next county while you're busy tweaking for an extra half second off a query time.

The process of database tuning consists of establishing a baseline, setting tuning goals, application of tuning techniques, and measuring their effects. This process is an iterative process. It is continually repeated and refined. It never stops.

Establishing a baseline

To improve the performance of your system, you must first be able to measure the performance of your system. Your users may come to you with vague complaints like "It just feels sluggish" or "My queries take too long." If you are to have any chance at improvement, you need to put a somewhat finer point on it. How long is too long? How fast should it run?

The way to do this is develop a process for gathering data about your system's performance. There are many possible ways to do this, so we'll look at just a few.

The `tbstat` utility provides the `tbstat -p` option that gives performance statistics. Since `tbstat` takes little in the way of system resources, it is feasible to run the `tbstat` utility in the background, directing the output to a logfile. If this can be done during a period of known load, you can analyze the statistics and evaluate the efficacy of any changes you may be making.

UNIX tools like `sar`, `top`, `systat`, `vmstat`, and `dkstat` are helpful in establishing your performance baseline. These tools should be run in parallel with your

Informix monitoring tools. The idea is to run in as controlled and monitored an environment as possible. Unless you are aware of the underlying performance of your UNIX system, any variations in your OnLine performance cannot be attributable to OnLine changes. Variations could be caused by the operating system load rather than the changes you are making in the database engine.

The application programs that you are running on your OnLine system may have methods for monitoring and logging system performance. If they don't, you may want to lobby for building in options for logging actions, query times, throughput, and the like.

Your users see performance through different lenses than you do. If they are working mainly with canned applications, the perceived speed at the application level may be the most important indicator of system performance where it really counts.

Another aspect of establishing the baseline is the development of benchmark applications. The most sophisticated benchmarking programs put a known load on the system and measure the results at different levels of load. These benchmarking programs are often developed as part of the process that makes the initial decision on purchasing the database engine. Save these benchmarks and benchmarking programs. They can be a very useful tool for monitoring the evolution of your system's performance.

A more common level of setting baselines simply requires that you develop a load profile of your system. For instance, if you know that your production system is heavily loaded on Friday afternoons and lightly loaded on Sunday mornings, you have important data for understanding your performance. Don't compare testing you did on Friday to changes you tested on Sunday.

If you are tracking performance data, plan on keeping it for a while. Sometimes performance issues take a while to develop or to manifest themselves. If you begin to feel like a disk hog with all the stuff you're keeping, run a UNIX `compress` on it. If that's not enough, save it to tape. Tape's cheap. Data is invaluable.

By the way, this same rule applies to all of your logs that are generated by OnLine. Oftentimes, you will be playing detective chasing down a performance or failure problem. Here, historical copies of your `online.log` can be very useful.

Setting your goals

After you've begun to track your system's performance, you will begin to see areas that you would like to improve. Your user community will be directing you towards areas that they would like to see improved. Once you've decided to work on something, try to quantify exactly what you'd like to accomplish. Check with the users. Will they be happy if their two-hour report finishes in an hour? Will they then expect it to finish in thirty minutes?

Database systems seem to follow the "80/20" rule. This rule says that 80 percent of the improvement can be achieved with 20 percent of the work. Usually, there are some simple changes that can make dramatic improvements. This is the easy 80 percent. The final 20 percent of possible improvement can take a lot of fine tuning and a lot more time to achieve. You get into a position of diminishing returns. Is that final 20 percent really necessary, or could you be better spending your time taking care of somebody else's 80 percent instead? The general rule is to go for the easy stuff first.

Try to isolate and dissect your performance issues. Don't try to make a lot of changes at once. Don't take a shotgun approach. Work on small, well-defined areas of performance and address them one at a time. Be aware that overall performance of the system is a trade-off between many factors. Don't go overboard on one area if it slows down the system in others. You need to try to balance the overall performance of the system.

Application of tuning techniques

In the process of setting goals for your tuning efforts, you will probably develop some theories about the root causes of the problem. Even if you have no clue about the root cause, you can apply some standard tuning knowledge or techniques. You should always look for concurrency problems, problems with the application code, poorly designed SQL statements, bad use of indexes, and the like. These are always good places to start.

As you apply these specific techniques, you will begin to develop a feel for what is working and what is not.

Measurement of the effects

You should always attempt to measure the effects of your tuning changes. Use the same tools that you use to develop your baseline. A lot of your tuning can be done by intuition and by "feel," but try to use a scientific method in the measurement. Only by documenting what is really working can you be certain that you'll be spending your time and effort making significant changes.

The other part of measuring the effects comes when you begin to notice the trade-offs you are making. You may succeed in making some activities faster while slowing up others. For example, you may greatly speed up a query by adding a new index but slow down updates and use up more disk space because of that index. Being able to measure your improvement in specific areas will allow you to quantify the overall improvements due to your tuning.

Another purely personal and selfish reason for measuring the effects of your tuning is to be able to document the brownie points that you gain for yourself by making the system work better. These things look great on weekly status reports. As a DBA you will tend to be invisible unless things are going badly. This may help make you visible when things are improving.

TECHNIQUES OF DATABASE TUNING

Once you have a feel for the general process of tuning an OnLine system, you are able to begin to apply specific tuning techniques. This section will point you in the direction of these specific techniques.

The order in which the DBA approaches the job of tuning an OnLine system is more or less one dictated by common sense. The key term is the word "system." OnLine is not just a database, it's not just an engine sitting out there in a vacuum. A database system is a tightly interwoven and highly interdependent symbiosis in which the computer hardware, operating system software, database software, system peripherals, and application programs have to live together and cooperate to allow the system to achieve its goals. Failure or poor performance in one area can make it impossible to identify, much less correct, performance problems in other areas.

It's important to get an overall view of the entire system. You need to appreciate the flow of work and data through a system. You need to know why and when things occur, and who uses the outputs. Taking a global view of the system can allow you to immediately identify redundancies, wasted effort, and poor procedures.

Oftentimes, it is possible to restructure the work flow or change operating procedures to cure performance problems. You could spend weeks trying to optimize a report for faster performance only to achieve the same results by having the report run overnight. Who cares if it takes a long time? It's there in the morning. Such common sense improvements are often the hardest for computer people to identify. We tend to try to solve everything with code.

Keep an open mind during your tuning process. Don't be afraid to ask stupid questions. Just because things have "always been done that way" doesn't mean that that's the best way. It may just be somebody else's kludge.

The procedural and timing issues are a good example of the 80 percent rule in tuning. Often, it's the easy and simple changes that can make the most, and most immediate, difference.

Assuming that the easy, "no brainers" have been taken care of, you are ready to begin your efforts at actually tuning the system itself. Tuning the system means first of all, getting the system running to the extent that you can begin to monitor its performance.

Tune the operating system first

Unless your UNIX system is operating with some degree of efficiency, you'll never reach your best performance. In fact, unless the operating system kernel is tuned to minimal specifications needed by Informix, you'll never even get the database running.

If you are starting out with a completely new computer system, don't try to install the hardware, install the database, and install the applications all at the same time. It makes much more sense to get your hardware and operating system working properly without the added complexity of the database. Make sure that all of your peripherals are working correctly, especially your tape drives. Check your disk access with your UNIX utilities and make sure that your system is using its resources with some degree of efficiency.

Let the system burn in for a few days. Put a load on the system. Have it create and delete files. Have it do some computations. Get it talking properly over the network and to its terminals. If you have other systems connected to the UNIX box, make sure that the network is working properly and that everyone can talk to everyone else.

Test things. In fact test everything. Don't rely on your hardware or Open Systems vendor who comes in, installs everything in a day and leaves. Make your vendor show you that everything works and that it works to specifications. If you are just purchasing the hardware, insist on a formalized acceptance testing program. You'll never get better service from a vendor than you will while you are doing acceptance testing of a system. You have the hardware, the software, and the money. If the vendor wants the money, he has to make the system work. Take advantage of this.

In other words, be sure that your platform is working properly before you even think about doing anything with OnLine. If you have been able to do this, you will then have confidence that your underlying platform is efficient and stable. If you run into complications later in the tuning process, you will be relatively safe in assuming that the problems lie further up in the system, above the UNIX and hardware levels, since you've already tested the lower levels of the system.

Get the database running

Once you have a stable underlying platform you can then concentrate on getting the OnLine system up and running. If you're new to Informix, you may have gone through a period of comparisons with other products to have gotten to the point of choosing OnLine.

Use the Informix salespeople. They have a vested interest in making you happy. After all, you'll be spending a good bit of money with them on their products. In your negotiating and evaluating process, make sure that the salespeople stand ready to provide installation and tuning assistance.

If you go through a competitive evaluation, you may have Informix gurus on site whose sole purpose is to tweak their system to make it perform better than the competition. Insist that they document and explain to you what they are doing. This is valuable information. Some of the tricks that the really advanced Informix people use cannot be found in any of the manuals. If possible, try to get a bit of experience with

OnLine before working with the Informix gurus. At least, go through this book first so that you'll have a chance of picking up some of their techniques.

Whether you have help from Informix or not, the first thing to do is to get the engine running reliably. Before you do anything, go through the installation worksheets that are in the manuals. Develop an idea for how you want to size the system, for how you want to lay out the databases, for how you want to lay out your chunks. This is a very critical time. If you make decisions now that you cannot live with later, you may very well have to completely reinstall the system from scratch. Use the Informix people here. Don't be shy about calling Informix Technical Support. They've done this many times before. They know what to look for and what the issues are. Don't depend on them to know everything, though. See if your hardware and UNIX vendors have any Informix gurus. They may know more about OnLine on your particular box than the Informix people do.

You may need to change some kernel parameters in UNIX if you haven't already done so. Once the system is running, let it run for a few days. If you or your programmers are new to OnLine, take this time to play around with the demonstration database. Check out the tools you have on site. Compile a few ESQL/C demo programs if you have this product. Make sure that everything is working normally.

The way to be sure that everything is working normally is to closely monitor the `online.log`. Every time you start or stop the system, check the log for error messages. If you see anything, look into it. The logfile is your early warning system.

Be sure to run a few archives and restores. It's much less painful to discover that your restores don't work at this stage than it is to find out after you have a month's worth of work on the system.

Once the system seems to be stable and reliable it is time to begin doing a little benchmarking and performance tracking. Get familiar with how long it takes to fill up a logfile if you're doing a large insert into a table. Get a feel for what normal operations of the database feel like. Of course, this is nowhere near what normal operations will really be like. You still have not even installed or began testing of your application code. Right now, you just want to document how long it takes to do some of the things you'll be doing later.

At this point, you have a stable, documented platform from which to work. The rest of the steps in the tuning process become much less linear. They tend to overlap a lot. These remaining steps include optimizing the database design, optimizing the application code, and tuning the engine. Changes in one area will probably affect performance in others. You can't approach the rest of this process as separate steps. It has to be viewed as a trade-off in which you as DBA must decide the directions in which you want to take your system.

Optimize the database design

The general area of optimizing database design is very important if you want to have a system that performs well. Optimizing the design consists of designing the table layout, designing the structure, choosing and creating appropriate indexes, and planning for the concurrent use of the database by multiple users.

Optimizing your design and optimizing your application code go hand in hand. These two steps are much more important to achieving good performance than is the actual tuning of the OnLine engine itself. The ratio is probably at least 10 to 1.

Optimizing the design is more important than optimizing the code. It's more important than tuning the engine. This one area can make or break your system. There are probably several ways of doing it correctly, but I can guarantee that there are many more ways of doing it badly. You can blow your entire project right here if you're not careful.

There have been many books written about database design, and any in-depth discussion of methodologies and techniques is far beyond the scope of this book. Suffice it to say that you should be very confident in your design before you commit to it. If you have little experience in this area and if your firm has not done this before, it would make sense to use outside consultants at this point.

Just because you have programmed with DBase™ or Paradox™ on a PC or because your people are converting a mainframe application to open systems does not mean that you have the requisite knowledge to develop a complex relational database application. One of the worst things you can do is blindly copy another system from an older legacy system and hope that it works.

Relational databases are a different breed. They have their own idiosyncrasies and they have their own traps. It's very easy to develop something that looks good on paper, that looks good with a few hundred rows of demo data in it, and that falls flat on its face when presented with live data. If you insist on going it alone without sufficient in-house expertise in database design, at least start out with a project that is not mission-critical. Start out with a few simple projects to get familiar with the tools and techniques, and then jump into something important.

At the very minimum, read a book or two about database design and try to take a class or two. It can't hurt.

Table layout and normalization

Assuming that the last few paragraphs have not scared you off and sent you scurrying in search of a database guru to design your project, you may be expecting me to give you some pointers on how to do it yourself. Maybe you took my advice and you're designing a simple application for the experience.

Your first job will be to develop a schema for the application's database. How will you lay out the tables? How many tables? How normalized do you need to be?

Table design is important, but it's probably not the most important issue. What it is, though, is a design issue that is difficult to change once you have decided to go down a particular path. Let's assume you have decided on a table schema and have developed your application around it. If you decide later that you've made a mistake, you'll have to change tables, indexes, reports, screens, processing steps, and just about everything within your system.

It's not impossible to change your table schema in mid-stream, but it's a serious hassle. It makes sense to do it right the first time. In this area, you may be able to get some help from some of the *CASE* (Computer Aided Software Engineering) tools on the market. Just about all of them can walk you through creating specifications for a system at a conceptual level and translating the requirements into a physical database design.

An advantage to using a CASE tool is that it can help you graphically envision the layouts and interrelationships between the elements of your data model. If you can create a visual representation of how everything fits together, mistakes and conceptual misunderstandings are easier to spot. We'll look at a few third-party CASE tools in the last chapter.

Whatever you do in the design stage, don't become a slave to database normalization. Find something that works and makes sense to you. If it has the additional benefits of fitting the Codd and Date model elegantly, so much the better. But remember, you have to be able to explain and to maintain this monster. Sometimes it makes sense to deviate from strict normalization to get better performance or to make the system easier to maintain.

Optimize the indexes

From a speed of execution standpoint, proper index design is the most important issue in performance tuning. Period.

If you have a limited amount of time to spend in improving your system performance, this is where you need to spend it. Indexes can make or break your system. An added advantage to tweaking your indexes is the fact that it is not as difficult to do as modifying your table structure. You can experiment with a new index. If it works, keep it. If it doesn't, find out why and drop it.

If you're designing your system from a conceptual standpoint, you will be able to easily see how your table should be joined to each other on the primary keys. This is a good starting place. As your joins get more complex, you may need to alter your indexing scheme to improve performance.

From a design standpoint, this is about as far as you can go before getting into your code. When you look at the code, you'll be looking at specific SQL statements to make further decisions about your indexes. Remember, it's all one big iterative process.

Ground rules for indexes

Index design is part science and part black magic. It is closely tied in with understanding the operations of the OnLine optimizer and understanding how to read query plans generated by the SET EXPLAIN SQL command. Sometimes it makes sense to try to work out the logic of the optimizer. Sometimes it's easier to just create an index and see if it helps.

Indexes have several purposes in a database. Understanding these uses will enable you to establish some general ground rules for when creation of indexes will be helpful.

Index your primary keys

If you are remaining relatively true to the theory of relational database design, you will strive to have a unique primary key for every table. These primary keys should have an index. A clustered index is often appropriate here, especially if the tables are relatively static. The clustered index will place the data in the physical order of the key. This can make access to the tables somewhat faster when you are accessing it in primary key order.

Use indexes or constraints to enforce uniqueness

For other cases in which you must enforce uniqueness, an index is needed. If you establish unique constraints in your CREATE TABLE statements, OnLine will create unique indexes to support the constraint. The first character of these indexes will be a blank.

Index columns used in joins

For cases other than primary and foreign keys you should have indexes on columns that are used to join tables. If you have not created the index yourself, you will find that the optimizer often will create the index on the fly, just for your particular join. After the join is over, the index will be deleted. If you see the optimizer creating temporary indexes when doing a join, these indexes are prime candidates for being made into "real" indexes. The only stipulation is that the join must happen with some degree of frequency. It doesn't make sense to create indexes to accommodate a join that only happens once a month.

Index columns used in filters

Filter expressions are evaluated on columns in WHERE clauses that do not create joins but that restrict the rows returned by the SQL statement. If a column is often used in filter statements, especially on larger tables, it is a candidate for an index. Such an index can often prevent full table scans in favor of indexed searches.

Whether or not this index will help depends upon the size of the table and the selectivity of the index. Index selectivity refers to how many unique values appear in the indexed columns. For example, you may have a column in a personnel database to indicate whether the employee is human or a Martian alien. The vast majority of the entries would probably be "H" (except in some areas of the country). This index would not be very selective and would be of very limited utility. Since the indexed access takes more reads than sequential access, the selectivity of the index should be such that no more than about one-fourth of the rows would pass the filter.

Basically, unless the index is pretty selective, it won't help a lot and may even slow the statement down.

Index columns used for ordering

When your statements call for ordering or grouping of large tables, the optimizer may choose to use an existing index to do the ordering rather than sorting the final results. Creating an index on a frequently used sort column can speed up your statements that use an ORDER BY clause.

Avoid duplicate keys

Although it sometimes makes sense to create indexes on columns that have a very few number of distinct values, this can cause you pain in updating the index. This is caused by the fact that in an index the values that contain any particular key value are listed in a list composed of node structures. Any time an update, change, delete, or insert is done, the engine must manipulate the entire list to update the index. If the index is not very selective, it is possible that updates to any one row may take a long time to update the index. For example, if a table allows "M" or "F" only in an indexed row and if the table has a million rows, approximately 500,000 will be in the "M" list and 500,000 will be in the "F" list. Any update to a row here would mean (in the worst case) that half a million index entries would have to be juggled.

If you have to have such an unselective index, you can make it much more selective by using a composite index. In the sample case, a composite index on (sex, SSN) would be much more selective. The optimizer would still use the first part of the index (sex) for its queries on sex, giving you the same performance as your original nonselective index, but updates would affect only a very few (probably only one) b+tree node, since (sex,SSN) would be much more selective.

Consider dropping indexes while updating

For the same reasons that dropping indexes during bulk loads can improve loading performance, dropping unnecessary indexes during mass updates, inserts, or deletes can speed up their respective processes. This is only practical if you are able to conduct these mass data changes during a time in which other users do not need to access the tables. If you can do this, you will gain in several areas.

First, the updates, deletes, or inserts will go much faster with fewer indexes. Second, recreating the indexes will place the data pages and index pages contiguously, as in the mass load example. Finally, the new indexes will be more efficient, since newly created indexes are more densely packed than indexes that have had lots of update and delete activity. Being more densely packed, they will have to access fewer pages to get to your data.

More densely packed indexes may show a slight performance degradation during inserts and updates because the engine may need to split and balance the b+ tree more if there are not sufficient nodes in the tree.

Concurrency issues

Another design issue is more concerned with preventing problems than it is with optimizing speed. This is the area of concurrency control. This is a "traffic cop" type of situation that governs what happens when a number of users want to do the same thing at the same time.

These issues often surface only after the system is designed, implemented, and begins to experience a user load. As more users begin to get on the system, performance degrades and some tasks fail. Proper design on the front end can alleviate many of these problems down the line.

LOCK MODE

When you create a table, you are able to use the LOCK MODE parameters in the CREATE TABLE statement to establish at what level you want the table to lock.

There are four usable lock modes available to your applications:

database locking	locks the entire database
table locking	locks the entire table
page locking	locks the entire page that a row is on
row locking	locks only the row

Of these four modes of locking, the page and row level locking options are available at table creation time. When tables are created with specific lock modes, all processes will observe these lock modes when they work with the table. Table locking is invoked by the SQL statement LOCK TABLE in EXCLUSIVE MODE. An entire database is locked appending the word EXCLUSIVE to the DATABASE command, as in:

```
DATABASE database_name EXCLUSIVE.
```

Locks are important for several reasons. First of all, they are a limited resource. If someone wants to modify every row of a million row table and that table uses row-level locking, your user will not have enough locks to do the job.

Second, locks can prevent other jobs from being able to happen. For example, suppose you have a table called `batch` that has about two hundred rows that get updated by every job in your system. Each row in batch is 20 bytes wide. This means that in a system with 2K pages, each page in the batch tablespace can hold about 100 rows (there's a little overhead). Thus, your batch table will occupy about two pages in the tablespace.

Now suppose that job A needs to update batch row number 1. It's on the first page. If the lock mode is set to the default, the table uses page-level locking. That means that while the update is being done by job A, the entire first page of the table (half the rows) is locked and not available to other jobs needing to update a row. This means that there is about a 50 percent chance that an update will be unable to acquire the lock and update his row in `batch`.

Contrast this to the situation in which `batch` is set up for row-level locking. Job A locks row 1 and holds the lock until the update is done. Meanwhile, Job B locks row 2 on the same page, does some work, and finally releases the latch. All of the jobs go through, and nobody is blocked.

On the other hand, consider what would have happened if each row in `batch` was 1000 bytes wide. Then a page would hold two rows and the locking problem with page-level locking would be much less.

A general rule to follow is that any table that gets updated frequently, has many rows per page, and does not have a lot of rows is a good candidate for row-level locking.

Why is it important that there not be a lot of rows? If you have a lot of rows, the odds of having a conflict on any particular update are less. But worse, the odds go up that some user will try to update or copy the table into another table and suck up all of the system locks trying to do it.

Unless you have a very disciplined, very aware user base, large tables with row locking are accidents waiting to happen.

If you absolutely must have large tables that use row locking, be sure that the LOCKS parameter in your $TBCONFIG file is set very high. The maximum allowable is around 250,000 locks.

Each lock only takes a few bytes of shared memory, so configuring your system with a large number of locks will not use up an excessive amount of the shared memory in your system.

Bottlenecks

A bottleneck is any table or any process that needs to be updated, inserted, or processed before other tasks can occur. This is almost always a situation that can be controlled by proper design and applications programming. Bottlenecks can also occur due to tuning problems with the engine. In these cases, proper tuning can go a long way towards eliminating these system bottlenecks.

Table bottlenecking can be illustrated by imagining a system that uses a global audit trail table to track the types of transactions that each data entry person does. Each time that the data entry person does something, the master audit trail is updated. If there are many operators, this type of table could quickly become a bottleneck. The solution would be to have individual audit trail tables for each operator.

Isolation Levels

Early in the development game, you must give serious thought to the proper isolation levels for your applications. You need to decide just how consistent you need your data to be, and just how much you need to guarantee that a particular piece of data does not change while you are working with it. After you've decided the proper isolation level for your own piece of the program, you need to consider how your chosen level of isolation will affect other users and other applications.

If you have chosen a very restrictive level of isolation, you will be using and placing a lot of locks on the data. If you really need the protection, fine, go ahead and use it. That's what the controls are there for.

On the other hand, if you can get by using a dirty read instead of cursor stability isolation level for a particular function, you'll benefit everyone, including yourself, if you go for the lesser level of isolation. Your job will complete more quickly and with less interference from other users.

In many cases, dirty read isolation is all you need. Even if you're doing some sort of numerical analysis on the data, it is possible that you don't need to have the latest, up-to-the-microsecond data. If you're taking a snapshot of the data, just say that the snapshot was taken when you pushed the button, not when the shutter snapped closed.

TUNING THE APPLICATION CODE

Tuning the application code is second only to proper database and index design in improving the performance of your OnLine system. I'm assuming that you are more or less stuck with the system design and are not free to redesign the system from scratch. The demands of a production environment often force this type of constraint upon you. Often, you'll be in a situation where everyone knows that the design of the database is not overly efficient, but the effort and downtime necessary to correct the design problems are prohibitive.

In this type of situation, you can usually change your indexing scheme and you can rework your SQL statements to use your resources more efficiently. There's a large overlap between tuning and database design. Analysis of your SQL statements may alert you to the fact that you need to add or modify your indexes. If you find this to be true, you can often create some spectacular improvements in your system's performance. Order of magnitude improvements in system performance are not unusual in these cases.

SQL do's and don'ts

SQL is a nonprocedural language, and that is a foreign concept to many programmers who cut their teeth on procedural languages such as COBOL, FORTRAN, and C. Not that it is necessarily any better or any worse, just different. You'll often see programmers writing SQL code as though they were dealing with flat files in a traditional programming language. Go to one table and get some data. Process it and go to another table and match a lookup. Take the result and filter it to provide some output.

This may work, and it may be a very straightforward way of approaching a programming problem, but it does not take advantage of some of the intelligence that is built into the database engine. If you want to use flat files, why spend all the money on buying a sophisticated database engine?

The other end of the spectrum is the programmer who has just fallen in love with SQL and tries to do everything in one fanciful, complex, horribly inefficient SQL statement. True, God probably created the Earth with one SQL statement, but I'll bet it wasn't as efficient as breaking it up into seven separate statements.

There are several general rules for writing good SQL. I'm not going into great detail on each one. If you think that some of these statements need more proof, feel free to experiment with them. Build some test cases. Run them with SET EXPLAIN ON. This is probably the best thing you can do anyway. If nothing else, you can use the practice in looking at alternate ways of doing things in SQL. Check it out for yourself. Some of these sweeping generalities may be totally invalidated by the next release of the optimizer. You don't want to take any of this as gospel. I don't.

Do

Avoid sequential scans of large tables.

This one's a no brainer. Any time you can reduce the number of disk accesses to a table by using an index, you'll be coming out ahead. Note that I specified "large tables." Small tables are defined as tables that have just a few pages and that will probably be found in the shared memory buffers. Under this definition, a table can be pretty large and still be considered a "small table," if it is so central to your application that you can be sure that it is always in shared memory. Any table that can be found in shared memory will take almost no time to access.

Avoid correlated subqueries.

A subquery is any query that includes another query in the WHERE clause. This subquery is correlated if there is a common column label both in the main SELECT list and in the WHERE clause of the subquery. As long as a subquery is not correlated, it is executed once and does not adversely affect the performance. When the subquery is correlated, it must be reevaluated for every value that the SQL statement inspects. This can amount to a significant amount of work. If you can avoid using a correlated subquery, it's worth the effort. Unfortunately, this structure is sometimes the only way to do something in SQL. One alternative that's a pretty desperate step is to do what you can without using a correlated subquery and then shell out to UNIX and do the rest.

Avoid initial wildcards on matches.

The SQL constructs MATCHES and LIKE are quite powerful string matching tools, but you need to remember that indexes are processed from left to right. If you are searching an indexed field for something that MATCHES a*, you'll use the index since the engine can go to the a's in the index and work from there. If you are looking for something that MATCHES *a, you'll not be so lucky. The optimizer will not use an index for a statement like this and it will do a sequential scan, even though you may have an index in place on the column.

Avoid substring searches.

Although SQL provides the string[x,y] operator to deal with substrings of a string beginning with the xth and ending with the yth character, it will not use indexes on string to resolve the statements, unless the x value is 1. This is similar to the initial match problem with wildcards. If you can avoid this type of statement on large tables, do so.

Use temporary tables to guide the optimizer.

Temporary tables can be used in many cases to force the optimizer to do what you want it to do. In the two examples above, you have been cautioned to avoid dealing with anything except the initial part of an index. This causes even more problems when the statements with the offending substrings are combined with joins. If you find yourself unable to live without using one of these less-than-optimal filters, you can often make the SQL more efficient by first doing your less-than-optimal selects into a temporary table and then doing your joins against the temporary table.

This technique of first selecting some data into a temp table can also help you manhandle the optimizer into doing something your way.

You may be absolutely certain that the most efficient way to do a join is to look at table A first and then table B and then table C. You may know this because you know that the data is skewed in such a way that some of the filters are more selective than others. When you run a SET EXPLAIN ON command, the engine insists on evaluating the query in CBA order.

By first selecting the salient data from A into a temporary table that is obviously smaller than the rest of the tables, you can persuade the optimizer to evaluate the rest of the query as you wish.

You can also avoid using ORDER BY clauses in your query if you first select your data into a temp table using a

```
SELECT XXX from source_table


WHERE YYY order by XXX into TEMP
    temp_name
```

This is especially useful in cases where you are having to do repeated queries against a table with each of the queries having the same ORDER BY clause. Creating an ordered subset of a table in a temp table will mean that you will only have to do a time-consuming ORDER BY once rather than for each subsequent query.

Don't

Tolerate long transactions.

Be careful with your use of the BEGIN WORK / COMMIT
WORK statements. Long transactions represent a lot of
wasted resources and can be fatal to your database. Note that
long transactions do not have to be within a formal
BEGIN/COMMIT WORK pair. An implicit long transaction
can be created with a statement like:

```
INSERT INTO new_tab SELECT * FROM big_tab
```

If you can, chop your transactions into atomic units of work so
that your transactions remain short. See the section on flutter
locks for more details on this.

Stop processes using job control.

This isn't really a SQL item, but it's still a no-no. Just because
you have stopped a SQL job using your job control facilities
does not mean that all is okay. Your job may be holding
locks, latches, or other resources. You may have started a
transaction and haven't committed it yet. You may put the job
in the background only to find out that you cannot "catch" it
again because it's parent has died and it is now a zombie
process. If it's in the background, you may forget about it and
exit your shell without cleaning it up or bringing it down
properly. If it's in a critical section of code or if it's holding a
latch, you could bring the database crashing down. Be very
careful stopping SQL processes using job control. I
recommend that you don't even let your users know that it can
be done.

Allow prime-time updates of busy tables.

This one's as much a matter of simple courtesy as anything
else. When you are doing updates, you will be placing locks
on the table and you may be locking out other legitimate users
of the tables. Save this for slow times.

Use extreme indexed range indicators.

This one's not immediately obvious and goes pretty deep into
the way that OnLine evaluates indexes. Suppose you have a
lookup table for say, the person's area code. These area codes
range from 100 to 999 and are evenly distributed over that
range. Suppose you had several out-of-range indicators that
you wanted to code into this number. For example, no area
code might be 000. A slightly questionable code might be 001.
An obvious fraud might be coded as 999999

The point is that you are using extreme values on the high or
low end of an indexed variable to indicate out-of-range or
warning situations.

When the optimizer is looking at the selectivity of an index, it
throws out the highest and the lowest value of the index,
knowing that programmers often use one high and one low
number as range indicators. If you are using more than one
high or low indicator, the optimizer will take the second-
highest and the second-lowest values of the keys as
representing the normal range of the keys and will make bad
judgments about the distribution of values.

This could possibly cause bad query plans to be created.
Remember if you want to use out-of-range values, use only
one high and one low value, because they'll be ignored as the
optimizer   evaluates the range of values in the index.

UNDERSTANDING THE ONLINE OPTIMIZER

The INFORMIX OnLine system uses a cost-based optimizer to determine how to best satisfy SQL statements. The optimizer analyzes the SQL request from the I-SQL or other client program and decides upon a query plan. The query plan is the optimizer's best guess as to which indexes (if any) to use and the best order in which to access the tables.

Optimizer design is continuously changing. It is probably the most dynamic area of database research. Specifics about optimizer strategies and techniques will change as the state of the art advances. The generalizations made here conform to the state of the art as expressed in the OnLine 5.XX product. Earlier versions of the product will use more primitive optimization strategies. Later versions will use more sophisticated optimizers. This is one area that changes quickly.

To estimate the overall cost of executing a query in a certain manner, the optimizer looks at several pieces of information that is culled from the system catalog tables. Pertinent information is:

- Number of rows in the tables
- Whether a column has a unique constraint
- Existence and types of indexes
- Number of disk pages used by data
- Efficiency of the indexes
- Number of disk pages in the index
- Uniqueness of the index
- Range of values in the index

This information is only updated in the system catalogs when the SQL UPDATE STATISTICS command is run. Since this information is the basis for the query plans that are actually used to access data, it is obvious that you must have fairly accurate data in your system tables. Whenever data changes drastically, it will pay to update your statistics, at least for the affected table.

Based on the information it gets from the system catalogs, the optimizer looks at various query plans and estimates the number of disk accesses required to satisfy the query plan. It looks at many query plans and chooses the one that it believes to be the most efficient. The optimizer considers several factors in estimating the costs. It looks at number of disk accesses, costs for CPU resources to examine the rows, and basic network accesses costs in the event of a query over the network.

The INFORMIX-OnLine 5.0 optimizer gives you a choice as to how much optimization the engine attempts to achieve. This is controlled by the SQL statement SET OPTIMIZATION. The default of HIGH optimization forces the engine to examine all reasonable plans for executing a statement. The LOW level of optimization eliminates some alternatives early in the process, thus taking less time to perform the optimization. The risk is that some of the more unlikely plans that were discarded by the optimizer may have actually been very efficient.

This is very similar in operation to the way that game-playing programs such as chess programs work. They look at all the possibilities they can think of and choose the one that best meets their requirements.

This greatly simplifies the task of writing SQL code. Unlike systems such as Oracle that use a rule-based optimizer, OnLine is not picky about how the query is worded. As long as the SQL statement is legal (i.e., is understood by the parser), the optimizer will choose appropriate indexes and join strategies to make the query most efficient. An additional benefit to the cost-based joins is that the query plan can vary according to the size and data distribution of the tables.

The drawback to a cost-based optimizer is that this optimization must be done every time a SQL statement is parsed. It is possible to avoid the additional costs of repeated parsing by using the PREPARE command to create and parse the SQL statement and then using the prepared statement many times. Code that is placed in stored procedures is also pre-optimized.

Using SET EXPLAIN

We've talked a lot about the OnLine engine's being a black box to the users. For most purposes, this is as it should be. Users usually do not need or want to know how the engine is doing what it does. They just want it to do what they want.

In other cases, though, the users need to know how the engine behaves internally. Any user who regularly writes SQL statements needs to know how to write those statements efficiently. SQL is a very powerful query language. As such, it can enable users to create statements of such complexity and monstrosity that they can overwhelm the system's resources. At best, these statements can take forever to execute. At worst, they can bring the system to its knees.

The tool that allows the users to peek into the engine is the SQL statement, SET EXPLAIN. If SET EXPLAIN ON is placed at the beginning of a query, as soon as the optimizer evaluates the query plan, it will create a file called `sqexplain.out` in the user's current directory. This file contains a copy of the query and an explanation of the process that the optimizer has chosen to satisfy the statement.

If the user is running `isql` or `dbaccess`, as soon as the status line says `explain set`, the user can press the CONTROL-C key to exit from the query and see what the engine would have done. It is not necessary to actually complete the query. The results of each SET EXPLAIN ON run will be appended to the `sqexplain.out` `file` so that you can track the improvements made by your changes. We'll use some of the examples in the demonstration database provided with the OnLine products. While these examples are fairly simple, they are a good place to begin looking at how to read a SET EXPLAIN output.

```
QUERY:
select c.customer_num, lname, o.order_num,
       order_date, call_dtime
       from customer c, orders o, cust_calls x
       where c.customer_num = o.customer_num
         and c.customer_num = x.customer_num
Estimated Cost: 10
Estimated # of Rows Returned: 7

1) joe.x: INDEX PATH
     (1) Index Keys: customer_num call_dtime    (Key-Only)

2) joe.c: INDEX PATH
     (1) Index Keys: customer_num
         Lower Index Filter: joe.c.customer_num = joe.x.customer_num

3) joe.o: INDEX PATH
     (1) Index Keys: customer_num
         Lower Index Filter: joe.o.customer_num = joe.c.customer_num
```

This sample query is a three-table join. Notice some of the important parts of the `sqexplain.out` output. The query is listed in the first section. The next section contains an `Estimated Cost` and `Estimated # or Rows Returned` section. These numbers are just that, estimated numbers. The information comes from the data in the system tables, so it is important that there be a fresh UPDATE STATISTICS before making decisions based upon the query plans. In fact, if you are testing a SQL statement using SET EXPLAIN, you may want to insert an UPDATE STATISTICS FOR TABLE XXX clause before the SQL you wish to test.

The `Estimated Cost` statistic uses as its baseline the amount of work necessary to make one disk access. Small differences are not really significant. These numbers are not really generalizable across different queries, so you cannot compare `query1`'s `Estimated Cost` of 10 to `query2`'s `Estimated Cost` of 10 on another query. The path taken to resolve either of the two queries could be totally different.

The `Estimated Cost` variable can be used within a query to see if the changes you are making to the query or to the indexes are helping. If you place an index on a table and the estimated cost of the query goes from 100 to 10, you can be pretty sure that you've improved the response time. The slow disk has to do only one-tenth the work with the index in place. To be absolutely sure, you should time the query.

Timing the query can be done in several ways. One of the easiest is placing a `SELECT CURRENT FROM dummy` statement at the beginning and at the end of the query. In this case `dummy` is either any table with only one row or is a special table in your database called `dummy`.

Creating such a dummy table is a good idea, since it will allow you to choose any of the internal variables such as USER, CURRENT, SITENAME, etc. from within an SQL query. The dummy table should have one column and one row. The actual type and value for the column and row does not matter.

The estimated number of rows returned will depend upon the actual distribution of the data within the tables and indexes. This distribution data is at best an estimate in OnLine versions up to 6.0, so don't be surprised if the estimated rows are way off base. OnLine 6.0 has added a robust data distribution capability.

The most important data is the actual query plan, which begins after the estimated number of rows. It shows the order in which the tables are accessed and the means by which they are accessed. For the sample query, which joins the `customer`, `orders`, and `cust_calls` tables, the engine has chosen to begin by reading the `cust_calls` table. Since the only items it needs to satisfy the query from the `cust_calls` table is `customer_number` and `call_dtime`, it is able to find all of the information it needs from `cust_calls` by using the index. Thus, it does an INDEX PATH search using the index only. This is indicated by the `(Key-Only)` notation. Key-Only index reads are the most efficient type of index reads, because the actual table data does not need to be read. All needed data is available from reading the index.

Don't take the Key-Only notation as an indication that the SQL is at its optimum efficiency. It is possible for a query to be retrieving its data only from the index itself and still not be running optimally. Even if all of the data in your SELECT clause is contained in the index, the engine may still be reading the index sequentially and thus be at less than optimum performance. This is often indicated by the presence of a filter statement immediately before the key-only index statement in the query plan.

The second step calls for joining the `customer_number, call_dtime` found from the `cust_calls` table to the `customer` table using an index on `customer_number` in the `customer` table. In this case, the index is not enough to satisfy the query, as we have to go to the actual row data to get the value of the `lname` variable which is returned by the query.

The final step joins to the `order` table on `customer_num` to get the `order_date`. This is also an INDEX PATH. join. Now, let's look at a small change in the previous query. Suppose we did away with the need for the `lname` in the query.

```
QUERY:
select c.customer_num,  o.order_num,
       order_date, call_dtime
       from customer c,        orders o,        cust_calls x
       where c.customer_num = o.customer_num
              and c.customer_num = x.customer_num
Estimated Cost: 8
Estimated # of Rows Returned: 7
1) joe.x: INDEX PATH
    (1) Index Keys: customer_num call_dtime    (Key-Only)
2) joe.c: INDEX PATH
    (1) Index Keys: customer_num    (Key-Only)
        Lower Index Filter: joe.c.customer_num = joe.x.customer_num
3) joe.o: INDEX PATH    (1) Index Keys: customer_num
        Lower Index Filter: joe.o.customer_num = joe.c.customer_num
```

Notice that in step 2, we now have a `Key-Only` INDEX PATH. Getting rid of the need to go to the data rows to get the `lname` field means that all of the information needed from the `customer` table is now available in the index. The estimated cost went down from 10 to 8. This is a marginal improvement in cost as measured in arbitrary disk access units. You may have noticed that making this change means that we really don't need any information from the `customer` table any longer. In fact, look what happens when we get the `customer_number` from the `cust_calls` table rather than from the `customer` table:

```
QUERY:

select x.customer_num,  o.order_num,
       order_date, call_dtime
       from orders o, cust_calls x
       where x.customer_num = o.customer_num

Estimated Cost: 5

Estimated # of Rows Returned: 10

1) joe.x: INDEX PATH
     (1) Index Keys: customer_num call_dtime    (Key-Only)

2) joe.o: INDEX PATH
     (1) Index Keys: customer_num
         Lower Index Filter: joe.o.customer_num = joe.x.customer_num
```

Notice in these three sample queries that the estimated number of rows differs. The queries returned nine rows in the actual runs. Remember that this number is only an estimate.

Now, just for the heck of it, let's make the query a little worse. Working from the very first query, suppose we decided that we needed the `call_code` contained in `cust_calls` along with the rest of the information. Here's the query plan:

```
QUERY:
select c.customer_num,  lname, x.call_code, o.order_num,
       order_date, call_dtime
       from customer c, orders o, cust_calls x
       where c.customer_num = o.customer_num
         and c.customer_num = x.customer_num

Estimated Cost: 12
Estimated # of Rows Returned: 7


1) joe.x: SEQUENTIAL SCAN

2) joe.c: INDEX PATH
   (1) Index Keys: customer_num
       Lower Index Filter: joe.c.customer_num = joe.x.customer_num

3) joe.o: INDEX PATH
   (1) Index Keys: customer_num
       Lower Index Filter: joe.o.customer_num = joe.c.customer_num
```

Look at the difference in the first step. Now that we need to pull the `call_code` from `cust_calls`, the existing index on (`customer_num`, `call_dtime`) is no longer sufficient to satisfy the query. The engine could have continued doing an INDEX PATH as in the first example, only going out to the actual row data to get the `call_code`. However, it decided to do a sequential scan of the `cust_calls` table instead. This is because the engine has to work less to do a simple sequential scan of this small table than it would to read an index page and then to read data pages.

These are pretty simple examples. They are here just to help you get a feel for how to read the `sqexplain.out  outputs`. The best way to fine-tune your skill is to pick a query from your system and work with it. Note that when we're talking about "queries" here, we could also mean any type of SQL statements. It's best to do the demonstrations with queries to avoid changing the data in the tables. The same type of optimization techniques will work for any types of SQL statements. If you can find a query that you believe is too slow, so much the better. Be sure to understand all of the tables involved. Have their schemas handy and know how the indexes are defined. Don't be afraid to experiment. Just don't do anything to live data that will get your users up in arms. If you decide to try building some indexes in your experimentation, be aware that the very existence of new indexes may affect the performance of existing queries. Note also that creation of indexes will place locks on system tables and can interfere with other DML (data manipulation language) statements being run while you are creating an index.

Until you are certain that new indexes do not adversely affect the rest of your system, you may want to delete them after your experiments are over. Better yet, do your experiments after hours and clean up after yourself.

Things to watch for in query plans

There are several red flags that occur in query plans. If you spot any of these, you may have located a place where your performance can be improved.

Sequential Scans

Full table scans are the bane of efficient database design. Unless the table is very small, you cannot assume that its pages will be accessible in shared memory. The engine will probably have to go out to the disk to read the pages. Any time that the engine has to go through an entire table looking for data it will probably be incurring a high cost in disk access. That's why indexes were invented, to prevent having to completely scan a table to find a few data items.

In looking at a query plan, the steps are hierarchical. That is, for each row found in the first step, the second step is done. This applies to nested loop joins of multiple tables. For each row found in the second, the third is done, and so on. You can see that item in the second, third, fourth, or lower steps may be executed many times, depending on the size of your queries. If you find sequential scans deep into the logic of the query plan, they may be happening thousands of times. These are prime candidates for tweaking. You may find that a particular query is doing many full table reads of relatively large tables to satisfy your SQL. Consider creating indexes or modifying your approach.

A sequential scan in the first position, while not as good as an INDEX PATH access, is not quite as worrisome. After all, the query has to start somewhere, and this scan will only happen once. If you have a million-row table in the first position, though, you may want to modify your indexes.

The problem with full table scans is that they don't know when to stop. You may get all of the data you need within the first two or three rows, but since there's no index, the engine has to laboriously read every row in the table just to be sure that there's no more data you need. Most of the tuning that you do with query plans is to eliminate sequential scans.

Autoindex Path

If you see this in your query plan, it means that every time the SQL runs, the engine builds a temporary index to satisfy the SQL statement. If this is a query you run often, this can be taken as a strong suggestion from the engine that you create a permanent index.

Temporary Files Required

If your SQL calls for ORDER BY or GROUP BY statements, you will probably see this notation in the early part of your query plan. When OnLine must do an ORDER BY or a GROUP BY, it often has to create temporary tables for the output and sort the final output. Sorts incur a cost both in processing time and in disk access time. Both times can be significant, so sorts are a fairly expensive task from an efficiency standpoint. The cost increases geometrically with the number of rows to be sorted.

As an alternative to costly sorts, the engine can choose to do its ordering and grouping by accessing an index, if the index is in the exact same order as the ORDER BY. For example, you may have an index on (lname,fname,initial). If you choose to order by lname,fname,initial, the index will be used to satisfy the sort. If you choose to order by lname,fname the index will also be used. However, if you choose to order by lname,initial the engine will create temporary tables and sort the results.

TUNING THE ENGINE

Tuning the actual parameters that control the operation of the OnLine engine can be done in two ways, modifying the $TBCONFIG file directly or changing values through tbmonitor. Using the $TBCONFIG file is the most straightforward and is the recommended method.

The $TBCONFIG file's name and location is located by the UNIX environment variable $TBCONFIG. It is possible to have several $TBCONFIG files. As an example, you may want your engine to behave in one fashion during ordinary operations and in a completely different fashion when you are doing bulk loads of your data. If you have such extreme conditions, you may want to have a tbconfig.bulk_load file that has different parameters from your normal operations file. This configuration would be invoked by taking your database system offline, changing the value of $TBCONFIG to the bulk_load configuration file, and restarting the database.

In $INFORMIXDIR/etc/tbconfig.std you will find the "standard" or distribution version of the control file. In some instances, changes made to the actual $TBCONFIG file may seem to just "go away" next time you restart the engine. This is because in some versions, if the parameter is not mentioned in the $TBCONFIG.std file, it will not be included in the $TBCONFIG file whenever the tbmonitor utility is used to modify a parameter. The moral is, make the changes in both files.

Changes made in the $TBCONFIG file or through tbmonitor do not become effective until the engine is shut down and restarted. When this is done, an informational message noting the changes in parameters is inserted into your online.log file. These tuning changes should also be placed in your system logbook for later tracking and analysis.

Tuning the OnLine engine takes some time. In the first place, since changing most tuning parameters means shutting down the engine, it becomes difficult to tune a production system. If you can do your tuning under an actual load but before you get into production, it will help matters. If you have to tune a production system, track your changes carefully, monitor the effectiveness of your changes carefully, and make your incremental changes anytime you have the database down. Don't try to rush the matter by making a lot of changes at once. Take a slow and methodical approach.

Tuning the shared memory buffers

Physical disk I/O is the slowest thing that your OnLine engine does. Minimizing this I/O is the key to achieving good engine performance. OnLine uses its shared memory buffers to cache recently accessed pages in memory in the hopes that these pages will be needed again. The engine will try to avoid a disk I/O with all of its attendant delays and instead get the data from a shared memory buffer, The more memory buffers the engine has available for caching, the better the chance that the page can be found in the buffer. The idea behind tuning the buffers is to find the magic number that is large enough to generate efficient caching figures and small enough to minimize overhead and leave enough memory for other applications to run. The trade-off here is to trade memory use for disk I/O.

The `tbstat -p` and `tbstat -P` commands are your main tools for buffer tuning. You'll find two statistics in the `tbstat` output that indicate how well your buffers are tuned. Both are labeled the same, `% cached`. The first is the percentage of times that a disk access is satisfied from a buffer on a READ operation. The second is the number of times that a WRITE operation can occur to a page that is already buffered without physically reading a page from the disk. The general guideline is that the read percentage should be 95 percent or better, and that the write percentage should be 82 percent or better. The `tbstat -p` and `tbstat -P` commands also have several indicators of overflow conditions that are important to your tuning efforts. These are the `ov` statistics, `ovtbls` (not enough tables), `ovlock` (not enough locks), `ovuser` (not enough users), and `ovbuff` (not enough buffers). These statistics show the total number of times that a process had to wait because it could not acquire a needed shared memory resource. If you are seeing consistent readings of greater than zero in any of these fields, you should probably consider bumping up the shared memory parameters. In tuning the buffers, if you see consistent positive numbers in `ovbuff`, this means that processes are having to wait to acquire a shared memory buffer.

To accurately analyze the performance behind these percentages, it is necessary to run the system under a "normal" load, whatever that means. When the system is initially brought from quiescent to online mode, it will have to read in pages until it fills up its buffer pool and begins having to swap them to disk. Statistics taken immediately after system startup, then, are not indicative of a normal load and are not very useful. Let the system run for a while, then run a `tbstat -z` command to zero out the statistics. The statistics that are generated under load after the zeroing will be more indicative of your real load. Note that if your system has periods of extremely high activity, you should tune your system to support the peak activity levels if possible.

The shared memory buffers are the most "expensive" of all the shared memory constructs. You can find yourself using up a lot of your computer's memory with buffers. You need to know how much total memory your system has available and roughly how much gets used by normal non-database activities. The best way to follow this is with UNIX utilities such as `sar` and `top`. You also need to be able to tell whether your system is getting close to a critical situation on memory and whether you are getting close to performing UNIX swaps to disk. Swaps are absolute killers of performance. If your shared memory usage gets so high that you are swapping, you've gone too far and need to back down on your shared memory size. If you're not sure about any of these factors, talk to your System Administrator or other UNIX gurus on the system.

The way to tune the buffers is to bump up the number of buffers and see if your cache hit rates go up. In this case, it is often better to use the `tbmonitor` utility to bump up your buffer numbers because you will get immediate feedback about the amount of shared memory required for that particular buffer count. If you are directly modifying the `$TBCONFIG` file, the parameter that controls the number of shared memory buffers is, not surprisingly, BUFFERS. When you reach the point that increasing the number of buffers does not improve your cache hit rates, you have enough buffers. If you are swapping at the UNIX level or if your utilities indicate that you are low on system memory, you may have gone too far.

In addition to the costs in memory, additional buffers require some system overhead. Having too many can actually slow your operations down. On the other hand, if you have occasional spikes of extremely high activity on your system, you may want to include a bit of a "fudge factor" in your buffer tuning to give your system extra capacity to handle heavier loads. System tuning is not an exact science. Like everything else with the OnLine system, it is the result of balancing often conflicting requirements. Get as close to optimal as you can, but don't kill yourself trying to squeeze out the last drop of performance. As soon as you get it perfect, your system's requirements will probably change, anyway.

As in all other tuning matters, none of this should ever be set in concrete. Even if you have your system tuned to perfection, the system can change over time. You need to continuously monitor your engine performance and be open to making tuning changes as your system evolves.

Tuning the log buffers

There are two log buffers to consider, the physical and the logical log buffers. Tuning each type is similar, with some differences in exposure to disaster should the system crash. Tuning the physical log buffer is simpler, as there is no danger of losing data in the buffer in the case of a crash.

The physical log buffer is a set of pages in shared memory that holds data that is being moved to the physical log on disk. Since the physical log gets a lot of write activity, it benefits the system to handle this writing in the most efficient, least expensive manner.

When the physical log buffer is written to the physical log, all the pages of the buffer are written to disk. It makes sense to have each buffer as full as possible during the writes to ensure that the maximum work is being done with each write. This also minimizes the number of physical writes that are needed.

The `tbstat -l` command is the tool that is used to tune the physical log buffers

```
/usr/informix> tbstat -l

RSAM Version 5.00.UC3    -- On-Line -- Up 19 days 18:01:00 -- 16080
Kbytes


Physical Logging
Buffer bufused  bufsize  numpages numwrits pages/io
  P-2   0         16       145799   10969     13.29
        phybegin physize  phypos   phyused   percentused
        1002ef   13500    9803     0          0.00


Logical Logging
Buffer bufused  bufsize  numrecs  numpages numwrits recs/pages pages/io
  L-2   0         16       8447086  386846   90106     21.8      4.3

address  number   flags    uniqid   begin      size     used
percentused
c13001d8 1        F------   0        1037ab     4000       0      0.00
c13001f4 2        U---C-L   1478     10474b     4000     573     14.32
c1300210 3        F------   0        1056eb     4000       0      0.00
c130022c 4        F------   0        10668b     4000       0      0.00
c1300248 5        F------   0        10762b     4000       0      0.00
c1300264 6        F------   0        400076     4000       0      0.00
```

The salient numbers here are the `bufsize` and `pages/io` numbers under both the `Physical Logging` and the `Logical Logging` sections. Looking at the physical logging statistics, take the `pages/io` as a percentage of `bufsize`. If this percentage is greater than 75 percent, it means that writes are not occurring until the physical log buffer is almost full. If this is the case, you may achieve some performance gains by increasing the size of the buffer in the hopes that there is additional data that can be stuffed into these writes. If so, you will reduce your number of I/Os to the physical log. Raise the buffer size and see if your `pages/io` to `bufsize` percentage goes down. If it doesn't go down significantly, raise it again until you begin to see it going down.

On the other hand, if the percentage is low, it means that the buffer is getting flushed to disk before it gets close to being filled, indicating that your buffers may be too large. You can possibly save a little bit of shared memory here by lowering the buffer size.

You have an additional concern in tuning the logical log buffer. This buffer gets flushed to the logical log files on disk based upon the type of logging selected for your database. If the database uses unbuffered logging, the log buffer will be flushed after each transaction, and you will have minimum exposure should you have a crash situation.

If you are using buffered logging, you will face some exposure in the event of a system crash. Since the logical log buffer is in volatile RAM, the contents will be lost if the system goes down. If you make your logical log buffer too large, you will increase your possibility of losing data in a crash. Another consideration is the logging status of all databases in your system. You may believe that since you have several of your databases using buffered logging for speed, that you are getting the full benefit of buffered logging. This is not necessarily true because the buffers are a shared resource. If you have one database that is using unbuffered logging and is getting significant activity, this database may be causing the buffers to flush after each of its transactions and you may not be seeing the benefits of buffered logging in the other databases. If this is happening, you will see that the `pages/io` will hover around 1.

Tuning the size of the logical log buffers follows the same methods as tuning the physical log buffers, with the caveat just mentioned if you are using buffered logging. Here, you will be using the `bufsize` and `pages/io` in the `Logical Logging` section of the `tbstat` output.

Tuning the page cleaners

The subject of page cleaning ties together many of the more obscure aspects of the Informix OnLine database engine. If you walk up to an Informix guru and hear him muttering incantations such as "LRU Queue," "FG Writes," and "Chunk Writes" you can be pretty sure that he's been dealing with the OnLine page cleaning mechanisms. If he bangs his head into a wall after every incantation, you can be absolutely certain.

Page cleaning refers to the several methods that OnLine uses to synchronize the pages in shared memory with the pages on disk. As pages are placed into the shared memory pool and used for such tasks as updating and inserting data, they become *dirty*. Dirty simply means that the contents of the pages in shared memory have been changed and no longer reflect what is out there on disk. At some point, these dirty pages need to be flushed off to disk so that the disk contents can be updated.

Eventually, this page cleaning will occur. The DBA has several options that can be manipulated to stipulate when and how it will happen. These options can make a marked difference in the way that the engine performs.

Page cleaning can occur in four different ways, each of which is quantified in the `tbstat -F` output.

```
/usr/informix> tbstat -F

RSAM Version 5.00.UC3    -- On-Line -- Up 19 days 20:06:10 -- 16080 Kbytes

Fg Writes      LRU Writes     Idle Writes    Chunk Writes
0              0              12720              166441
```

The four types of writes are:

Fg Writes

Foreground writes. The engine (the `tbinit` process) does these writes itself when it cannot obtain a clean buffer. This is the least efficient and most disruptive type of writes because the application has to wait until the write is finished.

LRU Writes

Writes done by the page cleaners after they have been awakened by the engine, either because of its having to perform foreground writes or because the LRU_MAX_DIRTY parameter has been exceeded.

`Idle Writes`

Writes performed by the page cleaners during normal operations or as the result of LRU_MAX_DIRTY having been reached.

`Chunk Writes`

Writes by page cleaners as part of a checkpoint.

Each of these types of writes has a purpose and they're each a little different. As a general rule, you want to completely eliminate any `Fg Writes`. A foreground write is a desperation move by the engine. It is telling you that it cannot find any clean buffers to use for new data. Processes that are supposed to insure an available buffer anytime it is needed have failed, and now the application has to wait while it goes out and cleans up a buffer itself.

`LRU Writes` nd `Idle Writes` are very similar to each other. They are significantly different from `Chunk Writes` even though all three types of writes are done by the page cleaners. `LRU Writes` and `Idle Writes` are done by the page cleaners in between checkpoints. The order of pages written in these two types of writes is random, and the writes can occur across the disks with no consideration as to which chunk it is in. As such, they can cause a lot of disk activity. On the positive side, `LRU Writes` and `Idle Writes` do not cause other processes to wait, as do `Fg Writes` and `Chunk Writes`.

`Chunk Writes` are a more planned type of page cleaner write and they are the most efficient types of write. The page cleaner first does a sort of the dirty page numbers, sorting them by chunk location and by their location within the disk. This means that page cleaning during checkpoints attempts to minimize disk head movement. This preplanning of chunk writes can also allow writes to several chunks in parallel during a checkpoint with each chunk being handled by its own page cleaner process.

The drawback to `Chunk Writes` is that no engine processes can change a page during a checkpoint. The user can experience a momentary freezing of the engine as the checkpoint is performed.

So, what kinds of writes are best? The answer depends to a large degree upon the type of environment in which you are running. If you are running in a batch processing mode with little concern for interactive screen performance, you may want to have most of your writes done by the more efficient chunk writes. This will allow a higher throughput and the occasional freezes caused by checkpoints will not cause your users to get up in arms.

If you are in an environment that requires fast screen response and has a high OLTP (On Line Transaction Processing) component, your users may find the checkpoint freezes to be disruptive. In OLTP, you usually don't worry too much about absolute throughput anyway. The slowest part of the system will be the speed at which your data entry people can type, and they have to type pretty fast to cause throughput problems. In this case, you may want to cut down on the Chunk Writes and use more of the LRU and Idle Writes, that do not cause an interruption in operations.

For you to gain by doing more Idle and LRU writes, you must be able to handle the additional possibility of disk contentions caused by the random nature of the writes. If you are already plagued by a thrashing disk, this might not be the way to go.

Another case in which you might want to cut down on Chunk Writes is if you have a system that is distributed across several systems. Distributed systems have to worry not only about delays on one system, but about delays on any of the systems involved. A SQL statement can run awfully slowly if it being performed on three separate systems and has to wait until a checkpoint is completed on each system. Sure, it's a worst case situation, but worst case situations happen.

Controlling the page cleaning

Given that you have decided on an optimal mix for your page cleaners, you need to know how to tune the engine to make your favorite page cleaners happen. The basic question is, do you want your page cleaning asynchronous, happening between checkpoints, or do you want them synchronous, with all of the page cleaning occurring during checkpoints?

There are two tuning parameters that must be accessed by modifying the $TBCONFIG file. These variables are not available through tbmonitor.

LRU_MAX_DIRTY   The maximum percentage of dirty pages that can exist in any
                         queue before the page cleaners kick in.

LRU_MIN_DIRTY   The minimum percentage of dirty pages that must exist on any
                         queue before the page cleaners go back to sleep.

What happens is that any time an LRU queue gets a sufficient number of dirty pages to cause it to exceed the LRU_MAX_DIRTY percentage, the page cleaner is fired off for that queue and it runs until that queue goes below the LRU_MIN_DIRTY percentage.

If you want to force more idle and LRU writes, lower the percentages significantly. They default to 60 percent and 50 percent. You can safely lower them to just about zero if you wish. Often, a good workable figure is 15 percent and 5 percent. Use the tbstat -R command to watch the activity of your page cleaners. I've found it useful to run a tbstat -Rr and watch the activity every five seconds. If you do this during an active time, you will find yourself beginning to get the feel for how your pages get cleaned.

Another parameter to tune is the number of page cleaners allocated for your system. How you set this up depends on whether you are going for idle/LRU writes or chunk writes. If you are going for the idle/LRU writes, you are wanting to have most of your page cleaning occur between checkpoints. Here you need to have one page cleaner for every LRU queue, as the majority of the page cleaning work will be fired off as the queues reach their LRU_MAX_DIRTY percentages.

If you are going for chunk writes, you want most of your page cleaning to occur at checkpoints. Since these types of writes can sort their work by chunk, you want to have one page cleaner per chunk, so that as much of the work as possible can happen in parallel. This is a maximum figure, as each spindle can handle many chunks. Informix recommends one page cleaner per spindle.

You also have the choice of specifying the maximum number of LRU queues in your system. Generally, you want this number as high as possible as having more LRU queues will reduce the possibility of having to wait on any one queue. Generally, you want more LRU queues as you increase the number of buffers. LRU queues do add overhead and it is possible to have too many, but there is no hard and fast rule for allocating number of LRU queues. This is an area in which you just need to experiment to find out what works best in your system.

Checkpoint frequency

The optimal frequency for checkpoints ties closely into the decisions you have made about the types of page cleaning you want.

If you are going for chunk writes, you are expecting most of your page cleaning to be during checkpoints. You are willing to put up with some delay while the checkpoint runs. In this case, it is better to have your checkpoints occur more frequently. The reason is that if your LRU percentages are set high enough that the checkpoints will be doing most of the work, a lot of work can build up to be done. If your checkpoints were very far apart, each checkpoint could take a lot longer, freezing the system up for a longer period of time. You don't want them to occur too frequently, because this will also cause a lot of waiting.

On the other hand, if you are going for LRU/idle writes, most of the page cleaning will be done asynchronously, independent of the checkpoints. If the LRU percentages are low enough, there won't be much work to be done at a checkpoint, and they will go faster. You can also make them occur at less frequent intervals to further minimize the freezing of the system.

The DBA must also take into account the amount of time that the system will spend in recovery should the system go down unexpectedly. With less frequent checkpoints, there will be a longer fast-recovery period, as much more log file data has to be applied.

The checkpoint frequency is controlled by the CKPTINTVL parameter in the $TBCONFIG file. Like other tunable parameters, it will not become effective until the engine is restarted.

Experimenting to find the correct checkpoint interval can be made a little easier by using a feature of the tbmode command. The tbmode utility has a -c option that will force a checkpoint. If you use this command, you can effectively take control of checkpoints away from the engine and give it to a script that you control. This way, you can change checkpoint intervals without bringing your system down.

To do this, you need to do three things. First, you need to set a very long CKPTINTVL in the $TBCONFIG file, on the order of one hour (CHKPTINTVL 3600). Second, you need to create a very large physical log file, large enough that it will not reach 75 percent full during the long checkpoint interval you have set. This could be a very large physical log file requirement. This is because a checkpoint will be automatically triggered by the engine when the physical log becomes 75 percent full. The third thing to do is to run the following script:

```
while true
do
        tbmode -c
        sleep $1
done
```

Invoke this script with your experimental checkpoint interval. When you want to change the interval, kill the script and rerun it with another interval. When you are happy with the performance, you can reset the CKPTINTVL to the magic number you have determined and reduce the physical log down to something that makes more sense.

Chapter 9

DBA Tools

For the last several hundred pages we've been talking about the OnLine engine, with all of its flexibility, its quirks, and its peculiarities. Now we will talk about the tools that are available to help the DBA do her job.

The job of monitoring and controlling the database is a major part of the DBA function. Often, the DBA has the responsibility of managing multiple, diverse database systems. Anything that can help the DBA with this function can be an important addition to the DBA's arsenal of tools.

It seems that the entire computer world is moving towards graphical environments. There's a reason for this, and one reason is that humans can get the "big picture" much easier by using graphical tools. It's true that "a picture is worth a thousand words." Actually, it would be more accurate here to say that a picture is worth a thousand numbers, since the output of the OnLine database monitoring tools consists mostly of numerical output.

Although OnLine has the sources of information, to date there is no graphical tool that can allow the DBA to get to the heart of the data without wading through pages of numerical output. Such tools are available for other database management systems. You can look through the pages of computer and database magazines and see graphical monitoring tools for OnLine's competitors in the market. These tools provide charts and graphs that show such critical items as free space, lock contention, buffer usage, checkpoint activity, and the like. A DBA can pull up a screen and see at a glance what is happening inside the system. These graphical tools can be indispensable in the job of tuning and troubleshooting.   Not having these tools places Informix at a distinct disadvantage when it comes to ease of management of the database.

Granted, these are basically luxuries. They don't do anything that we are not doing with plain old shell scripts. All that they are really doing is putting pretty GUI wrappers around the same type of shell scripts that we've been looking at for the first two hundred pages of this book.

Luxuries or not, graphical tools can be great timesavers for the DBA. Rather than spending an entire morning chasing through pages of numerical output looking for a problem, the GUI-based DBA often has the problem literally jump off the screen at her.

As more demands are placed upon the DBA's time, anything that can make the function more efficient and more focused can be a real lifesaver.

It's not as though Informix was completely bereft of graphical tools. They have several means for providing graphical DBA management tools, if they could see the benefit in doing it. Perhaps they should ask where the developers and users get most of their information about Informix.

I'll bet that they will get a lot of "from the DBA" answers. If Informix wants to penetrate the Oracle and Sybase market, they have to woo the users and the developers. If these users and developers saw flashy GUI screens whenever they walked into the DBA's office, my bet is that they would demand the same types of interfaces for themselves.

INFORMIX TOOLS

Informix itself may hold the best hope for getting some decent monitoring tools. The specifications for Version 6.0 and above call for a systems monitoring interface (SMI), which consists of a series of tables that collect and dispense performance information.

This is essentially the same type of system that we have patched together throughout this book that turn `tbstat` and `tbcheck` outputs into usable data. SMI will take that concept a lot further and place the monitoring information where it should have been all along, in the database.

SMI tracks:

- database names, owners, and logging status
- information on users waiting for resources
- performance profile information
- user and system CPU usage
- disk space information
- logical logging information
- dbspace information
- lock usage information
- extent usage information

If this information can be kept relatively up-to-date, it will be much easier to monitor the databases by using data from these tables. With all the data in one place, maybe someone will develop the visual tools needed to help DBAs visualize the data instead of just digging it out with SQL statements.

INFORMIX-HyperScript Tools

One of the most promising graphical tools in the Informix corporate arsenal is their INFORMIX®-HyperScript® Tools toolkit. Several years ago, Informix came out with a spreadsheet that could talk directly to their engines.

This spreadsheet, INFORMIX-WingZ, was introduced with all the hoopla and flair of a Broadway musical. Informix gave out the best canvas tote bags ever seen at several UNIX trade shows. WingZ was a client application running on windowed operating systems such as Microsoft Windows and IBM OS/2. WingZ had a macro language called HyperScript that was very flexible and allowed the user to generate slick graphic interfaces to their spreadsheets, making the spreadsheet seem more like a custom program than like a spreadsheet.

Although WingZ was an underwhelming performer in the spreadsheet wars and has since bitten the dust, Informix has repackaged the product as a graphical and spreadsheet toolkit called HyperScript Tools. This toolkit contains all of the pieces of the old WingZ product in the form of widgets that can be used together in conjunction with the HyperScript language to give windowing workstations access to Informix databases, both SE and OnLine.

HyperScript Tools allows a developer or an advanced user to design graphical interfaces running on windowed workstations that communicate with OnLine servers. Versions that I have seen have been slow and somewhat limited in capacity, but at least it is a step in the right direction.

Informix seems to be using their own HyperScript Tools in their internal development. These tools could be an invaluable tool to the DBA who wants to develop graphical applications, either for his own needs in monitoring and controlling the databases or for external needs such as providing data access to nontechnical users.

Two relatively recent products from Informix show that they are moving in the direction of providing easier access to data for nontechnical users. These two products, INFORMIX-DBA and ViewPoint, are used together to provide ad hoc data access to users.

INFORMIX-DBA

INFORMIX®-DBA is an application developed to solve some of the problems inherent in letting users have direct access to databases. INFORMIX-DBA works in conjunction with the ViewPoint product and attempts to make data available to ordinary users. INFORMIX-DBA exploits what they call *superviews*.

A superview is a simplified view of data. It hides such details as actual table location, keys, joins, and physical layout from the user. What the user sees is controlled views of the database. These superviews look like flat files to the user. The user uses these superviews in the ViewPoint product to create his own reports, screens, buttons, and other graphical objects. Informix DBA is the tool that sets up these superviews for the user.

The Database Administrator or developer decides which information should be made available for ad hoc users and sets controls upon how the information can be accessed and used. It may be decided that a particular user should have read-only access only to a few tables. This is easily accomplished by creating superviews on the tables. These superviews are then made available to users who are using ViewPoint to create applications to meet their own needs.

One of the most powerful aspects of the superview concept is the ability to set resource limits on the users. The DBA may limit the number of rows that a particular user may return in a query, she may limit the CPU time, or she may set limits on other resources. This serves to protect the system from uncontrolled users and goes a long way towards making ad hoc user access to the database a workable proposition.

INFORMIX-ViewPoint

The client side of the ad hoc database applications from Informix is ViewPoint. ViewPoint is a graphically oriented form generator, report writer, and query builder that runs on windowed client systems usually connected over a network to an OnLine server.

Using superviews generated in INFORMIX-DBA, the ViewPoint user is given a point-and-click interface that allows her to paint her own data entry forms, design her own reports, and generate ad hoc queries. All of this assumes a very limited knowledge of the underlying database structure and little or no knowledge of SQL. The simplified view of the database provided by superviews allows the nontechnical user to do meaningful work in the database. The superviews also protect the database system to some degree from the user, as it has the capability to limit resource utilization by any particular user.

Forms generated by ViewPoint can use multiple tables and superviews. The coordination between master and detail sections that can sometimes get so complicated is handled automatically by ViewPoint. The screen forms can be made more appealing by such features as custom drawing tools and a wide spectrum of user-interface objects.

Reports generated by ViewPoint can use custom grouping, sorting, and page breaks. They can contain normal data as well as formulas and expressions. These reports can be invoked from within ViewPoint forms as well as from the command line with command line parameters accepted as well.

The graphical query builder supports query by example and query by form. Queries can be named and reused in other areas.

The user is in the position of being able to actually create local applications without specific knowledge of programming. This is one of those "blurry" applications, in which the line between the user and programmers is hard to identify. Here, the user is given a toolkit of layout and drawing tools, custom buttons and controls, and objects representing data in the database. This type of application will become more and more popular as users get more sophisticated and as IS backlogs continue to increase.

THIRD-PARTY TOOLS

It is surprising that the Informix marketplace has not attracted more third-party support in the DBA tool market. There are over a half million Informix licenses out there and some of the largest corporate databases in the world are running on OnLine engines.

This is not to say that people are not developing for the OnLine marketplace. Informix has received quite a bit of support in the applications area. There are "canned" packages written by third parties that will do just about any job imaginable, from running a doctor's office to running a chain of hotels. Applications have never been a problem.

What's missing are the tools to help with the kinds of tasks that drive DBAs crazy, like designing systems, handling backups, and doing things that are not directly supported by Informix.

There are a few good tools out there, both in the commercial marketplace and in the public domain. This is by no means a comprehensive list. It is just a description of some of the tools that I have found useful.

We'll look at commercial and public domain software. It may be surprising to some that the public domain software may be the most stable and best supported products you will find. If a significant number of people are using PD software, and if you have the means of communicating with them, you will find that the PD software often matches or exceeds the commercial software. And you can't beat the price!

S-Designor
SDP Technologies, Inc.
One Westbrook Corporate Center, Suite 805
Westchester, IL 60154
Tel (708) 947-4250
Fax (708) 947-4251

S-Designor is a CASE (computer aided software engineering) product that supports the OnLine environment, as well as many other database systems. You don't usually look at CASE as a DBA tool, but S-Designor has several features that are of real utility to the DBA.

CASE tools are a lot alike. Just about all of them give you a graphic environment in which you can design and visualize your databases. They allow you to create diagrams that show the relationships between various data elements and to create the entity/relationship diagrams so dear to the hearts of database theorists. Based upon the entities, attributes, and relationships entered, a good CASE tool will help you to check your design for completeness and will help you design a normalized physical database schema.

S-Designor fulfills all of these basic requirements in a Microsoft Windows-based environment. Network versions are available that will allow a project to be broken up into separate modules with different analysts working on different parts. The system contains programs that will allow the merging and splitting necessary to manage multi-developer environments.

Since S-Designor supports many different database systems, it is possible to create a design for one system and easily port it over to another. Note that this system does not generate any code. It does not create screens or reports. What it does is manage the conceptual and logical design of database systems.

One of the things that makes S-Designor an excellent tool for the DBA, even if he is not actually doing the database design, is the reverse-engineering capability built into the product. The user can take a schema from an existing database and feed it into S-Designor. S-Designor then analyzes the schema and creates the entity/relationship (ER) diagrams for both the conceptual and for the physical data models. S-Designor will also generate reams of documents showing table layouts, index structures, data domains, constraints, and cross-references. This capability is a godsend to the DBA.

I'll wager that every DBA in the country has a bullet point in her job description calling for her to "Document the database." Typically, a database system just sort of appears out of nowhere or is converted from another system. You can be assured that everyone before you who was associated with the database system had the same bullet point in his job description, too. Think of how surprised everyone will be when you actually do it. Not only will you document the database, but you will do it in style. You'll have overall table layouts, lists of indexes, lists of join columns, ER diagrams, the works. And it won't take you forever to develop it.

The documentation feature alone probably justifies its cost. As systems get more and more complex, someone has to understand and more importantly, to be able to explain the structure to others. Having a well-documented, rigorous model to refer to and to work from makes this job much easier. As you are training new personnel, discussing modifications, or just troubleshooting the system, you will find that the physical and conceptual models created by S-Designor will be indispensable.

The product also allows you to make changes in the database from within S-Designor. Once you are sure of the changes, S-Designor will generate the SQL code to modify the database.

Intelligencia

DCC/4GL
1256 Cabrillo Avenue, Suite 250
Torrance, CA 90501
Tel (310) 320-4300
Fax (310) 320-3579

Intelligencia is an enhanced backup and restore tool for Informix OnLine systems, offering performance and features that can be very helpful in the administration of an OnLine database.

The `tbtape` utility that is provided with OnLine has many drawbacks. One of the major drawbacks is that it is an all-or-nothing proposition. In versions prior to Version 6.0, archiving and restoring is done at the instance level. There is no finer control. If you lose a few critical rows from a table or if you lose an entire table, or even if you lose an entire database, you have only one option. That option is to restore the entire instance from tape. If you have ten separate databases running in an instance of OnLine, you restore all ten or you restore none at all.

In Version 6.0, this will change, but users of earlier versions have had to struggle with this since OnLine came out. You will see DBAs exporting critical tables or whole databases to flat files to avoid catastrophic loss of data. Until Intelligencia, this was the best solution.

The Intelligencia product allows the DBA to archive at the table or even at the row level. Rather than simply being a technique that dumps flat files, Intelligencia actually goes into the Informix data structures and pulls out the information needed to do its backups. They claim that the performance is on the same level as the Informix `tbtape` program.

This product does not replace the `tbtape` program. Intelligencia does not understand logging and how to apply logfiles to bring a database up to date from the last archive. The need to do this is the reason why `tbtape` has the limitations that it has, and Intelligencia does not attempt to provide the same capability as `tbtape`. It also does not have the capability of insuring consistency. If changes in one table also create changes in another and if you have transactions that span tables, Intelligencia will not be able to insure data consistency if you have to restore unless you have been able to halt all operations on your system for the duration of the backup.

Where Intelligencia does excel, though, is as a substitute for the `dbexport` and `dbimport` programs. If you have critical tables that must be maintained and aren't too picky about the consistency between tables, or if you have the ability to shut your system down to allow a full Intelligencia backup, you may find this product a useful tool.

DB-Privileges

Advanced DataTools Corporation
4510 Maxfield Drive
Annandale, VA 22003, USA
Contact: Lester Knutsen
(703) 256-0267

DB-Privileges is an interface to Informix database privileges. It allows a database administrator to quickly change user database, table or column permissions using a data entry screen without any programming. DB-Privileges is easy enough that a non-technical security officer can maintain database privileges.

DB-Privileges is the first product that allows a database administrator to create and manage groups of users with common Informix database permissions. Add a user to a group and the user instantly inherits all the group database permissions. Remove a user and all their privileges will be automatically revoked.

DB-Privileges is available as INFORMIX-4GL code that may be customized to meet your specific requirements. An enterprise version of DB-Privileges is available that controls database privileges across multiple database servers.

BreakAway Technologies toolkits

BreakAway Technologies
P.O. Box 681092
Schaumburg, IL 60168
Tel (708) 582-3512
Fax (708) 582-3515

BreakAway Technologies provides several inexpensive toolkits that can be helpful to the DBA. There are some things that simply cannot be done without getting into the OnLine shared memory or directly into the disk structures. Without the ability to go directly into the engine, we have to rely on utilities such as `tbstat` and `tbcheck` to tell us what's going on inside the black box.

The problem is that Informix is very protective of their black box. They do not encourage anyone poking around in their disk structures or in their shared memory. Information about data structures and Informix internals are not published.

BreakAway Technologies has developed several utilities that can get into these areas. If you need the particular features, these toolkits provide the means of accessing them. BreakAway has 3 separate products for OnLine:

DBToolkit-1
Prices run from $150 to $250 depending on platform
Contains:

SQL	A command line editor for SQL query statements
schema	Enhanced `dbschema` includes table sizing information and dbspace information.
OAR	A `sar`-like performance and activity monitoring tool
4gltags	Creates a `vi` tags file from 4GL code

vie   Integrated `vi`-like editor for 4GL

ecmake   Generates the framework of an ESQL/C program based on a
                    database and list of tables

dbnames   Generates a list of databases in an instance

extent   Estimates extent sizes for a given number of rows

runprog   Allows programs to be run as a specific UNIX user ID

DBToolkit-2
Prices run from $150 to $250 depending on platform
Contains:

dbdiff   Compares two Informix databases and generates SQL
                    statements needed to make them the same

olrpt   System reporting utility for OnLine. Includes table and sizing
                    data and other space utilization data

mvdb   Renames an OnLine database

nodb   Prevents databases from either being created or dropped by
                    users

dosql   Runs SQL statements on multiple databases

4glc   A useful function library for 4GL and RDS

Source-Trak:
Prices run from $399 to $499 depending on platform
Contains:

source-trak   A source-code analysis and formatting tool for 4GL. Checks
                       and reports on 4GL code and gives `lint`-like diagnostics and
                       function-call reports. Contains a `vi` tags generator and a full
                       screen text-mode interface

PUBLIC DOMAIN SOFTWARE

`ISQLPERL`

The `perl` programming language is one of the major "cults" in the UNIX world.
The `perl` (Practical Extraction and Reporting Language) program was developed by
Larry Wall for personal use and evolved over a period of years into a powerful and
flexible language in itself. If you get involved with Internet, you will find that
`comp.languages.pcrl` is one of the most active of the USENET newsgroups and
that people are using this language to do amazing things.

The `perl` language can best be imagined as a combination of all that is good from
all of the UNIX utilities, Take the best features of `grep`, `awk`, `sed` and all of the shells.
Throw in the ability to control processes and to talk directly over sockets. Mix it in with
sophisticated interactive and scripting capabilities and you have what is being touted as a
"systems administration language."

How does this tie in with Informix? The `perl` language has "hooks" built into it
that will allow it to work with other products. Several programmers have used these
hooks to tie `perl` into routines that will allow it to talk to OnLine. This modified
version is called `ISQLPERL`.

Dealing with `perl` is not a job for the meek. Dealing with `ISQLPERL` is even more daunting, but in the right circumstances might pay off handsomely. The `perl` language is available by anonymous `ftp` from various sites on the Internet. As with most other software you will find on the Internet, you will get source code and makefiles. You're expected to modify it and compile it yourself. You've got to realize that the Internet is vast. There are hundreds of different types of computers out there. There may be a hundred separate versions of UNIX out there, each one a little different. Any attempt at writing code that will run without change on all versions of UNIX would be a massive undertaking. If you are not on intimate terms with your C compiler and if you don't have access to a C guru who dreams in C, you may want to wait a while on `perl`.

Of course, if you're lucky, someone has probably ported `perl` to your system. If you can get a copy, your job will be much easier. If you're really lucky, your UNIX system administrator has already placed a copy on your system. Getting `perl` is only the first step.

After you get `perl`, you have to get `ISQLPERL`. `ISQLPERL` is usually distributed as a patch to `perl`, so you have to have a few of the object and source files that are distributed with `perl`. If you've managed to get executables from someone else, you may need to go back and get the needed source and object files. Get a copy of `ISQLPERL` first and read through the documentation. Then you'll be able to be sure and get what you need from `perl`.

To get `perl` and `ISQLPERL`, you need access to the Internet. If you don't have direct access, check around with some of your cohorts. Odds are, someone already has access and they'll be glad to help you out. You'll have to be prepared to be preached to though. Internet users are evangelistic about the net.

`comp.database.informix` archives

There are several locations on the Internet that contain archives of past activity from the `comp.databases.informix` USENET discussion group. These archive sites contain old messages as well as several useful DBA management programs that have been placed in the public domain.

The main source at this time for archived data is `mathcs.emory.edu` (`128.140.2.1`). As with anything else on such a fluid, changeable medium as the Internet, this location is highly subject to change. The sure way to find the location of an archive site is to check the `comp.databases.informix` newsgroup. You can search for either the keyword `archive` or FAQ, which is the "Frequently Asked Questions" file. If you do not find either reference, you have a couple of options. The best is to use the `archie` program. Just type `archie informix`, and `archie` will return a list of `ftp` sites that have the word `informix` in their directory structure. You can `ftp` out to any of these sites and look around for archive files. If you are more patient, you can post a question on `comp.databases.informix` asking for the current archive site.

Once you have the name and/or Internet address of an archive site, you can then `ftp` out to the site. At the login prompt, login as `anonymous`. When it asks for your password, just give it your e-mail address. You can now submit UNIX (or DOS-like) commands to the `ftp` program. The main ones you will use are `cd`, `dir`, and `get`. Some of the programs that I have found available on the `comp.databases.informix` archive include the following.

`dbbeauty.sh`	Capitalizes reserved words in an INFORMIX-4GL program. Ignores words that are quoted.
`dbinfo.sh`	Provides table information ala the SQL INFO command.
`dblist.sh`	This program dumps the contents of a table to `stdout`. It has the ability to select an index to sort by and also provides the ability to start at a specific place in the file. This program requires I4GL to compile, not ESQL/C.
`dbloader.sh`	This program generates SQL statements to load unloaded tables into a database. When compiled, `dbloader` should be linked to `dbunloader`. The `dbunloader` program generates SQL statements to unload tables.
`dbreserved.sh`	This program will scan a table and print all reserved words to `stdout`. There are currently 400+ words that are checked.

`dbsyntax.sh`	This program checks the syntax of SQL statements without actually executing them. If a file is not specified on the command line, `stdin` is used instead.
`db4glgen.sh`	This package is a PD INFORMIX-4GL code generator. It is at version 3.17 for right now. Grab this file if you run a version of Informix-4GL newer than 4.00.
`db4glgenOLD.sh`	This package is a PD Informix 4GL code generator. It is at version 3.17.4 now. Grab this file if you run a version of INFORMIX-4GL older than 4.10.
`dbform.sh`	This package generates "quick & dirty" data forms. It requires that INFORMIX-SQL be installed on your machine.
`vie.sh`	Vie will allow you to view and correct an INFORMIX-4GL source/form error file using `vi`.
`dblist.sh`	This program dumps the contents of a table to `stdout`. It has the ability to select an index to sort by and also provides the ability to start at a specific place in the file.
`4gltags`	shell/awk script to generate `vi` tags file for 4GL source code
`appstart`	program to run Informix applications `setuid`
`arrdemo`	4GL and C routines to demo a method of displaying 4GL arrays

`areacode`	utilities and data for north American telephone area codes
`blob_char`	C function to convert a TEXT type to a CHAR type
`dbamon`	shell script to monitor OnLine engine performance
`dbastruct`	shell script to generate C structs for database tables
`dbxref`	C program to cross-ref 4GL variables, labels, and functions
`esqlutil`	ESQL/C program to generate C structs for database tables
`fgl_run`	functions to run commands without 4GL `run` statement
`get_user`	function to return current login-ID
`inferr`	shell/awk script to scan `.err` files for error messages
`kw`	prints 4GL source file with keywords in upper case
`make_sccs`	examples for using `make` and `SCCS` with 4GL
`msg_pmpt`	4GL function to display message box and let user choose option
`rpt_awk`	functions to control `awk` reports like 4GL or ACE

`soundex`	C and 4GL utilities for generating Soundex codes
`sql_yacc`	an SQL parser based on `lex` and `yacc`
`asql_yacc`	an ANSI-compliant SQL parser based on `lex` and `yacc`
`calx`	4GL routine that pops up a calendar pick-list
`check_prt`	check printing program
`dbnames`	ESQL/C program to get list of visible databases
`easter`	several methods of calculating Easter for a specified year
`emacs_4gl`	4GL mode file for emacs
`esql_proto`	header (`.h`) files containing ESQL/C function prototypes
`iedit`	simple text editor
`m4gl`	macro to provide `define`/`include` for 4GL
`ppcc4gl`	shell script to preprocess 4GL source using `cpp`
`privproc`	ACE report to print privileges for stored procedures
`reform_sql`	awk script to reformat I-SQL output to 1 wide line per row

`rpt_size`	C functions to change 4GL report dimensions at runtime
`shar`	shell script to make shell archives (`shar`'s)
`updblob`	generic ESQL/C program to update BLOB fields
`vgrind_4gl`	`vgrind` definition file for 4GL
`xref_4gi`	4GL RDS program to cross-ref 4GL functions, cursors, etc.
`xtbload`	X application that displays OnLine status similar to `xload`
`sqlcmd`	multipart distribution (part00-part06) of a program that interprets SQL commands against an Informix database. Suitable for placing in shell scripts
`termcaps`	`termcap` entries submitted by Informix users or grabbed off of the Net grouped into files loosely based on equipment or environment supported

As you can see, there is a lot of software out on the Internet that can help you in your OnLine administration. Most of what's out there may not be directly usable in your projects, but the ideas they present are almost always adaptable to specific needs. If there's nothing out there that fits your needs, post a message on `comp.databases.informix`. Odds are, someone will have just what you need, or will know where to get it.

If you get onto the Internet, feel free to drop me a line. My current Internet address is:

```
jlumbley@netcom.com
```

Or, just get onto `comp.databases.informix`. I visit there at least once a day.

INDEX

—b—

—c—

—d—

—m—

—n—

—o—

—p—

—q—

—t—